# Remembering
# Sepharad
**Jewish Culture in Medieval Spain**

Organized by

**Sociedad Estatal**
**para la Acción Cultural Exterior**

In collaboration with

# Remembering
# Sepharad
## Jewish Culture in Medieval Spain

Text by ISIDRO G. BANGO

Washington National Cathedral
May 9 - June 8, 2003

STATE CORPORATION FOR SPANISH CULTURAL ACTION ABROAD

*SOCIEDAD ESTATAL PARA LA ACCIÓN CULTURAL EXTERIOR DE ESPAÑA*

**ORGANIZED AND FINANCED BY**

State Corporation for Spanish Cultural Action Abroad, SEACEX

**COLLABORATORS**

Ministry of Foreign Affairs of Spain

Ministry of Education, Culture, and Sport of Spain

Embassy of Spain

Washington National Cathedral

**CURATOR**

Isidro G. Bango

**COORDINATION**

Illana Bango

Genoveva Fernández

**EXHIBITION DESIGNER AND SUPERVISOR**

Macua & García Ramos, Equipo de Diseño, S.A.

**AUDIOVISUALS**

LUNATUS. Comunicación audiovisual, S.L.

**DOCUMENTATION AND GRAPHIC INFORMATION
FOR THE AUDIOVISUAL "JEWRIES OF SPAIN"**

Clara I. Bango

Illana Bango

**SCALE MODELS**

HCH Model, S.L.

**TRANSPORTS**

T.T.I. Técnicas de Transportes Internacionales, S.A.

**INSURANCE**

Axa Art Versicherung AG. Sucursal en España

Aon Gil y Carvajal, S.A. Correduría de Seguros

**WITH THE COLLABORATION OF**

*IBERIA*

**VOLVO**

# Acknowledgements

Miguel Ángel Albares Albares; Sidney Alpert; María Ángeles Alonso Cacho; Marcelino Angulo García; Xavier Aquilué; Rita Barberá Nolla; Nathan D. Baxter; Margarita Becedas González; Ralph Block; Carlos de la Casa Martínez; Emilio Cassinello; Pere Castanyer; Belén Castillo Iglesias; Miguel Castillo Montero; Diana Cohen Altman; Jaime Coll Conesa; Concepción Contel Barea; Julie Cooke; Natividad Correas; María Luisa Cuenca; Christopher Dodd; Antonio Domínguez Valverde; Christina Dykstra Mead; Cristina Emperador Ortega; Carmen Escriche Jaime; Genoveva Fernández; Álvaro Fernández Villaverde y de Silva, Duque de San Carlos; Carlos Fitz-James Stuart, Duque de Huéscar; Cayetana Fitz-James Stuart y Silva, Duquesa de Alba; Dennis Fruitt; Jesús Gaite Pastor; Rafael García Serrano; Jay Garfinkel; Jane S. Gerber; Carmen Godia; Jorge González; Carmen González de Amezua; Luis A. Grau Lobo; Nadia Hernández Henche; Ramón del Hoyo; Jason Isaacson; Joel S. Kaplan; Karl Katz; Teresa Laguna Paúl; Josep Vicent Lerma; Ana María López Álvarez; Vicente Malabia Martínez; Alicia Manso; José Marín; Juan José Martinena Ruiz; Rocío Martínez; Juan Carlos de la Mata González; María del Carmen Muñoz Párraga; Michael Neiditch; Santiago Palomero Plaza; Consolación Pastor Cremades; Eduardo Pedruelo Martín; Luis Racionero; Miguel Ángel Recio Crespo; Jaime Vicente Redón; José Luis Rodríguez de Diego; Julia Rodríguez de Diego; María Jesús Ruiz y Ruiz; Javier Rupérez; Teresa Sánchez; Ramón Sáenz de Heredia; Jerry Schwarberd; Julio Segura Moneo; Juan Sell; María Pía Senent Díez; Naomi M. Steinberger; Mark E. Talisman; Elías Terés Navarro; José Luis del Valle

American Jewish Committee; Archivo Diocesano de Cuenca; Archivo General de Navarra, Pamplona; Archivo General de Simancas, Valladolid; Archivo Histórico Nacional, Madrid; Archivo Municipal de Tudela, Navarre; Archivo de la Real Chancillería, Valladolid; Ayuntamiento de Ágreda, Soria; Ayuntamiento de Valencia; Biblioteca General de la Universidad de Salamanca; Biblioteca Nacional, Madrid; The B'nai B'rith Klutznick National Jewish Museum and B'nai B'rith International; Sevilla Cathedral; Consulado General de España, New York; Embajada de España, Washington; Fundación Casa de Alba, Madrid; Fundación "El Conventet", Barcelona; The Jewish Theological Seminary of America, New York; Musefilm and Televisio; Museo de Burgos; Museo de Teruel; Museo Arqueológico de León; Museo de El Greco, Toledo; Museo Numantino, Soria; Museo de Santa Cruz, Toledo; Museo Sefardí, Toledo; Museu d'Arqueologia de Catalunya-Empúries, L'Escala; National Building Museum; Obispado de Cuenca; Ohev Sholom Talmud Torah Sinagogue; Patrimonio Nacional, Biblioteca del Real Monasterio de San Lorenzo de El Escorial, Madrid; Project Judaica Foundation, Inc.; United States Senate

Of the very many strands, studied and disseminated in varying degrees, from which Spanish history is woven, the history of the Sephardic Jews is undoubtedly one of the most fascinating and in greatest need of revision. The vicissitudes of a people who, for centuries, professed an unfailing love of the land and traditions of the kingdoms of Spain, where they had settled since late antiquity, bear witness to the loyalty of those compatriots of ours, to whose tenacity and creativity we owe some of our greatest cultural accomplishments.

It therefore falls to us to analyze this past with scientific rigor, although we should not overlook the unique dramatic force of the historical adventure of the Sephardic Jews. This essential facet of our past is the subject of this exhibition, which has been organized by the State Corporation for Spanish Cultural Action Abroad in accordance with the guidelines established by the Spanish government for spreading the cultural legacy of our country across Europe, America, and throughout the world. This exhibition testifies to the value of cultural dissemination as a means of addressing the challenges of the present by bridging a political and cultural gap that is perhaps wider in appearance than in reality, as evidenced by the fact that our country was once the home of diverse beliefs and civilizations.

Sepharad and its history and art, the collective dream of a community unfairly marginalized and expelled after centuries marked by chronic tensions, prompt us to reflect on the ups and downs of a past shared by many communities across various continents. These communities still provide, rather than a relic, a challenge to scholars and a living testimony to the beauty of late-medieval Spanish culture, frozen by the tragedy of dispersal but enriched by the varied contributions of the lands that took in the exiles. By mapping out the course of this exceptional human history before and after its turning point, the expulsion edict of 1492, this exhibition presents visitors with a comprehensive and unbiased view of the history of collective loyalty to a faith and to a land; of a cultural splendor that remained intact even in the most adverse circumstances; and of the constant need for understanding others — a need that can never be stressed sufficiently — as the sole means of fruitful interaction based on the ties that bind peoples together and run deeper than sterile and artificial divisions. This special opportunity to present to the American public a smaller version of an exhibition previously shown in Spain's historic city of Toledo is therefore intended as a new tribute to the understanding between our two countries.

**Ana Palacio**
Spanish Minister of Foreign Affairs

Sepharad — the name, steeped in legend, which the Spanish Jews gave the Iberian peninsula hundreds of years ago — is a fascinating historical adventure from its origins in Roman antiquity up until the dawn of the modern age. As a collective experience handed down over the centuries from generation to generation in the form of a dream sublimated by the trauma of expulsion and dispersal, this name denotes a host of social, economic, political, and artistic facets that are almost impossible to embrace. This exhibition aims to provide a comprehensive and thought-provoking approach to these realities, in order to enhance the knowledge of specialists and of society of a whole, helping us decipher the keys to our past and showing their potential for building a future based on unbiased knowledge, freedom, and tolerance.

As an indissoluble part of Spanish history, Sepharad and the legacy of the Sephardic Jews pose a challenge to research and to the necessary dissemination of a history that, in many aspects, is still alive in the many communities scattered around the world, who preserve the memory of this heritage. An unbiased analysis of the historical facts is the best tribute that can be paid to the accumulated experience of these communities, which were closely involved in the complex process of shaping the concept of Spanishness in a shared time and space. Therefore, any effort to reinstate the historical memory of the Sephardic people and, accordingly, of the Spanish people as a whole, is an essential part of the program designed by the State Corporation for Cultural Action Abroad, one of whose priorities is to disseminate the legacy of Spain throughout Europe and the world.

In accordance with these aims, this exhibition sets out to summarize the main aspects of the historic universe of Sepharad: fragmentary testimonies to daily life, marked by the liturgical calendar and the solemn splendor of feast days; collective attitudes toward death; the sacred and profane places, both public and private, that occupied the most diverse urban centers of the Spanish kingdoms; and, naturally, the artistic techniques and sensibilities that were shared with people of the other faiths but gave rise to a specifically Sephardic creativity, which also occurred in the sciences and other branches of knowledge, where the significant progress made by Jewish scholars helped change the West's view of the world.

Together with the unquestionable achievements of a civilization closely linked to other Spanish cultures — Islamic and Christian — the exhibition also traces the conflict that increasingly cast a dark shadow over the coexistence of these cultures and finally erupted into expulsion and exile. The growing prejudice and intolerance culminated in the establishment of the Inquisition which sprang from complex ideological roots that were both Spanish and European.

The archaeological pieces, furnishings, codices, sculptures, and paintings are accompanied by scale models, maps, and a host of audiovisual aids designed to help explain the various stages in this ambitious journey into the memory and legacy of that other fertile Spain that lives on in the descendents of the Jews of the Diaspora and in Spain's own heritage, and shaped the dream of Sepharad. We owe this glimpse of Sepharad to the conscientious cooperation of all the institutions and lenders who have made this exhibition possible and to whom I wish to express my sincerest thanks.

**Felipe V. Garín**
President of the State Corporation for Spanish Cultural Action Abroad

# Contents

בְתָנוּהַצִילוּ וַיִּקְרַהַנָּסוֹ וַיִּשְׁתַּחֲווּ

מַעֲשֵׂה חֹרֶשׁ

שָׁאנוּ

אוֹכְלִין

מַהֶעַל

יִשְׁלֹא

עַל שׁוּם

שׁוֹבר

הַסְפִיק

בְּצֵקָם

# By Way of an Introduction

In recent years, history, overly concerned to satisfy the interests and geopolitical trends of today's society, has attempted to reinterpret the concept of Sepharad. This endeavor has given rise to the idea that Sepharad does not denote Spain, but rather al-Andalus or Castile taken in their broadest sense. The problem is that a number of historians, instead of objectively analyzing the facts, have elaborated their own versions of history that are biased by nationalistic sentiment — whether pro- or anti-Spanish. Some would have us believe that Spain has always been a single nation; these scholars even deny that it was made up of various kingdoms during the Late Middle Ages. Others, obsessed by that same plurality that emerged at the end of the first millennium, ignore the fact that Roman Hispania became Europe's first nation after the fall of the Roman Empire, and that this left an indelible imprint on the inhabitants of the peninsula. The various states that sprang up after the Muslim invasion were undoubtedly shaped by the laws and geopolitics of the peninsula, but the feeling of being linked by a common past and of belonging to Spain lived on in all of them.

Sepharad should be regarded as the Hebrew word for Spain. The concept of Spain/Hispania varied, depending on the period. In ninth-century Asturian chronicles, Hispania encompassed the whole of the territory under Muslim rule. Although this definition changed considerably during the Christian reconquest, the idea that the old Roman Hispania and, particularly, Gothic Spain were made up of many different kingdoms never varied. The term Sepharad/Hispania has the same meaning in Hebrew sources.

*Remembering Sepharad* sets out to paint a picture of the Spain in which the Jews lived from the perspective of their own experiences, though on many occasions we have had to include Christian or Muslim references. The dramatic expulsion and the equally dire activities of the Inquisition erased many aspects of Hispano-Jewish heritage. This has obviously weakened the memory of Jewish culture in Spain, but we should not be deceived: the Jews became so well integrated into Spanish life that Jewish history and Spanish history are practically inextricable. In this respect, it is only fair to point out that many apparent gaps in the history of the Spanish Jews are not what they seem; rather, in these instances it is impossible to differentiate between Jewish and Spanish heritage.

Not only did Jewish culture suffer the same vicissitudes as Spanish culture during the fifteen hundred years of Jewish presence in Spain; it became fully integrated. Only one aspect of Jewish tradition, religion, would remain

"Ornamental reproduction of an unleavened loaf", *Golden Haggadah*, fol. 44v, Barcelona, 1320. London, The British Library (Ms. Add. 27210)

15

unchanged — at least, so it seemed. However, even in this respect the Sephardic Jews developed certain characteristics of their own that set them apart from other Jewish communities in exile. Moses Arragel, the rabbi of Alcarria who translated the Alba Bible, stated in the first half of the fifteenth century:

> Most of the glosses we Jews of today have on the law and on their laws and rights and other sciences were composed by the wise Jews of Castile, and today Jews throughout the kingdoms to which they migrated are governed by their doctrine.

The Jews' stay in Spain was enriching both for them and for Spaniards. Neither the Sephardim on the one hand, nor the Spanish Christians on the other would have been the same without the long period during which they lived together. However, that prolonged experience was marked by bright light and by dark shadows, which left a lasting imprint on both groups. In the patches of light, a culture flourished that was unmatched by any other contemporary community of the Diaspora, and during that period the human condition of Jews was respected in Spain as in no other place in Europe. But in the shadows there was deep suffering, which the collective memory of a people finds difficult to forget.

This book undertakes to place on record both the light and the shadows, knowledge of which could be conducive to greater understanding and tolerance of the attitudes of each party. If all forms of cultural expression — except that of religion — tended to blend together into an inextricable whole, why did lack of understanding gain ascendance? Obviously, when we look back at the past, we must interpret it in accordance with the norms of the time. No society — not even the hypocritical society in which we live today — can stand up to the moral judgment of coming centuries.

In order to have an opinion about the Sephardic human and cultural phenomenon, we need to know the facts (see the sections on "The Historic Background," "Jews, Moors, and Christians," "History of a Conflict," and "The Inquisition"), take a close look at their lives ("The *Judería*"), and get to know their inventions and creations ("The Jews and the Arts and Sciences").

Before continuing, I wish to comment on the writing of this book. I wanted to allow the men of the time to do the talking as much as possible. Therefore the narrative is continuously interrupted for the insertion of texts from each particular period. As far as possible, these texts adhere to their original form; their verbal, colloquial, and conventional structures give us more and better information about the ideas of the time than do the contents themselves.

# THE HISTORIC BACKGROUND

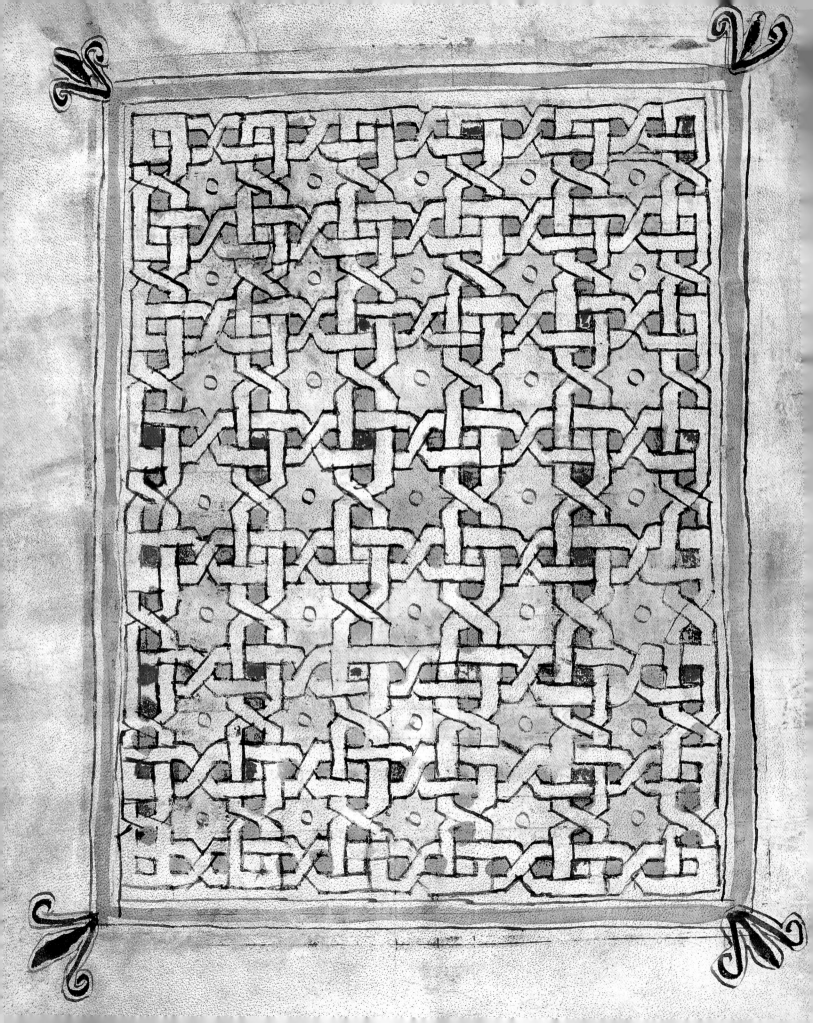

# The Historic Background

"Carpet page," Bible fol. 163r
(Castile, 1279–mid-fifteenth century).
Cambridge, University Library
(Ms. Add. 3203)

[1] This legislation against the Jews will
be discussed in the chapter on the
"History of a Conflict."
[2] They can be classified into two groups
— one formed by two coins from the
reign of Herod I (37–4 B.C.) and Herod
Archelaus (4 B.C.–A.D. 6) and the rest
from the time of the Procurators under
Augustus and Tiberius.
[3] García Iglesias, 1978.

Coins from Ampurias. 1 B.C.–A.D. 1
bronze. Ampurias, Museu d'Arqueologia
de Catalunya–Empúries (inv. no.
MAC–Empuries 6343–6352)

## THE HEBREWS SETTLE IN HISPANIA, AN ANCIENT ROMAN PROVINCE IN THE WESTERN MEDITERRANEAN

If we dismiss the old stories about the origins of Hebrew settlement in Spain, nothing certain in this respect can be affirmed until the first century. We know that was when the apostle Paul talked about coming to the western Mediterranean to preach. Paul's evangelizing activity was focused at that time on the Jewish communities scattered around the world. The Council of Elvira (300–306), considered to be the first expression of an organized Spanish Christian church, drew up a large number of its canons against the Jews. Jewish settlement in Spain must already have been considerable during that period; otherwise it would be difficult to understand the synod's concern.[1]

Archæological material from that Roman period gives us different clues to Israel and the Israelites. A collection of Roman coins from Judea, found at Ampurias, provides evidence of legionaries passing through from the East.[2] A certain Justinian died at Merida and an altar stone, a second-century work in marble, bears his epitaph. Justinian was born in Flavia Neapolis, that is, the *Siquem* of the Jews, the current Nablus. According to García Iglesias, he was probably a Samaritan.[3]

Mystery surrounds one of the most important Jewish artifacts of that time: the trilingual *pileta* (trough or basin). The specialists have not reached an agreement about its meaning or function.

Trough *(pileta)* with inscriptions in three languages, fifth-seventh centuries (?), White marble. From Tarragona. Toledo Museo de Santa Cruz (inv. no. 80)

Orihuela tombstone, sixth century. White limestone. Orihuela, Museo Arqueológico Comarcal (inv. no. HEB–0000001)

This outstanding piece (stones with inscription in three languages are a rarity) appeared when some houses were demolished on Calle Enladrillado in Tarragona, very near the Jewish quarter, where it had been reused as a kitchen sink. Rectangular in shape, with two water outlets, it is difficult to attribute to any particular period.

It bears an inscription, together with different symbols on the front face: in the center is a *menorah*, the seven-branched candelabrum, flanked by the tree of life to the right and *šofar,* to the left. The composition is completed by two peacocks facing each other, as a symbol of the resurrection; one of them seems to be pecking the fruit from the tree. Above the peacock to the left can be read in Hebrew, "Peace on Israel, on us and on our children!" and above that to the right there are the words in Latin, "PAX FIDES." Below this can be read, with difficulty, three Greek letters "MAH," whose meaning escapes us. Whereas some people consider that this is a ritual basin, others think it is a child's ossuary or sarcophagus. The universality of the images and the rudimentary technique of the incisions do not allow for precise dating, although there are undeniably similar techniques on certain funerary reliefs of the fourteenth and fifteenth centuries. A more delicate work is the Orihuela tombstone. Although it is broken, it is possible to make out a *menorah* under which two birds are pecking. We continue in the same ideological world as that of the *pileta* — a universal language representing souls refreshed by food and sheltered by divinity, which is indicated by one of its symbols: the candelabrum with seven branches.

## SPAIN OF THE VISIGOTHS

When the Western Roman Empire drew to a close in the fifth century, Spain experienced a long period of political inchoateness. From the start of that century barbarian peoples started to arrive who converted the towns into dangerous places. When the Visigoths were definitively established in Spain from the year 506, a long process of cooperation began between Hispano-Romans and invaders. The process would end in the creation of a Spain governed by Goths, which has been considered the foremost nation in Europe after the fall of the Roman Empire. The consolidation of a kingdom based on a monarchy anointed and protected by God required the Catholic Church to play a decisive role. A dominant alliance of two thus arose whose declared enemies were the Jews. Luis García Iglesias gives a very good description of the causes of the persecution of the Jews:

> The true reasons are religious and political, which are inseparable from each other: the pursuit of unity for the kingdom and the defense of Christianity in all its purity, dominance and unicity; in other words, the heritage of a very ancient anti-Judaic tradition of the Church, which was competitive and protectionist, and stirred up by Messianic dispersing movements.[4]

A long period of conflict now began, which would be interspersed by considerable periods of tolerance but which would not end until the definitive expulsion of the Jews in the fifteenth century.[5] The laws promulgated by the kings were so harsh that when the Islamic invasion took place in 711, the Jews welcomed the Muslims as true liberators.

## THE GREAT REVOLUTION OF JEWISH CULTURE UNDER MUSLIM HEGEMONY

The Jews enjoyed an untroubled situation under the Muslims compared with what they had suffered under the Gothic monarchy, although they were also subject to certain restrictive rules. Public expression of their religion was limited, and the old Roman laws that prohibited the building and renovation of their synagogues were reintroduced.

Slowly a process developed that would lead to the Arabizing of the Jewish minority. This process culminated in the appearance of an exceptional person, Abu

[4] García Iglesias, 2002, p. 39.
[5] This conflict will be the subject of detailed analysis in other chapters of this book.

Yusuf Hasday ben Yishaq ibn Saprut (ca. 910–970), one of the most influential figures at the court of the Caliph Abd al-Rahman.

Centuries later, the Jews themselves acknowledged the enormous influence of Islamic culture in the subjugation of the Hebrew language:

> "The language of the Israelites," he said, "was made the slave of the Arabic language… Prostrate yourself so that we may pass over you… The Arabic language blackened it and, like a lion, tore it to pieces. A wild beast devoured it. Everybody despised the Hebrew language and loved Arabic."[6]

The great poet Abraham ibn Ezra (1089–1164), in his poem on various peoples, conveys the following view about them through his poetic compositions:

> The poems of the Ishmaelites, on love and pleasures;
> Those of the Christians, on wars on vengeance;
> Those of the Greeks, on science on cunning;
> Those of the Hindus, on parabolas on enigmas;
> Those of the Israelites, on canticles and praise
> To the Lord of the armies.[7]

This is a stereotyped and commonplace view. Undoubtedly all Hebrew poetry, without Muslim contacts, would have met these criteria, but, as we shall see later, the great poets at that time composed the most beautiful love poems, full of sensuality. Judah Halevi (ca. 1070–1141) demonstrated his lyrical gifts as follows, not as a Hebrew poet, but rather as a Hebrew Andalusian:

> The hind washes her clothes in the waters of my tears,
> And hangs them out in the sun of your splendor.
> Having my eyes, she does not ask for springs,
> Or for sun, given the beauty of your face.[8]

Language, poetry, good taste, and culture in general, all became Arabized under Muslim rule. But precisely because this Arabization led to such great progress in the cultural education of the Jewish sages, they felt a need to apply their recently-acquired knowledge to learning about their own language and culture. However, this research into Hebrew was for the most part conducted from an Arab perspective. Ibn Saprut, who became a *nasí*, prince of the Jewish communities of al-Andalus, converted the Jewish community of al-Andalus (Muslim Andalusia) into the most flourishing of the Diaspora. Jews from the East and North Africa flocked to Cordoba, which had already become a byword as a center of culture. In this way Sephardic civilization began to take shape. Within the continuity of the religious tradition, it would eventually become something very different from the rest of the Jewish communities.

[6] Text by Yehuda al-Harizi quoted by Alfonso, 2002, pp. 78–79.
[7] Sáenz-Badillos, 1991, p. 149.
[8] Ibid., p. 137.

Tapestry of the Creation
(detail of Jews), twelfth century,
Gerona, Tesoro de la Catedral

With another *nasí*, Samuel ibn Nagrella ha-Nagid (993–1056), the definitive step was taken towards cultural integration into Islam, without abandoning the principles of the Jewish religious tradition. He lived in a palace befitting his status, at the Alhambra, and as Vizier of Granada participated in the military campaigns against neighboring kingdoms. In the following portrayal by ibn Daud we can see how he was transformed into the great patron and protector of Jewish civilization:

> He favored Israel in Spain, in the Maghreb, in Africa, Egypt, Sicily, and even at the Assembly of Babylon and in the Holy City. All the sons of the Torah in these countries enjoyed his possessions. He bought many books… Anyone who wished to make the study of the Torah his profession, whether in Spain or in the above-mentioned countries, could count on being paid by him. He had

secretaries who copied the Misnah and the Talmud, and he gave these copies to the disciples who could not afford to buy them, both in the academies in Spain and in those of the aforementioned countries. Every year olive oil sufficient for the synagogues in Jerusalem came from his house.[9]

The dominant role achieved by the Andalusian Jews in the entire Diaspora can be perceived from these words. Their integration into the history of the *taifas* (smaller Muslim kingdoms in Spain) conferred social prestige, cultural leadership, and economic power on them, but also led them into the same crisis that brought about the downfall of some *taifa* kings. The following biographical sketch of the son of the *nasí* Nagrella — Joseph — records a tragic end, which would constitute the first act of the final disaster:

> He was envied so much by the Berber princes that both he and the whole community of Granada and all those who had come from far-off countries to see his law and dominion were assassinated on the Sabbath.[10]

Tribes of zealots from Africa arrived on the Iberian peninsula and finished off all those who did not become Muslims:

> The rebels in the Berber kingdom traveled from the Maghreb over the sea to Spain after leaving not a single Israelite alive from Tangiers to Al-Mahadiya... That is what they wanted to do in all the Ishmaelite countries of Spain.[11]

The intransigence of the Almoravids, Spain's Berber rulers, put an end to any religious expression other than that of Islam. Jews and Christians were victims of the most terrible scenes:

> Some were taken prisoner by the Christians and sold themselves in order to escape from the Ishmaelite country. Others fled walking, naked and without shoes, hurting their feet in the high wooded countryside; "the children asked for bread and there was nobody to give it to them."[12]

The poet Abraham ibn Ezra wrote this deeply-felt epitaph on the end of the Jews in al-Andalus:

> Alas! onto Sepharad misfortune has fallen from the sky,
> From my eyes water flows.

[9] Abraham Ibn Daud, *Libro de la Tradición*, ed. Ferre, 1990, p. 92.
[10] Ibid., p. 93.
[11] Ibid., pp. 104–105.
[12] Ibid., p. 105.

## THE CHRISTIAN KINGDOMS WELCOME THE JEWS HOSPITABLY

When the Islamic invasion took place in the eighth century, some northern territories remained in the hands of resisting Christians who refused to recognize

the new hegemony. In time these pockets of resistance formed a new geopolitical structure, basically consisting of three kingdoms: Castile-León, Navarre, and Aragon.[13] For centuries these territories were progressively enlarged southwards by means of reconquest. This process of expansion ended with the final defeat of the Muslims through the conquest of Granada in 1492 — the same year in which the Jews were also expelled from Spain.

But let us return to our story. At the end of the eleventh and beginning of the twelfth centuries, the Almoravids seized control of Andalusia and

[13] The Catalonian counties were attached to the kingdom of Aragon.

threatened the Christian kingdoms. When those who had fled from al-Andalus arrived on Christian territory, they were welcomed and found themselves with co-religionists who had been living there since the tenth century in freedom that put them on an equal footing, except in certain religious matters, with their Christian neighbors. Nevertheless, the living conditions of Jews and Christians were not the same as those which the people from the south had enjoyed in the Andalusian cities. It is not surprising that a man who had lived in the splendor of Nagrella's Granada should be so critical of those who welcomed them in the north:

> They are wild men in need of a little knowledge,
>     lacking the waters of faith.
> They think they are philosophers but they are architects of destruction,
>     they err and they make the innocent err.
> They believe themselves to be wise, but they are not;
>     they predict the future without being prophets with visions.
> The wind of their love is no use for cleaning
>     nor for blowing away particles of dirt, as is the pure air.[14]

However, their suffering had been so great, that the majority of Jews were exceedingly happy to feel that they were safe under the protection of Christian kings. The chroniclers spared no praise when referring to them. The words of ibn Daud about Alfonso VI are an example of this climate of cordiality:

> The expulsion of the heretics in Castile: Don Alfonso, son of Raimundo, king of kings, reigned justly and imposed his power on all the Ishmaelites who were in Spain and levied a tax on them. And in his own kingdom Yahweh granted him rest from all the enemies around him. (II Sa. 7: 1)[15]

From that time on, and independently of the constantly shifting relations between Christians and Jews, the latter always appear at crucial times during the Reconquest — in support of the Christians and against the Muslims. On most occasions, at least during the twelfth and thirteenth centuries, they benefited from the Reconquest. When King Ferdinand III took the city of Seville in 1248, accompanying the monarch was a numerous group of Jewish courtiers who received houses and mosques for transformation into synagogues as a reward for their help during the conquest. As late as 1492, the Jews not only commemorated the conquest of Granada, a few weeks before their expulsion, but took advantage of those feast days to attack the beliefs of the Muslims, thus demonstrating their collective resentment that dated from the end of the twelfth century. Rabbi Yehudah related these incidents as follows:

[14] Sáenz–Badillos and Targarona, 1988, p. 162.
[15] Abraham Ibn Daud, *Libro de la Tradición*, ed. Ferre, 1990, p. 104.

When I was in Sepharad, at the time when the holy communities (Jews) were organizing festivities on the occasion of the conquest of the great city of Granada, I ordered the Jews of my community ... to make an effigy of Mohammed, the prophet of the Ishmaelites, and to drag it along the ground. It was dragged along and thrown into the markets and streets.[16]

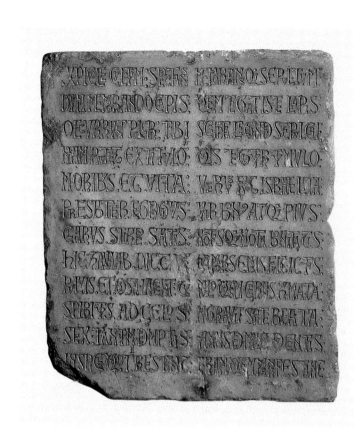

Epitaph of Havaab, 1156. Marble.
From the church of San Miguel el Alto in Toledo. Toledo, Museo de Santa Cruz (inv. no. 235)

## THE JEWISH ARISTOCRACY AND THE CENTURIES OF TOLERANCE

During the twelfth and thirteenth centuries, the Jews experienced a long period of tolerance in the Christian kingdoms. A result of this situation was the close collaboration that bore fruit in the form of economic and cultural progress that benefited both communities. The powerful families that governed the Jewish quarters, and who provided courtiers for the Christian kings played an important role in this relationship. This situation was not new, since it had also been true under Muslim rule. Let us recall here some names of those figures who were very important not only in the history of their own people: Joseph ibn Selomó ibn Sosan, Alfonso VIII's *almojarife* (tax collector), contributed decisively with his own financial resources to the organization of the campaign of Navas de Tolosa. Çag de la Maleha was an important figure at the court of Alfonso X, although, as was the case so often in the stories of these Jewish courtiers, this one had a fatal ending. In Aragon under Peter III (1276–1285) we find Yehudá de la Caballería and the Ravaya family of the Jewish quarter in Gerona; Jews even participated in the military campaigns, for example Muça de Portella and Samuel Alfaquim.

## FROM THE FOURTEENTH-CENTURY CRISIS TO THE FINAL DECISION

Although there had also been some shadows over Christian-Jewish relations during the previous period, co-existence had been good and in no way comparable to the situation of the Jews in the rest of Europe. Things began to change markedly at the start of the fourteenth century.

The calamities and misfortunes that rained down on Europe during the fourteenth century proved a decisive influence in shattering the reasonable

[16] Quoted by Castaño, 2000, p. 58.

balance that had been established in the Spanish kingdoms until then: people were fearful in the face of so many disasters; half of society was deeply in debt to the Jews; the Church switched its policy from attempted evangelization to forced conversion — all this made it too much to expect the masses not to engage in violence against those whom they accused of deicide, the ritual murder of children, usury, and, in short, all the suffering of their human condition. The entire fourteenth century was punctuated by violent incidents in the Jewish quarters. Anti-Jewish riots in Seville, instigated by the cleric Ferrand Martínez in 1391, spread like wildfire throughout Spain's Jewish quarters. Terrified, many Jews converted, some fled, and the few who persevered in their beliefs were reduced to forced confinement in the Jewish quarters, which progressively became ghettos. In any event, the drawing up in 1432 of the Valladolid Ordinances, consisting of a general law for the internal government of the Jewish quarters of Castile, provided a short-lived breathing space before the final decision that would come in 1492 with the expulsion of the Jews.

# THE *JUDERÍA*

# The *Judería*[1]

**"Baking unleavened bread,"** *Hispano-Moresque Haggadah,* fol. 88r, Castile, 1300. London, The British Library (Ms. Or. 2737)

The Jews of the Diaspora tended to settle in communities that were confined to particular areas of the towns and cities they lived in. This bound the group together, made it easier for them to practice their religion, and gave them a certain amount of power that ensured their survival as an ethnic minority.

*Judería* (Jewry) is the generic name given to the districts where Jews lived in medieval Spain. Jewries which had the characteristic institutions and related community buildings (synagogue, school, ritual pool, cemetery, etc.) were called *aljamas*.[2] Other names were also used during the medieval period. In Catalonia Jewries were frequently known as *cal de los judíos*, a term that originates from the Hebrew expression *qal* or *qahal,* meaning meeting or congregation. In urban centers we find names such as Jewish quarter. A document from Gerona dated 1284 refers to the *"barri d'Israel."*[3] Jewries were often simply called "Israel."[4]

Given our current knowledge, it is practically impossible to paint an exact picture of life in the Jewish quarters during the almost fifteen hundred years the Jews lived in Spain. Historians have gone to great lengths to define and identify patterns in the layout and structure of the streets surrounding the principal buildings. However, the results are not very satisfactory and may never be, as there was probably never a particular type of structure that can be classified as specifically Jewish.[5]

## FROM TOWN DISTRICT TO CLOSED AND ISOLATED ENCLAVE

Various circumstances, many related to twentieth-century history, have given rise to the idea that the Jews of medieval Spain lived in ghettos. This opinion is supported by documents such as Doña Catalina's *Pragmática* of 1412 demanding that the Jews be isolated by confining them to a particular area of their respective towns. However, we should bear in mind that this was not a new idea, since similar laws had been systematically drawn up over the previous two centuries — which in itself indicates that they were not very effectively enforced. Even when Spain's Jewish communities were struggling to survive in the fifteenth century, the rules of 1412 were not actually put into practice. The provincial church synods found themselves obliged to issue constant reminders of the regulations establishing that Jews should live in separate communities. Even the Cortes (Parliament) of Toledo in 1480 reiterated these restrictions.

[1] Much of this chapter is based on the article by Clara Bango, "Un barrio de la ciudad: la judería," in *Memoria de Sefarad*, 2002, pp. 63–70.

[2] Muslims also had their own *aljama*. For a view of the Jewry as an urban area and its organization, in addition to the classical works by Cantera and Lacave cited frequently in this catalogue, a very interesting work on account of its interpretation of archaeological information is the short article by Izquierdo Benito, 1998, pp. 265–290.

[3] Planas, 2002, p. 58.

[4] The use of the generic term "Israel" to denote the Jews of a Spanish town/city or territory in the Middle Ages is frequently found in both Christian and Jewish documentary and narrative sources.

[5] The regulations drawn up by the Jewish authorities in this respect (water systems, size of streets and public areas) do not differ from the Christians' municipal laws.

The Jews lived in neighborhoods of their own which are difficult to define accurately. What started out merely as a preference for living together owing to their religious affinity often became an obligation imposed by the law from late Roman times onwards. The well-known letter of Bishop Severus of Minorca (418) mentions Christians and Jews living in different towns.[6]

In medieval Spain the obligation to live in separate districts applied to Jews, Muslims and Christians at various times, depending on the ruling power. A community generally occupied just one neighborhood, though in larger towns and cities it could extend to several districts. Throughout the Reconquest the Jewries of the formerly Muslim towns remained in the same location under Christian rule, as is the case of those of Cordoba and Tudela, to name two.

Owing to various aspects of relations between Christians and Jews, certain Jewries were moved to different parts of cities. Factors such as social tensions, economic interest, demographic movements, and constant pressure from the Church to isolate the Jews prompted these changes.

In the major cities and towns, the Jewish quarters had their own wall, which was built onto the wall surrounding the whole urban area. We know that some Jewries, as well as giving onto the neighboring Christian districts, had another gate leading out of the city, called the *puerta de los judíos* or Jews' gate.[7] The Jewries in Muslim territory were walled. In Islamic Toledo the Jewish population lived outside the Muslim and Mozarab Christian area in the "city of the Jews" or *madinat al-Yahud*, which, according to an Arab chronicler, had been walled in 820.[8]

The walls enclosing the Jewries were no different from those separating the various Christian districts that made up the urban centre. It is a well-known fact that certain economic or social disputes commonly led to violent clashes between Christian districts, requiring them to be protected by enclosures and palisades. Parish churches often became neighborhood bastions.

There is one aspect in which the fortifications of the Jewries differ from those of the Christian districts: documentary sources refer to the "Jews of the castle" living in Christian towns and cities. Some historians have taken this to mean that there were castles or fortress-like buildings within Jewries. Although the subject is confusingly dealt with by some specialists, what the term basically signifies is that the king's castle provided protection to "his Jews". By locating the Jewry close to the castle, the king's officials could easily protect the Jewish community. In other instances the Jews built their dwellings inside the fortress grounds. There are references to this as early as the twelfth century. Upon issuing charters for the Jewish *aljama*, Alfonso VIII granted the Jewish community the castle of Haro.[9] In 1170, the Jews of Tudela went to live in the grounds of the town's castle with the approval of King Sancho the Wise, who gave them permission to sell the houses they left behind in what had been their district.[10] The town thus came to have two Jewish quarters, an old one and a new one. Both coexisted for a time

[6] This situation is discussed in the chapter entitled "History of a Conflict."
[7] There are many documented cases of Jewry gates connecting the district to the rest of the city. The oldest are possibly those of Cordoba's Jewish quarter. Saragossa's city walls had a "Jews' gate." This arrangement is found in the Muslim towns and cities conquered by the Christians (Torres Balbás, 1985, I, pp. 210–211).
[8] Levi-Provençal, 1973, V, p. 127.
[9] González, 1960, doc. no. 962, pp. 660 *et seq.*
[10] Yanguas y Miranda, 1964, I, p. 516.

would have belonged to the synagogue complex. They required running water from a spring and drainage. The illustration of the *mikvah* in the so-called *Hispano-Moresque Haggadah*, a fourteenth-century Castilian work, showing women washing glass objects, recalls the atmosphere of the one at Besalú: an enclosed space with sturdy walls, stone arches, and a system for channelling the water.

### ALCAICERÍA

The *alcaicería* is a covered market of Muslim origin. These markets with stalls were regulated. They were only allowed in Jewries of a certain size. The Jewish shopkeepers originally rented establishments in the town *alcaicería*, along with Christians. However, over time, Jewish markets sprang up. The records often mention how many Jews attempted to set up their stalls outside the Jewry to make them more accessible to Christian customers. Miniatures and Gothic

"Pharmacy of a Jewish alfaqui," *Cantigas de Santa María*, fol. 155r, detail (facsimile edition of the copy held in the Biblioteca del Real Monasterio de San Lorenzo de El Escorial, Madrid)

paintings provide very enlightening illustrations of these shops: an alfaqui's
pharmacy, a shoe shop, a textiles warehouse, the workshop of a metalsmith, and
a "pawnbroker's."

## PUBLIC OVENS. UNLEAVENED BREAD

Documentary sources also mention the existence of ovens for baking bread in the
Jewish quarters. Although the wealthier members of society had their own ovens,
public ones were obviously required to cater to the needs of ordinary folk. For a
long time Jews shared the public oven with Christians. The dough was prepared
at home and then taken to the community oven to be baked;[44] this task was
normally carried out once a week.

The obligation to avoid leavened bread during the Passover called for *massah*
(matzo), an unleavened bread that is flattened or wafer shaped. This custom had
its origins in Exodus:

[44] Inventories of household furniture
refer to troughs for kneading dough.

Unleavened bread shall be eaten for seven days; no leavened bread shall be seen with you, and no leaven shall be seen with you in all your territory […] "It is because of what the Lord did for me when I came out of Egypt." (Exodus, 13: 7–9).

Bakers had to guarantee the purity of the process of making the unleavened bread, which began with harvesting and milling the grain. A seal confirmed that this had been carried out according to the regulations. One of these bronze seals with ears of corn and bird motifs has survived; they normally bore the following inscription in Hebrew:

In peace for seven days you shall eat unleavened bread.[45]

Several miniatures from the *Hispano-Moresque Haggadah* show a sequence of preparations for the Passover celebrations, including the kneading and decoration of the *massah* and its baking. The illustration of the baking shows an interesting genre scene inside a bakery with women holding the bread on wooden boards and men placing the dough in the oven. Despite the painter's technical shortcomings, both the oven and the shape and position of the baker's tools, and the decoration of the breads are depicted with expressive realism.

## BUTCHERS' SHOPS

Meat consumption was in accordance with the rules on things clean and unclean laid down in *Leviticus:*

> These are the living things which you may eat among all the beasts that are on the earth. "Whatever parts the hoof and is cloven-footed and chews the cud, among the animals, you may eat. Nevertheless among those that chew the cud or part the hoof, you shall not eat these: The camel, because it chews the cud but does not part the hoof, is unclean to you. And the rock badger, because it chews the cud but does not part the hoof, is unclean to you. And the hare, because it chews the cud but does not part the hoof, is unclean to you. And the swine, because it parts the hoof and is cloven-footed but does not chew the cud, is unclean to you. Of their flesh you shall not eat, and their carcasses you shall not touch; they are unclean to you." (Leviticus, 11: 2–8)

[45] Various seals of this kind survive. One of the best preserved is held in the Museu de la Vida Rural, L'Espluga de Francolí (Tarragona).

As long as Christians showed a tolerant attitude, Jews were able to put their rules on cattle and grazing into practice. Christian laws even banned herds of pigs from crossing or coming near Jewries.

In addition to abiding by the traditional rules on the slaughtering of cattle and sale of meats, Jews had to prepare their meat in accordance with religious criteria. The whole process was monitored, from selection of the animal to cooking. The slaughterman had to slit the animal's throat by making a sharp, clean incision in the jugular using a knife without notches in the blade. The "bleeding and slicing of the entrails" then followed. Bleeding was essential, since the Torah prohibited the consumption of blood: "Only be sure that you do not eat the blood" (Deuteronomy, 12: 23). The entrails had to be sliced open to check for disease, lesions, or defects. The Talmud established eight types of defects that made meat unfit for consumption.

The larger Jewries had a slaughterhouse where the slaughterer approved by the community performed this task. Nearby were tables where the meat was displayed to the public. One of the miniatures in the *Golden Haggadah* depicts one of these medieval butcher's shops.

Christians did not approve of this manner of handling meat. Indeed, it was described as abhorrent in the new laws of the *Fuero Juzgo:*

> The Jews err in their ways and uphold the bad law and are the dirtiest of the dirty, they leave some meats and eat others, separating some from others.[46]

On some occasions, particularly towards the end of the period, Jewish and Christian butchers sold meats to customers of different religions. Bearing in mind

[46] "Los judíos que son en yerro, é mantiene la mala ley, é son mas sucios que todas las suciedumbres, lexan las unas carnes, é comen las otras, departiendo las unas de las otras." (Ley VII).

**"Slaughtering and roasting the lamb,"**
***Rylands Haggadah,* fol. 19v, detail.**
**Manchester, John Rylands University**
**Library (Ms. Ryl. Hebr. 6)**

the theory set forth in the *Fuero,* it is not surprising that this practice was severely punished. The Madrid law code provides some information on the conditions under which meat could be sold to Jews:

> The butcher who sells the meat of the Jews, *trifá* or other meats that are exclusive to them, shall pay twelve *maravedíes* and, if he does not have the money, he shall be hanged.[47]

## TAVERN

The Valladolid *taqqanot* contain some information about Jewish taverns, which had to supply wine that was suitable for consumption by Jews:

[47] "El carnicero que vendiera carne propia de los judíos, trifá u otra carne alguna exclusiva de ellos, pague doce maravedíes, y si no los tuviere, sea ahorcado." (Quoted by Sánchez, 1963.)

That in places where ten or more heads of households live, they shall see to it that there is a tavern supplying kosher wine in their midst, both for them and for passers-by.[48]

These places were also appropriate settings for playing cards, dice, and other games. These sessions often ended in brawls, when players under the effects of alcohol were carried away by the excitement of the game.[49]

## SCHOOLS

One of the main concerns of the Jewish communities was the study of the Torah. The Valladolid *taqqanot*, the first chapter of which is devoted to this theme, bear witness to its importance:

> The first of our commandments and the principle of our *taqqanot* is to strengthen those who study our Torah, because the Torah is what sustains the world.[50]

The chapter goes on to provide measures to encourage children to study the Torah and to arrange for the payment of teachers. When referring to schools in the Jewries, we naturally mean establishments where the Torah was taught. These places were located near the synagogues.

In the village of Biel, the records refer to the public building used as a school as follows: "District of the synagogue with the house called the boys' school."[51] Nothing is known of these places, though we do possess a good knowledge of the rules and standards governing the organization of these schools. Girls did not attend; since they did not have to study the Torah, there was no need for them to learn Hebrew. Higher studies were at the *yeshiva* (academy of Talmudic learning) or at the rabbi's home.

These schools are often represented in *Haggadot* by a picture showing the rabbi Gamaliel and his pupils. The pupils are depicted sitting opposite their teacher, as in any modern school.

[48] "Que en el lugar do moran o moraren diez cabezas de familia o más, que fagan en manera que exista entre ellos taberna de vino kaser, asi pora ellos como pora los transeúntes." (Quoted by Moreno Koch, 1992, p. 65.)
[49] Blasco, 2002 (2), pp. 103–133 and p. 131.
[50] Ibid., pp. 21–23.
[51] "Barrio de la sinoga con la casa clamada la escuela de los mocetes." (Quoted in *El legado judío*, 2002, p. 88.)

# Household Items

S ome of the least familiar aspects of the day-to-day lives of Spanish Jews in the Middle Ages are their household items, in the broadest sense of the term.[1] We have a very complete collection of diplomatic accounts describing the various utensils of daily household life. Furthermore, the Spanish *Haggadot* provide a variety of information about the dining rooms and kitchens, and to a lesser extent the bedrooms, of Jewish households. In addition to these sources, archaeological excavations have provided us with numerous tableware and kitchenware items, some of which are in excellent condition.

Illustrations in the *Haggadot* give us a close look at the extraordinary Passover *seder* tables and the household kitchens as they prepare the food for the feast. The household's best dishes and platters are laid out on the table along with glasses, wine pitchers, knives, etc. These items look very similar to many of the pieces excavated at Teruel. However, in spite of the appearance of luxury that the painters of these miniatures wished to convey, these items pale by comparison with the gold and silver items used in the homes of some of the wealthier Jewish families. The silver plates and spoons of the Briviesca service are worthy of palatial surroundings, such as those depicted in the *Rylands Haggadah*.[2] These silver plates are the most important pieces of this type of Spanish medieval service in existence. Because so many objects made of precious metal were looted or used as collateral, few have survived to this day. Certainly the wealthiest Jews probably owned a set of gold plates such as the one depicted in the *Sarajevo Haggadah*. But as we descend the social scale, the quality of the ware decreases. Later on, we will examine the ceramic dishes that were typical of those used by the well-to-do classes as we deal with some of the more significant pieces from Teruel's Jewish quarter. The pieces found at Burgos are generally of lower quality. And further down the scale are the crude peasant utensils of ordinary earthernware or wood.

In illustrations depicting wealthier homes, the rooms that have been transformed into dining rooms contain very luxurious trappings. The room depicted in the illustration of the Passover *seder* of the *Barcelona Haggadah* is particularly attractive. There is a beautiful rich green cloth with gold decorative motifs hanging on the wall in the background. Many of these cloths were Oriental. Jews dominated the trade in these textiles in Christian cities.

The pictures from the so-called *Hispano-Moresque Haggadah* from the mid-fourteenth century give us a close view of a livelier folk atmosphere. Here we see various kitchen items: pots and pans, the large Spanish mortars used to grind nuts, spices, and wine in preparing the *kharoset*, and the large soup pots. Although we will

[1] Although sources are both numerous and very rich in information, experts in this field do not abound. Of great significance is the research by Martín, 1988, pp. 93–115 and 309–345. Brief, but with a good overall view, is the article by López Álvarez, 1998, pp. 219–246.
[2] We will examine this dishware and the silverware in the chapter on ceremonial feast day rituals (the Passover *seder*).

examine only ceramics in this chapter, the kitchens were certainly stocked with many metal utensils as well. This is apparent from the following description of the metal items in a fifteenth-century Aragonese Jewish kitchen:

> Six small skewers of iron, four pans, and one of copper, a small copper bowl for drinking water, old, a small pot about half a jug in size, made of copper with an iron handle, two iron spoons, a copper pot about half a jug in size, also a load of firewood, also a table with its feet [...] a chamber pot.[3]

Another type of miniature, Christian in origin, shows us various aspects of Jewish households: two men sitting playing chess in the garden of a house; the living room of a house; a wake scene in a bedroom with the family gathered around the corpse and a group of mourners; an office, etc. We find no overtly Jewish features in any of these rooms or their furniture, dishware, or household items, except for the occasional Star of David. This symbol is what identifies the bedroom of a Jew in one of the *Cantigas* of Alfonso X. This codex contains a number of illustrations of bedrooms, all of which are identical except for this one, which belongs to a Jew and is decorated with the star.

## JEWISH SYMBOLS AND MOTIFS ON OBJECTS

Excavations in Jewish quarters have provided us with a large number of household items. It would be impossible to classify most of them as Jewish simply by their markings, technique, material, shape, or iconography. Only a few can be tentatively identified as such by certain ambiguous iconographic motifs. We can identify the ceremonial lamps because of their obvious function.

[3] "Seis espedos de hierro, chicos, cuatro sartenes con una de alambre, chicas, una calderica chica de alambre, de beber agua, vieja, un calderuelo chico, demedio cántaro poco más o menos, de alalmbre con asa de hierro, dos cucharas de hierro, una olla de alambre, de medio cántaro poco más o menos, item una carga de lenya, item una tauleta con sus piedes [...] un orynal."

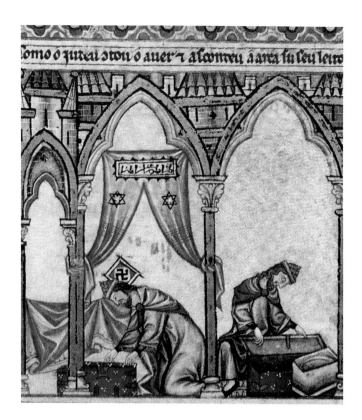

Cantigas de Santa María, fol. 39r
(facsimile edition of the copy held in
the Biblioteca del Real Monasterio de
San Lorenzo de El Escorial, Madrid)

We say ambiguous motifs because they were common to several religious cultures in medieval Spain. The Star of David was probably the most common symbol used by Jews, Moors, and Christians alike. The fleur-de-lis, a heraldic symbol sometimes associated with certain royal households, can be confusing and can prevent identification of an item as Jewish unless it is part of an identifiable context. The ceramic ware from Teruel's Jewish quarter displays a host of variations of this motif. The fleur-de-lis stands out elegantly and subtly against the white background of a small bowl, and is bold and expressionistic on another bowl. On the fragment of a late fourteenth-century Valencia platter, the fleur-de-lis is combined with a lion rampant, following a well-known heraldic model.[4]

The Jew's room illustrated in the *Cantigas* represents a paradigm within this universal language of symbols. The curtains are embroidered with the Star of David, and there is an inscription in what looks like Hebrew characters. On the bed is a cushion with a large embroidered swastika. The swastika symbol belongs to the family of crosses with curved or bent arms, used primarily by cultures with an astral god, or one that could not be depicted. This last characteristic led it to be used by Jews and Christians alike.

But in the case of the Valencia saltcellar[5], the symbols are so ambiguous that they are completely indecipherable, even to the experts, because there is no additional context. The bottom of the object is decorated with a design that could be interpreted as a *hamsa* or Hand of Fatima, with a Star of David on the palm. We might think that this was a typically Islamic item, but these symbols are also prevalent in Christian and Jewish iconography. The hand is an ancient iconographic device symbolizing the divinity that cannot be represented. The large size of the hand is a conventional representation of the importance of the presence that it symbolizes.

## TERUEL CERAMIC WARE

A considerable number of ceramic pieces that have been attributed to Jewish households[6] were unearthed in the area of Teruel's former Jewish quarter. Except for a few specific objects that are obviously Jewish because of their function or iconography, they are otherwise identical to items used by other Teruel households during the fourteenth and fifteenth centuries.[7]

[4] Found during excavation of the square of Teruel's Jewish quarter.

[5] This is either a saltcellar or spice bowl and is part of a set of tableware characteristic of fourteenth-century Valencia.

[6] Located in an area near the Alcázar Real.

[7] This type of ceramic ware was studied by Ortega, 2002.

Dish or carving platter, second half of fourteenth century. Teruel ceramic ware, green/purple series. From Teruel city centre. Teruel, Museo de Teruel (inv. no. 7156)

Bowl, mid fourteenth-mid fifteenth century. Ceramic. From the cloister of the church of San Pedro in Teruel. Teruel, Museo de Teruel (inv. no. 7577)

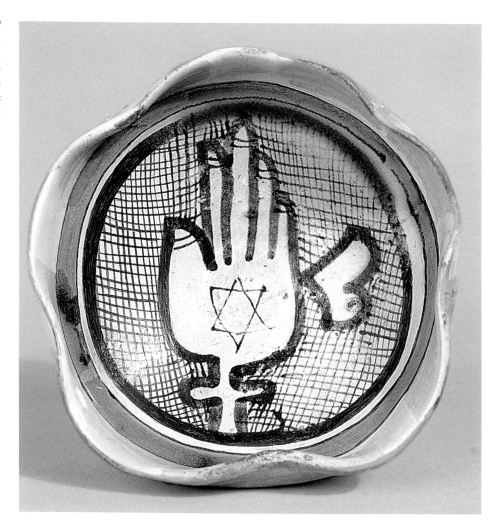

These sets of ceramic ware include pieces that were made for storing or transporting foodstuffs, such as unglazed, painted jugs, although there are also a number of glazed green and honey-colored pieces. The most important kitchen utensils are the round red-glazed pots, glazed bowls, and lead-glazed pots for collecting fat from roasting meat.

The main pieces of tableware are dishes, spice containers, bowls, and carving platters. The dishes, which were used for soups and broths, measure between 14 and 15 centimeters (5.5 to 6 inches) in diameter. The earliest pieces, from the thirteenth and fourteenth centuries, are decorated in the characteristic greens and purples of Teruel ware. Schematic floral patterns are very common. Some of the most impressive objects on account of the subtle effects achieved with minimum resources are the bowls decorated with simple green strokes on a white background.

The shape of the plates used for carving or slicing meats (beef, poultry, or fish) is very characteristic of the fourteenth century. These large pieces, between 27 and 34 centimeters (10.5 to 13 inches) in diameter, are completely covered with decorative

Dish or carving platter, second half of fourteenth century. Teruel ceramic ware, green/purple series. From the site of the Archivo Provincial de Teruel. Teruel, Museo de Teruel (inv. no. 5053)

Bowl, late fifteenth century. Teruel ceramic ware, blue series. From the Plaza de la Judería, Teruel. Teruel, Museo de Teruel (inv. no. 5297)

Bowl, late fourteenth century. Teruel ceramic ware, green/purple series. From the Casa del Judío, Plaza de la Judería, Teruel. Teruel, Museo de Teruel (inv. no. 2225)

Plate, second half of fifteenth century. Teruel ceramic ware, blue series. From Teruel city center. Teruel, Museo de Teruel (inv. no. 7710)

Dish or carving platter (fragment), late fourteenth century. Ceramic. From the Plaza de la Judería. Teruel, Museo de Teruel (inv. no. 5290)

Bowl, late fifteenth century. Teruel ceramic ware, blue series. From the Plaza de la Judería, Teruel. Teruel, Museo de Teruel (inv. no. 5298)

Mortar, late fourteenth–early fifteenth century. Teruel ceramic ware, green/purple series. From Calle Amantes, nos. 15–17–19, Teruel. Teruel, Museo de Teruel (inv. no. 18452)

Jug with spout, second half of fifteenth century. Teruel ceramic ware, green/purple series. From Teruel city center. Teruel, Museo de Teruel (inv. no. 7317)

Mortar, late fifteenth century. Teruel ceramic ware, green/purple series. From the Plaza de la Judería, Teruel. Teruel, Museo de Teruel (inv. no. 5251)

Pot, thirteenth-early fourteenth century. Common ceramic kitchenware. From Santa María la Blanca (Burgos). Burgos, Museo de Burgos (inv. no. 8.796/11.2)

Pot, thirteenth-early fourteenth century. Common ceramic kitchenware. From Santa María la Blanca (Burgos). Burgos, Museo de Burgos (inv. no. 8.796/11.1)

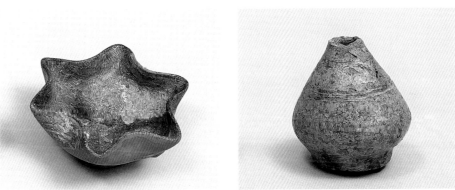

Lobed bowl, fourteenth century. Glazed ceramic tableware. From Santa María la Blanca (Burgos). Burgos, Museo de Burgos (inv. no. 8.796/16.1)

Ointment jar (?), fourteenth century. Glazed ceramic. From Santa María la Blanca (Burgos). Burgos, Museo de Burgos (inv. no. 8.796/17.2)

designs which are far more intricate than those found on the other pieces of tableware. The designs are remotely Oriental in origin. In fourteenth-century Spain, these motifs were not unusual and had been used in Christian and Muslim designs for centuries.[8] Eloquent examples of this are the basilisk on one of the most well-known carving platters and another piece depicting two birds with outspread wings pecking at a tree. Gazing at these objects, we might think that the craftsman experienced a kind of *horror vacui* and filled every available space with logical or gratuitous decorative motifs. Actually, the lavish embellishment was intended to disguise the effects of wear on the plate from cutting meat. The Passover *seder* tables illustrated in the *Hagaddot* usually show only one utensil, the knife, which was used by the diners to cut their meat on the platter; they would then eat the slice of meat with their fingers.

The mortars had to be very strong to withstand the stress of grinding foodstuffs. Some of them had spouts for drainage, while others did not. Their cup shape is very characteristic of fourteenth-century ware.

According to various illustrations, the vessels used for liquids were made of ceramic, metal, or glass. The Teruel finds include only ceramic. Aside from

[8] The claim that this is Moresque decoration is therefore absolutely unfounded and distorts the reality of Spanish culture.

Jug/pitcher, fourteenth century. Glazed ceramic tableware with teardrop decoration. From Santa María la Blanca (Burgos). Burgos, Museo de Burgos (inv. no. 8.796/18)

conventional pitchers, there are also several pitchers that appear to have been modeled after metal pitchers, with round bodies, truncated cone-shaped necks, flat handles, and protruding spouts.

The presence at this site of ceramic pieces from nearby Valencia with characteristically Jewish decorative motifs can be explained by their having been imported as ceremonial objects specially manufactured for the Jewish community. This fragment could therefore be from a Passover *seder* platter.

## POTS FROM THE JEWISH QUARTER OF BURGOS[9]

The ceramic wares discovered in Burgos were discarded objects used as fill during the building of the church of Santa María la Blanca in the heart of the Jewish quarter of the so-called Villavieja (Old City). The church was built at the end of the fourteenth century during a period of decline in the Jewish quarter, which subsequently became a Christian neighborhood.

These pieces are a type of ceramic ware that was very popular in Castile in the second half of the fourteenth century. Here we do not encounter the fleurs-de-lis or stars as at Teruel. Only the fragments of ceremonial lamps are typically Jewish. The Burgos ceramics comprise cheap, metal-glazed dishes, or higher-quality ones with honey-colored glazes and engraved designs. Common kitchenware is represented by typically shaped pots. The most interesting items are a series of small green glass objects: a lobed dish and an attractive, teardrop-shaped ointment jar with engraved bands.

A particularly important pitcher, of which unfortunately only a few fragments remain, is more refined in its decoration. This piece was cast in a mould and is light green (lead glaze); its surface is covered with large teardrop shapes that create a swollen effect. Although distant origins have been suggested for pieces of this type, they are in fact simply a well-known variation of the techniques and shapes produced in Castile during that period.

There are also a number of amusing small metal-glazed items that scholars describe as toys. The money box and the little jug barely six centimeters (2.5 inches) high suggest children's playthings from the Jewish quarter. These items are no different from similar toys used by the city's Christian children.

[9] A study of the Jewish sites and an analysis of the discoveries can be found in Ortega Martínez, 2002, pp. 133–140.

# Personal Appearance

Judging by certain images of Jews in medieval Christian art, we might think that the Jews adopted a particular look that made them easily identifiable. We might term these clichéd depictions the "image of the other" — Jews as they were seen through the biased eyes of the Christian population.[1] The iconography shows a caricature-like stereotype that allows us to identify them as Jews immediately without requiring any further explanations: particular facial features (prominent nose, black beard), a pointed hat, etc. Such are the Jews depicted in collections of images like the *Cantigas* and the *Libro de Ajedrez*, not to mention other traditional legal works such as the *Vidal mayor* or strictly religious works such as illustrated bibles. This chapter will deal with real image of the Spanish Jews, that which they adopted voluntarily or otherwise.

Although at times they had to wear a mark or endured restrictions imposed by law on their dress or physical appearance, generally speaking nothing in their attire or adornments distinguished Jews from the rest of the society they lived in. They adapted totally to the prevailing Islamic or Christian environment of the time.

## A MARKED PEOPLE

At some point, Christians and Muslims decided that the Jews should be easily identifiable.[2]

One of the many restrictive measures imposed on the European Jews by the fourth Lateran Council (1215) was the obligation to wear badges or different clothing from the rest of society to make them distinguishable in public. Unlike the rest of Europe, the Spanish kingdoms were highly reluctant to accept this rule, which popes Innocent III and Gregory IX were so eager to enforce. Indeed, it was always applied very laxly in Castile.

James I of Aragon had asked the pope to excuse the Jews in his kingdom from complying with the Lateran rule of wearing a distinctive sign, since they were perfectly recognizable by their clothing. Honorius III replied to the archbishop of Tarragona and his bishops that, so long as Christians and Jews could be distinguished by their dress, the Jews need not bear any distinctive sign.[3] In 1233 pope Gregory IX urged King Sancho VII, the Strong, to compel the Jews of Navarre to dress differently from the Christians.[4]

[1] See the section entitled "Image of the Other" in the chapter on "History of a Conflict."

[2] This section will deal with the signs imposed by the religious and civil laws of the Spanish Christians, though there were also prohibitions of this type in Muslim al-Andalus: Lévi-Provençal discusses them in his history book.

[3] "*Eos* [judíos] *a christianis habitus sic distinguit*" (Honorius III's bull of 1220, Carrasco *et al.* 1994, vol. 1, doc. no. 61). See the section on "Church versus Synagogue."

[4] Ibid., doc. no. 62.

[5] "Cómo los judíos deben andar señalados porque sean conocidos. Muchos yerros et cosas desaguisadas acaecen entre los cristianos et los judíos et las cristianas et las judías, porque viven et moran de so uno en las villas, et andan vestidos los unos así como los otros. Et por desviar los yerros et los males que podrien acaecer por esta razón, tenemos por bien et mandamos que todos quantos judíos et judías vivieren en nuestro señorío, que trayan alguna señal cierta sobre las cabezas, que sean atal porque conozcan las gentes manifiestamente quál es judío o judía. Et si algunt judío non levase aquella señal, mandamos que peche por cada vegada que fuese fallado sin ella diez maravedis de oro; et si non hobiere de que los pechar, reciba diez azotes públicamente por ello," *Partida*, VII, título XXV, ley XI.

[6] For more information on the distinctive marks Jews were made to wear, see the section on the "Image of the Other."

[7] "Que los judíos e las judías que troguiessen ssinal de pano amariello enlos pechos e enlas espaldas ssegunt lo trayan en Francia, porque andassen conocidos entre los cristianos e las cristianas."

[8] The Council of Arles (1235) established the round yellow badge measuring four fingers in diameter that became widespread in Europe.

[9] Although, as we have seen, James I opposed the use of these signs, they began to be worn in his kingdom at the end of the thirteenth century.

[10] ("Teneantur in veste superiori rotulam panni coloris dissimilis dicte vesti consuram portari"), Carrasco *et al.*, 1994, doc. nos. 214 and 215.

[11] *Llibre dels privilegis*, 1988, privilegio del Rey Pedro, no. 144, p. 182.

[12] Owing to security problems, the Aragonese Jews were exempted from wearing the sign by Alfonso the Magnanimous: "quels jueus e juyhias no porten roda per cami per esquivar peril."

[13] "Que en aquellas partes donde los judíos no llevaren a la presente tan claro y manifiesto el signo referido, como disponemos en esta constitución, lo muestren eminente, fijo y partido de color rojo y amarillo, los varones en el traje ó prenda exterior sobre el pecho," Amador de los Ríos, 1875–76, pp. 983–984.

In Castile and León the papal rules were known and acknowledged in the *Partidas*, of which law no. 11 is devoted entirely to this issue:

> How the Jews must be marked so that they be recognized.
> Many faults and unjust things occur between Christian and Jewish men and between Christian and Jewish women, because they live and dwell as one in towns and dress like each other. And in order to avoid the faults and evils which could occur for this reason, we consider and order that all Jews and Jewesses living in our domain wear some sign on their heads so that people may know clearly who is a Jew or Jewess. And if any Jew should not wear that sign, we order that for every time he be found without it he pay ten gold *maravedís*; if he is unable to pay, he shall receive ten lashes in public.[5]

The lawmakers say that the Jews must wear a sign on their heads, but do not indicate what kind.[6] The idea was to prevent Christians from mingling with Jews owing to an inability to identify them. These rules were not put into practice in Castile and León, for at the beginning of the fourteenth century, the meeting of the Cortes in Palencia (1313) demanded of the king that Jews be made to wear distinctive clothing as they did in France:

> That Jewish men and women wear a badge of yellow cloth on their chests and backs as they did in France, so that they could be distinguished from Christian men and women.[7]

The sign that the Cortes was calling for is a *"roella."*[8] This is the circular badge that European Jews and those of Navarre and Aragon had worn since the thirteenth century.[9] James II of Aragon exempted his physician Ezmel de Ablitas, a Navarrese Jew, and his family from the obligation to wear the *"rotula panni"* as a sign of their religion".[10] We find various descriptions of what the badge should look like. It was the size of the palm of the hand, and yellow and red in color.[11] There is even mention of Jews wearing a round cape and a hood. The rules for the Jews of Valencia establish that they are to be worn "in the same way that the Jews of Barcelona wear them."

So often were the Jews exempted from having to wear their badges[12] that the regulations were constantly reiterated. Benedict XIII stressed this in his famous anti-Jewish bull of 1415:

> That in those parts where the Jews do not wear the sign as clearly as established in this canon, the men shall display it clearly and securely in red and yellow on the front of their clothing or outer garment.[13]

Indeed, we find so many repetitions of these orders and express references to the failure of the Jews in Castile to comply with the laws on identification that it is

[14] Concerned to prevent carnal knowledge between Christians and Jews, the ecclesiastical authorities stressed the need for compliance with the regulation at the councils. The following canon of the Council of Ávila in 1481 illustrates this very well: "Because in some parts, Jews and Moors should be distinguished from Christians by their different clothing" Christians mistakenly "know Jewish and Moorish women and Moors and Jews know Christian women." So that there could be no excuse the synod established "that henceforth all Jews and Moors shall wear signs, the Jews red ones, as is customary, and the Moors yellow hoods with blue crescents and their women blue cloth crescents." (Quoted in *Sinodicon Hispanaum,* 1993, p. 204.)

[15] A bull issued by Sixtus IV, in 1484, expresses the pope's displeasure at the failure to comply with rules on Jews in Spain: "In the kingdoms of Spain, and particularly in the province of Andalusia, Jews and Saracens lived together with Christians and wear the same kind of clothing as them." (Martínez Díez, 1998.)

[16] "E mandamos otrosy que traygan continuamente la dicha señal de paño bermejo en el ombro derecho según que enlas leyes antes desta se contiene." Title III (Book Eight) is devoted entirely to Jews and Moors.

[17] "Capirotes con chías luengas."

[18] "Las chias cortas fasta un palmo, fechas á manera de embuo é á tuerto cosidas, todas en derredor fasta la punta," "Pragmática de la Reina Doña Catalina, Gobernadora del Reino durante la minoridad de Don Juan II, sobre el encerramiento de los judíos de Castilla y régimen de las juderías." (Quoted in Amador de los Ríos, 1875–76, pp. 965–970.)

[19] "E otrosí que trayan sobre las ropas ençima tabardos con aletas, é non trayan mantones." The rules set out in the Montalvo code make similar statements about headgear and tabards.

[20] "Que todas las judías [...] trayan mantos grandes fasta los piés [...] e trayan las cabezas cobiertas con los dhos mantos doblados."

[21] "Non se fagan nin manden façer las barbas á nabajas nin a á tixera, salvo que las trayan largas, como les creciere, ni se cercenen nin corten los cabellos; é que anden, segun antiguamente solian andar." "Pragmática...," no. 18.

most likely that this practice was very limited. Provincial synods repeatedly stress the need for compliance with the rules,[14] and even the pope is called upon on occasions to ensure that they are abided by.[15] Although they were far from observed in practice, the rules came to be reiterated almost automatically in the various law codes at the end of the Middle Ages, as the Montalvo *Ordenamiento* of 1484 illustrates:

> And we furthermore order that they constantly wear the badge of crimson cloth on their right shoulders as established in the laws prior to this one.[16]

## BENEATH THE JEWS' HABIT

The previous section examined the badge that marked and identified the Jews. However, there were also a number of rules on the type of clothing they were supposed to wear and their physical appearance. Taking as a reference the stereotypical images that had gradually taken shape on the basis of the Holy Scriptures and the longstanding Church/Synagogue controversy, some ecclesiastical authorities attempted to have the Jews dress in a particular type of attire and established specific rules for their beards and hairstyles.

In the thirteenth century French Jews were forced to wear a round cape which was soon introduced in the kingdom of Aragon. The *capa rotunda* or *redondel*, as it was called, included a hood. Similar rules in Castile refer to an overgarment and headgear, but the repeated issuing of these rules suggests that little attention was paid to them.

As for their headgear, according to the rules enacted by Doña Catalina, Jews were not allowed to wear long *capirotes* (hoods)[17] though shorter *capirotes* were permitted provided that the sides hung down as far as "a palm's breadth, were funnel shaped and stitched together on the wrong side as far as the tip."[18] The outfit was completed with an outer garment: "and furthermore over their clothing they shall wear tabards with sleeves and they shall not wear mantles."[19]

Doña Catalina's regulations also refer to women:

> All Jewesses [...] shall wear long mantles down to their feet [...] and cover their heads with the said folded mantles.[20]

As for hairstyle, the rules were inspired by what were assumed to be ancient laws:

> They shall not shave or trim their beards, but wear them long, as they grow naturally; nor shall they trim or cut their hair; and they shall go about as they did in ancient times.[21]

## THE IMAGE OF DIGNITY

Among the Jews there was always a select minority with a sense of ethics and dignity regarding their personal appearance. Despite their wealth and social position, their appearance was sober and discreet. In a dialogue between the most prominent members of the late-medieval Spanish Jewry and their king, the latter reproaches these Jews for their arrogance and for the fact that they dress like free men. The following reply given by the famous Benveniste the Elder provides a very interesting insight into the appearance of Jewish dignitaries of the time: "Our King, have you ever seen me, your vassal, even when I have all the affairs of Castile on my hands, dressed in silken robes?"

The reply of the delegates of the *aljamas,* Abraham Benveniste, Yosef Nasí, and R Samuel ben Susén, is very similar: "We, messengers of your people and the richest members of our people, although it is only fitting to don rich clothing in the presence of the king, come in cheap black robes."[22]

This dialogue, skilfully written by Solomon ben Verga, clearly illustrates two truths, one obvious and the other more subtle: while one group of Jews complies with the rules on personal appearance, one infers from the king's words that those who enjoy a certain status dress like the rest of the population. Benveniste and his colleagues show they are responsible subjects by abiding by the rules on luxury and the constraints imposed on them even when in the king's presence.[23]

The pictures of Rabbi Moses Arragel of Guadalajara in the *Alba Bible* convey the spirit of law-abiding dignity that Solomon ben Verga attributes to the royal envoys: no matter how solemn the event in which he is participating, he is

[22] This dialogue is recreated by Solomon ben Verga in one of his well-known works. Here it is cited from Baer, 1998, p. 699.

[23] The next section examines sumptuary laws. As part of the general restrictions on dress, in the case of the Jews, these also applied when they were in the presence of the king: several provincial synods establish that when the Jews go to welcome the monarch, only the person bearing the Torah may wear rich garments. The Montalvo code also refers to these measures: "henceforth when Jews go out to receive us they shall not wear linen vestments over their clothing except for he who carries the Torah."

"Interior of a synagogue," *Barcelona Haggadah,* fol. 65v, Barcelona, 1350. London, The British Library (Ms. Add. 14761)

depicted wearing a simple tunic and purple mantle with the red circular badge as laid down by the rules.

Extant fourteenth-century illustrations of Jews at the synagogue in both Hebrew and Christian works show them dressed, as the rules established, in long tunics and roomy mantles that are sometimes worn over their heads. Curiously enough, although the artist has taken a certain amount of care in depicting the voluminous mantles, these are not the characteristic *taled* — the compulsory attire in European synagogues during the period.[24]

### ON ADORNMENTS AND ELEGANCE IN DRESS

Considering the regulations compelling Jews to wear distinctive clothing, the image of dignity sought by certain groups, and the garments required during services at the synagogue, one might conclude that Jews were not interested in

24 A white woollen shawn, with eight-strand fringes, also woollen, hanging from each corner.

fashion, luxury, or enhancing their personal appearance with jewelry and adornments. However, this was not the case. Men and women followed the fashions of the society they lived in. Perhaps the Muslim domination of al-Andalus marked a decisive step in this direction. Like literary tastes, culture in general became deeply Islamicized during this period. In many instances this caused Jews to shed some of the characteristic features of their tradition and to cultivate a taste for material possessions and sensuality. This is clearly displayed in the practice and customs of Jewish dwellings and dress. In one of his poems, Abraham ibn Ezra (1089–1164) of Tudela conveys the clichés on the attitudes of the communities:

> The poems of the Ishmaelites, on love and pleasures
> Those of the Christians, on wars and vengeance [...]
> Those of the Israelites, canticles and praises to the Lord of the armies.[25]

The poet is not aware how untrue this is of Hebrew poetry during the Muslim rule. The woman described in the following lines by the poet Todros Abulafia (1247–1306), although in a very beautiful figurative language, shows a desire to take great care over her personal appearance down to the slightest detail, including makeup to emphasize her sensuality:

> She painted her eyes with the black [ash] of my [scorched] heart;
> The luster of her teeth she took from the pearls of my tears;
> She painted her face in white and crimson
> With my greying hair and the blood of my entrails.[26]

Their contact with Islam led Jewish women to cover their heads with mantles. This distinguished them so clearly in public that, as we have seen, the Christian religious laws compelled them to dress in this manner in public regularly. The Muslims' veiled women also influenced Jewish attitudes. The fact that Jewish women showed their faces in public was considered improper in some periods and social environments of medieval Sepharad, as this poem demonstrates:

> Her face is like the genitals exposed publicly, / which must be covered with shawls and veils.[27]

The appearance of the couple illustrated in the *Rylands Haggadah* speaks for itself about the ideal of elegance that many Jews aspired to. They have donned their finest clothing to celebrate the Passover feast. The attire of both the man and the woman show the same sensuality that Todros's poem conveys. However, such pride in one's appearance was not merely vanity or presumptuousness — which it obviously could have been — but also a religious recommendation: "The glory of God is in men and

25 I quote from Sâenz-Badillos, 1991, p. 149.
26 I quote from Rosen, 1998, p. 128.
27 Ibid.

**"Passover scene,"** *Rylands Haggadah,*
**fol. 19v, detail. Manchester, John Rylands**
**University Library (Ms. Ryl. Hebr.)**

the glory of men is in their dress" (Yevamot, 63 b). A fourteenth-century father advised his sons:

> Accustom yourselves and your wives, sons, and daughters to always wear beautiful and appropriate clothing, in order that God and men may honor you.[28]

The golden buttons and headdress of the Rylands lady give an idea of the richness of the courtly attire for a woman of the time, no matter what religion she belonged to. The same can be said of the Jewish nobleman who assists the poor during the Passover preparations shown in the *Golden Haggadah*. It has sometimes been said that these pictures are not lifelike depictions of Jews but conventional illustrations borrowed from Christian art. I have no doubt that the Jews followed the fashions for their particular social class; the extant material evidence does not contradict the images or prove me wrong.[29] Further on, in the section on archaeology, we will see the tomb of a Teruel Jew who, like fourteenth- or fifteenth-century Christians of a certain social status, was buried with gold rings with gemstones adorning each finger of his left hand and a silver ring on his right hand. The archaeological finds at Briviesca known as the Tesorillo I include somewhat less flamboyant versions of the elegant gold buttons worn by the Rylands lady.

The restrictions imposed on the luxury of Jewish dress have been referred to on many occasions. In order to analyze this subject properly, we should bear in mind that such restrictions were also applicable to Christians. These rules sprang from thirteenth- to fifteenth-century economic and fiscal policy.[30] Although at times the political theory underpinning these rules was used to bolster specific anti-Jewish measures, they were generally observed by Jewish and Christians society alike.

The oldest references, which date from the thirteenth century, illustrate the restrictions on types of cloth.[31] The Jews who drew up the Valladolid *taqqanot* of 1432 provide us with very clear information on the garments worn during that period and the related restrictions. The justification for these restrictive laws was the same for both Christians and Jews, and the type of clothing mentioned is identical to that of any Christian household of similar status.[32] What kind of textiles are we referring to? What sort of jewelry and adornments? Judging by the following description, the clothing and accessories worn by the Rylands lady and

[28] Metzger and Metzger, 1982, p. 149.
[29] Leafing through the illustrations found in the Hebrew codices, we find that the types of dress worn by the different classes in Jewish society are fully consonant with those worn by the equivalent groups in Christian society.
[30] Sempere and Guariños, 1788.
[31] Cortes of Valladolid (1258) and Jerez (1268).
[32] See the excellent edition of these rules by Moreno Koch, 1987.

Shields (possibly buttons). Gilded silver. From Tesorillo I, found at Briviesca in 1938, near the current cemetery. Burgos, Museo de Burgos (inv. no. 735)

Shields (possibly buttons). Gilded silver. From Tesorillo I, found at Briviesca in 1938, near the current cemetery. Burgos, Museo de Burgos (inv. no. 736)

the wealthy Jew of the *Golden Haggadah* would have been classified as ostentatious according to the criteria of the sumptuary laws:

> Women shall not wear golden or oriental cloth or sendal or silk or camlet, and their clothing shall not bear linings of rich or golden or oriental cloth, nor shall they wear brooches of gold or jewels, or pearls, or strings of pearls adorning their foreheads, or a train that trails longer than thirteen *varas*, etc.[33]

The list of fabrics and garments continues, ending with the statement that certain ornaments are allowed, but of limited weight: "silver and enamel brooches and ribbons of silver or anything else, as long as each one of them weighs no more than four ounces."[34] But there were also exceptions to these rules: young people or during solemn events as "in times of rejoicing or receiving the lord or lady, or at dances."[35]

The laws were equally restrictive on the adornments of horses' tack and knights' costume: "saddle with a border of neither gold nor silver."[36] Further restrictions refer to the "harness of neither gold nor silver, and spurs of neither gold nor silver."[37]

[33] "Las mujeres no debían vestirse de paño de oro nin de azeituni nin de çendal nin de seda nin de camelote nin traya en su ropa forradura de pania rica, nin de paño de oro, nin de azeituni; ni traya brochadura de oro, nin nin de aljófar, ni sartal de aljófar puesto al comienzo de la frente, ni cola en ropa alguna que arrastre mas de treçea de vara de medir, etc."

[34] "Brochadura de plata e esmaltes de plata e çintas de plata o cualquier cosa de ello, de manera que aya en cada cosa dellas fasta peso de cuatro onças e non más," "Capítulo Quinto acerca del vestir" (Ibid., pp. 93–95).

[35] "En tiempo de alegrías o recibimiento de señor o señora, nin en danças."

[36] "Siella de barba dorada nin argentada," Cortes of Valladolid, 1258.

[37] "Freno dorado nin argentado, nin espuelas doradas nin argentadas," Cortes of Jérez, 1268.

To give an idea of the objects that would have made up a late-fifteenth-century Jewish trousseau, the following extract lists the items sold at an auction in Granada according to a document dated 8 September 1495. The variety of materials is perfectly in keeping with the objects one would expect to find among Christians:

> Fine scarlet silk bed linen embroidered in fine gold thread. Another set made of colored silk. Some blue braid used to fasten small pearl buttons. A trimmed silk *hamya*. A blouse with trimming, all in yellow silk. A yellow *farba*. Another red *farba*. A silk *namat* as a bedspread. Four silken girdles of which those with gold are called *many*. An *adud* of six silk tassels, with pearl. Another without a pearl, all in silk. Two 19-carat gold earrings. A large gold ring with a coarse stone that is worthless. Another ring with a false turquoise. Another ring with a seal with 22-carat gold enamel. Another ring with a stone that is worthless. Another cheap ring that looks like gold but is tin, with a glass imitation gem. Four 18-carat enameled beads. A 21-carat golden bead without enamel. Two more 16-carat gold beads without enamel. Two 18-carat gold tubular beads without enamel that are called *tutes* and ten grains of gold. A small skein of gold thread, old. A piece of silver earring. Laces with silver adornments. Two more laces like the aforementioned. Set of headgear with golden spur, all old.[38]

## DECORATIVE ARCHAEOLOGICAL PIECES

The items listed in this short archaeological catalogue are a good illustration of the Jewish trousseaus that have survived to this day. However, the problem is that what has survived is by no means representative of the valuable pieces owned by the great families of Sephardic Jews.

While the information gleaned from historical documents provides an insight into the types of costume worn by the Jews, which, as we have seen, were not at all different from those of the Christians, we generally have a very limited knowledge of their jewelry and adornments. Museums are beginning to acquire a fair number of gold and silver objects that originally belonged to Jews, but the quality of the materials and the workmanship is not very high. All these pieces hail from archaeological digs which have unearthed tombs and hoards stashed away for fear they would be stolen.

Excavations of Jewish burial sites have long been carried out in Spain. Twentieth-century finds have supplied us with a good deal of personal items. However, we should recall that, although for pious and sentimental reasons, people were buried with some of their most treasured possessions, the family kept the most valuable precious metal items. Although the results of these digs are

[38] "Una ropa de carmesí de grana de lavores con alcarchofas de oro fino. Otra axedría de zarzahán. Unos cordones azules que eran los botones de aljófar menudo. Una hamya de seda orillada. Una aljuba con orillas toda de seda amarilla. Una farba amarilla. Otra farba colorada. Una namat de seda como colcha. Quatro çeñidores de seda que llaman many del de con oro. Un adud de seys borlas de seda, con aljófar. Otro sin aljófar todo de seda. Dos çarçellos de oro de XIX quilates. Una sortija de oro grande con una piedra çamorra que no vale nada. Otra sortija con una turquesa falsa. Otra sortija de un sello con un esmalte de oro de XXII quilates. Otra sortija con una gorgoça que no vale nada. Otra sortijuela que paresçie de oro y salió de latón, con un doblete de visrio. Quatro quentas esmaltadas de a XVIII quilates. Una quenta de oro sin esmaltar que es de XXI quilates. Otras dos quentas de oro sin esmaltar de XVI quilates. Dos canutos de oro sin esmaltes que se llamen tutes de a XVIII quilates e dies granos de oro. Una madexuela de oro de baçin hilado, vieja. Un pedaço de çarçillo de plata. Unos cordones con perillos de plata. Otros dos cordones como los susodichos. Unas cabeçadas con una espuela dorada, vieja todo." (Quoted in Martínez Ruiz, 1977–79, pp. 357–367.) For an analysis of Jewish inventories to glean information on personal and household items, see López Álvarez, 1998, pp. 219–246.

**Set of seven pins, twelfth-thirteenth century. Bronze. From the Cerro de los Judíos necropolis, Deza (Soria). Soria, Monasterio de San Juan de Duero, medieval section of the Museo Numantino (inv. nos. 81/1/614–620)**

often a matter of luck, the burial sites do at least indicate the size of the Jewish quarter in question. The excavations at the cemetery of the modest Jewry of Deza (Soria), located by the wall, unearthed a very paltry selection of funerary objects. Jewish women were buried with their hair fastened by modest bronze pins. The coarsely made silver and bronze jewels of Deza are a far cry from those of the wealthy Jews buried in larger Jewish quarters such as those of Teruel and Barcelona.

The items discovered in family hoards are a different matter. The fourteenth century witnessed very hard times for the Jews. When rioting occurred for days on end, they feared not only for their lives but also for their estates, particularly their money and valuable objects. Families would hastily fling all their valuables into an earthenware jar and bury it. On occasions, the violent death of all the members of a family prevented them from retrieving their hoard, which remained hidden until unearthed by chance. Of these treasures, those found in the town of Briviesca in Burgos are particularly outstanding.[39]

Briviesca's Jewry sided with King Peter of Castile in his dispute with the pretender Henry of Trastámara. The quarrel ended in the assault and destruction of the Jewish quarter in spring 1366. Trastámara's troops stormed into the quarter, unleashing a bloodbath and leaving behind them a trail of destruction, which is dramatically described by ancient historians:

> They slaughtered the holy and innocent community of Briviesca [...] of the two hundred patriarchs who lived there not a single one remains, and they fed their corpses to the birds of the skies and to the beasts of the earth.[40]

These gruesome events spurred some members of the Jewish community to conceal their treasures to prevent them being stolen. Some owners did not survive to retrieve them, and several findings were made during the twentieth century, known by archaeologists as the Tesorillos ("little hoards") of Briviesca. Tesorillo I was unearthed in 1938; it is comprised of the jewelry described at the end of the chapter, plates from a silver dinner service, and a considerable number of coins.[41] Tesorillo II was found when a street was dug up in 1985. Tesorillo III was discovered in 1988 during the course of road works. This third find contains coins and, in particular, four silver plates and two spoons. Some scholars believe that the first of these treasures was concealed by a family, while the second consists of ritual vessels used at a synagogue. I believe that both are family treasures. We will return to this theme when we deal with Passover.

How do we classify metalwork items as Jewish? There are only two reasonably reliable grounds for classifying an object as Jewish metalwork: excavation from a Jewish cemetery; and the presence of Hebrew inscriptions. Certain symbols are also taken as indications — six-pointed stars (*Magen David*) — though these are

[39] The third most economically powerful Jewish community in the province after Burgos and Pancorbo, according to the *Padrón de Huete* (census).

[40] For an up-to-date view on the Tesorillos de Briviesca see Castillo, 2002b, pp. 181-185.

[41] Jewelry and coins (298) found inside a copper vessel which was buried one meter beneath the ground in the center of a room.

Lot of 298 copper coins and four reales of Peter I. From the Tesorillo I, found at Briviesca in 1938, near the current cemetery. Burgos, Museo de Burgos (no. inv. 8850/1)

also found on Christian or Muslim objects.[42] In this connection, the colored bronze belt clasp and horse's bit which have been classified as Jewish could hail from the other medieval Spanish cultures. At any rate, they are not of fine quality. On the other hand, the surviving illustrations and other documentary sources indicate that a large number of Jews engaged in different types of metalwork and that their products were greatly appreciated by medieval society. It is therefore quite likely that some medieval Christian pieces of metalwork are actually Jewish, and vice versa. We should bear this in mind when viewing the following objects:

### RINGS AND SEALS

As pointed out earlier, Jews were just as fond of jewellery as any other social group in medieval Spain. There is sound evidence of their taste for wearing many rings on their fingers, as in the case of the wealthy citizen of Teruel.

The seals are of the same kind (featuring four lobes and a shield) as those used by Christians. In many instances the motifs are identical and difficult to classify if there is no inscription. The bronze seal from Toro (Zamora) housed in the Museo Sefardí carries the image of a very conventional castle and Jewish fleurs-de-lis. If it

42 See the chapter on art and iconography.

69

Seal, Toro, fourteenth century. Bronze. Toledo, Museo Sefardí (inv. no. 216)

Seal, Al-Andalus, 1145. Bronze. Edinburgh, National Museums of Scotland (inv. no. H.NM 51)

were not for the Hebrew inscription (Abraham bar Moses Crudo), it would be practically impossible to link it to a Jew.

But Jews also adapted their seals to those of Muslim Spain. One, dated 1141, displays a turbaned figure surrounded by inscriptions in Hebrew and Arabic. The Hebrew inscription reads: "Solomon son of Isaac." The Arabic states: "May Allah protect him to whom the turban was given."[43]

**Set of six rings from Deza** (twelfth-fourteenth centuries). Very simply shaped and of low-grade metal, these four silver and two bronze rings are decorated with Hebrew inscriptions, which are difficult to read. One is glazed. Although it has been suggested that they date from the twelfth and thirteenth centuries and may be related to Aragonese metal workshops, caution is required as both the design and the technique were common until the end of the medieval period.

**Gold rings from Montjuïc necropolis** (thirteenth-fourteenth centuries). The rings held in the Museo Sefardí in Toledo, which hail from Montjuïc necropolis (Barcelona), not only display better workmanship and material (they are made of gold); aesthetically they are of a higher standard. One of them bears an inscription with the name of its owner. The ends of the ring are shaped into heads of two animals which support the piece bearing the Hebrew inscription: "Most blessed of tent-dwelling women be Astruga."[44] Astruga was a fairly common women's name among Catalonia's Jewish community. The other ring, although the stone is missing from the setting, displays a subtle design and simple vegetal motifs that make it highly suitable for a young girl.

**Rings from Briviesca** (fourteenth century). The four silver rings from Tesorillo I found at Briviesca illustrate a range of typical thirteenth- to fifteenth-century jewelry: a very simple and modest band; a thicker band set with a reddish agate; a

[43] This seal is believed to have belonged to a Jew who was forcibly converted to Islam. This may be the case, though there is no specific evidence to suggest a forced conversion.

[44] According to scholars, this is a reference to Judges (5: 24) (see Cantera and Millás, 1956, p. 376).

Ring with inscription. twelfth-thirteenth century. Silver. From the Cerro de los Judíos necropolis, Deza (Soria). Soria, Monasterio de San Juan de Duero, medieval section of the Museo Numantino (inv. nos. 81/1/568-572, 574)

reinforced, double circular band set with a silver hemispher; and one with a raised setting for a green stone.

**Rings from Teruel** (fourteenth century). Two rings from the Teruel necropolis[45] are quite impressive on account of the thickness of the gold and the contrasting effect of the stones: one is blue glass, and the other a garnet.

**Silver necklace from Teruel** (fourteenth century). It is a shame that this silver necklace from Teruel is so badly deteriorated, as it must have been quite exquisite. It must have of consisted of clusters of veined, lanceolate leaves interspersed with small round beads. The delicate workmanship of the leaves indicates that the silversmith was an accomplished designer with considerable technical skill.

### HARNESS ORNAMENTS, PENDANTS AND BUTTONS

As mentioned earlier, like Spanish Christians, Jews were also fond of richly adorning their horses' harnesses. We have seen pieces made from colored bronze; gear was probably fashioned from higher quality metals too. I doubt whether the Briviesca emblazoned escutcheons are really harness ornaments as such; they may be personal adornments. In either the case, although these are Jewish treasures, the

[45] The cemetery or "honsal" of the Jews was located in the hills to the north of the city.

Ring with Hebrew inscription, thirteenth-fourteenth century. Gold. From the Montjuïc necropolis (Barcelona), tomb no. 51. Toledo, Museo Sefardí (inv. no. 83)

Ring, thirteenth-fourteenth century. Gold. From the Montjuïc necropolis (Barcelona), tomb no. 88. Toledo, Museo Sefardí (inv. no. 82)

Ring, fourteenth-fifteenth century. Gold. From the Llanos de Santa Lucía Jewish necropolis (Teruel). Teruel, Museo de Teruel (inv. no. 594)

Ring, fourteenth-fifteenth century. Gold. From the Llanos de Santa Lucía Jewish necropolis (Teruel). Teruel, Museo de Teruel (inv. no. 595)

Ring. Silver. From Tesorillo I, found at Briviesca in 1938, near the current cemetery. Burgos, Museo de Burgos (inv. no. 738)

Ring. Silver and reddish agate. From Tesorillo I, found at Briviesca in 1938, found at Briviesca in 1938, near the current cemetery. Burgos, Museo de Burgos (inv. no. 740)

Ring. Silver. From Tesorillo I, found at Briviesca in 1938, near the current cemetery. Burgos, Museo de Burgos (inv. no. 739)

Ring. Silver. From Tesorillo I, found at Briviesca in 1938, near the current cemetery. Burgos, Museo de Burgos (inv. no. 741)

Pendant. Silver and traces of enamel. From Tesorillo I, found at Briviesca in 1938, near the current cemetery. Burgos, Museo de Burgos (inv. no. 734)

Dentiscalpium (toothpick). Silver. From Tesorillo I, found at Briviesca in 1938, near the current cemetery Burgos, Museo de Burgos (inv. no. 733)

Sphere. Silver. From Tesorillo I, found at Briviesca in 1938, near the current cemetery. Burgos, Museo de Burgos (inv. no. 742)

**Necklace, fourteenth-fifteenth century. Silver. From the Llanos de Santa Lucía Jewish necropolis (Teruel). Teruel, Museo de Teruel (inv. no. 597)**

coats of arms they bear are Castilian and Christian.[46] The silver and enamel pendant depicting a seated lady is very unusual.

Although they are usually described as harness ornaments, I believe that the circular silver shields with a castle in the center are buttons, one of the silver or gold "fastenings" that are frequently cited in historical documents.

### DENTISCALPIUM (TOOTHPICK)

This curious pieces was an instrument of personal hygiene, with a ring enabling it to hang from a chain worn around the neck. Tenth-century Andalusians and Christian knights of the early Middle Ages used to wear them around their necks as a status symbol.

[46] Items of this kind made from precious metals could have found their way into Jewish hands as deposits for loans, merchandise, etc.

# The Administrative Structure of the *Aljama* and the Law

The communities of Spanish Jews (called *aljamas, juderías,* or Jewries) were independent of each other; each had its own administrative and legal system. The fact that they were dependent on the king — by law they were considered the monarch's property — might lead us to think they were all equal, though we should bear in mind that they belonged to different Christian kingdoms: Castile, Navarre, and Aragon. Nonetheless, as they all shared the same religious-legal tradition, the administrative structure of the *aljamas* was fairly similar. In fact, the system greatly resembled that of Christian society, as different towns had their own law codes, the *fueros*.

The *aljamas* were controlled by minorities: families who exercised their power over all aspects of everyday community life, generation after generation. José Luis Lacave, a leading expert on Jewish Spain, provides a shrewd analysis of the significance of this group of oligarchs in the history of the Jewries of Sepharad:

> In each Jewry, particularly the large ones, there were marked class differences. On the one hand there were a few families who formed the oligarchy: these people were rich, powerful, and influential, even at the royal court, and were also the learned families from which the chief rabbis hailed; and then there were the rest of the Jews. Those influential and powerful families to an extent formed another closed society. They almost only mixed with each other; they married each other, formed business partnerships, were neighbors, etc. And since, in addition to being rich and powerful, they generally gave rise to outstanding figures in Hebrew literature and rabbinic scholarship, their members held the posts of authority in the *aljama*. As a rule, the "subjugated" Jews accepted this system, the all-embracing power of a few families over the rest, as something natural, for these privileged families not only produced the experts in Jewish law, who were able to interpret their laws and judge their claims, but also those who, on account of their background and culture, could defend them at court when there were problems between Christians and Jews.[1]

Hebrew literature is full of references to the power and prestige afforded by membership of a recognized lineage and possession of wealth. Sem Tob ben Yoseph (ca. 1380–1441) refers to lineage as follows:

> In order for a man to prove his nobility he must fulfill three requirements: be of pure blood, be associated with noble persons, and not be poor.

[1] Lacave, 1991, p. 37.

To supervise the *aljamas*, the king appointed a *rab de la Corte* or *rab mayor*[2] (chief rabbi), the highest authority over all the Jewries in the kingdom. The *rab de la Corte*, an institutional post, was not the Jews' delegate but a royal official in charge of the affairs of the "King's Jews." He was not only entrusted with the administration of the *aljamas*; he was the highest legal authority to which appeals could be addressed.

This chapter will deal with the internal laws of the *aljamas*: the laws of the Jews drawn up for the Jews. The laws made by Christians for the Jews to abide by, that is, what the Jews called the "laws of the kingdom", are examined in a different chapter.[3]

## THE ADMINISTRATIVE BODIES

The *ma'amad* was the assembly responsible for making decisions on all affairs relating to the *qahal* (community of the *aljama*). Its main duties were to draw up the rules regulating life in the Jewry, particularly on the distribution of the tax burden and the election of people to administrative posts. This assembly usually met in the synagogue.

The *guedolé* of the *qahal* (or elders of the *qahal*) made up the *ma'amad*, a pressure group which controlled the *aljama*. Its members always belonged to the powerful families described by Lacave. The following extract from the Tudela *taqqanot* (laws of the Jewish Community) of 1287 gives an idea of the high esteem in which these families were held:

> [The *aljama*] furthermore agreed that henceforth no rule or regulation drawn up and passed by the *aljama* from this feast day of *Sukkot* shall enter into force until it is signed by eight men from the eight families who regularly participate in the assemblies of the *aljama* together with the exercising administrators at the time. And these are the eight families: bené Falaquera, bené Abasi *(Abenabez)*, bené Pesat *(Evenpesat)*, bené Soeb *(Enxoeb)*, bené Daud *(Evendeut)*, bené Menir *(Evenminir)*, bené Camiç and bené Orabuena; and no rule shall be made unless...[4] [members of the families] who participate regularly in the assemblies of the *aljama* are present.[5]

The *guedolé* were also known as *zeqené ha-ir* (elders). In Navarre they were called *mayores* or *mayorales*. As a result of the fierce social clashes that began to erupt towards the end of the thirteenth century, the different social classes of the *aljama* gained representation in the communal government and various subdivisions emerged: *mayores*, the most powerful; *medianos*, equivalent to today's middle class; and *menudos* or *pequeños*, who were widows, orphans, and poor people. These social divisions were exactly equivalent to the Christian social structure. Although

[2] Given some of his functions, he was also known as the Chief Justice.

[3] The section "The Legal Conflict: The 'Law of the Kingdom' and the Religious Principles of the People of Israel" can be found in the chapter entitled "History of a Conflict."

[4] This blank space was filled in with the number of representatives; the figure varied depending on the population of the *aljama*.

[5] Lacave, 1998, pp. 42 43.

this achievement marked a social triumph for the most underprivileged sectors, it signified few changes in practice: the *mayores* continued to control the *aljama* with an iron fist, aided by the *medianos*. The laws give a good idea of the methods used to silence dissidents:

> In addition [the *aljama*] agreed that anyone who stood up in the synagogue to oppose any aspect of the matters of the Jewry or anything else, and was told by two of the senior members of the congregation of that synagogue to remain silent about the said matter and took no heed of them, should pay the king's treasury 5 *sueldos* of Sancho.[6]

The number of representatives varied, though most Jewries had seven. In Barcelona, as many as thirty were elected, following the example of the Christian Council of One Hundred. When the population of the *aljamas* began to dwindle, the rules were progressively amended to adapt to the new situation, as the Tudela *taqqanot* of 1391 state:

> In addition, the *aljama* agreed that, since only a few of us remain of the many, eleven men shall suffice where this bylaw establishes twenty, including any administrators present at the time.[7]

It is moving to read how, after their community was decimated by the violence and forced conversions of the fourteenth century ("only a few of us remain of the many"), the Jews of Tudela considered it necessary to halve their number of representatives.

The *berorim u-memunim*, the true rulers of the *qahal*, were elected by the majority vote of the *ma'amad*. The *muqademim* (*adelantados* or administrators) were in charge of liaising with the court; their main task was to supervise taxes and share the tax burden among the members of the *qahal*. The *ne'emanim* (faithful) were responsible for lending and collecting taxes. The money was then handed over to the *meayenim* (supervisors and inspectors). Sometimes the same person held both posts of *ne'emanim* and *meayenim*. While tax collection was in progress, a treasurer *(gizbor)* was appointed.

Although important, all these posts were unpaid. Wages were paid to the *rab, sofer, kazan, tabah* and *melammeb*.

The *rab* was elected for a specific term; this was often a hereditary post. The *sofer* was the public scribe whose duties included recording lawsuits. The *kazan* was the synagogue cantor. The slaughterer or *tabah* was entrusted with the task of slaughtering cattle in accordance with civic and religious regulations. The schoolmaster was the *melammeb*. According to the laws, it was advisable for masters not to have more than twenty-five boys in their class; when the number of pupils exceeded that limit, they had an assistant or *res dukana*.

[6] The whole of *taqqanah* no. 3 deals with measures against those who oppose the bylaws established by the *ma'amad* (*Taqqanot* of 1287, Lacave, 1998, p. 32).

[7] Lacave, 1998, p. 365.

**TAXES**

The Jewish communities had to resort to imposing hefty fines and "moral" and civic punishments on their members to prevent them from seeking royal privileges exempting them from paying certain taxes to the *qahal*. This lack of solidarity was so widespread in Tudela that the punishment, in order to deter such practices, consisted in totally isolating the guilty party, as if he had died:

> Shall pay our lord the king, his majesty be praised, 1000 gold *maravedís*, and shall be anathema to this town and to the whole of Israel for twenty whole years: his food shall be the food of a Gentile, his wine, wine that is forbidden to the Jews; he shall not be called upon when three or when ten Jews are needed to pray; nobody who lives in this town shall have any contact with him, nor shall they speak or negotiate with him; however, if he were involved in a lawsuit with anyone, the plaintiff and the witnesses involved shall be permitted to speak to him, but after the suit is settled they shall refrain from talking to him; and nobody shall do business or trade with him, nor eat nor drink at the same table as him, nor fulfil duties in his company, neither circumcision nor weddings nor mourning, nor accompany him at a burial; rather, they shall behave towards him in the same manner that one behaves towards someone who has died.[8]

The Valencia *taqqanot* hit a raw nerve:

> The [Jewish] taxpayers who are obliged by law to pay shun their obligation and burden other Jews with it.

However, despite censuring this practice, the above law is less strict than that of Tudela.

There were two types of taxes: those levied by the *aljama* and those payable to the king.

The main source of income of fifteenth-century Castilian *aljamas* was the direct taxes or *alcabalas* on meat and wine. The rate varied depending on the needs at the time. Sizeable profits were also made from circumcisions, weddings, and burials. However, we know of one tax system that was based on more diverse criteria. The surviving records of the *alcabalas* in Huesca provide an insight into the taxes levied by the *aljama* in 1389: the *cabezaje*, which was paid per capita; the *brazaje*, a tax on earnings and professional activities; a tax on income from capital and real property; the *mercaduría*, a tax on sales and purchases; and the *forniment*, levied on acquisitions of consumer goods.

The general taxes were those paid to the king: of these, the *pechos* were regular payments, while the *servicio* and *medio servicio* were special taxes. *Pechos* were paid annually by each citizen in recognition of the protection afforded by the king. Although the Jews were good about the king's taxes, they were always somewhat reluctant to pay the special taxes.[9]

[8] *Taqqanot* of 1305 (Lacave, p. 40).
[9] For the Jews' attitude to taxes, see the chapter on the law of the kingdom.

In Castile, the *servicio* and *medio servicio* generally amounted to a set total of 450,000 *maravedís,* to be raised by the different Jewries. The distribution of the tax burden was carried out by the *rab de la Corte* with the help of some representatives of the *aljamas.*[10]

In many towns and cities it was customary to employ a mixed system of taxation: half of the tax burden was divided among the number of inhabitants, and the other half was allocated in proportion to each citizen's estate. The following lines describe how some special taxes were raised according to the Tudela *taqqanot* of 1287:

> In addition [the *aljama*] agreed that all expenses and losses arising from these matters in future would be paid equally by the *aljama,* half per capita and half according to the estate of each person, as it had been customary to pay previously, per capita and according to each person's estate.[11]

But we should not be deceived by this criterion: by no means was the tax system governed by a sense of equality. Indeed, it was not even proportional.

## A SYMBOL OF AUTONOMY: *BET-DIN* AND *TAQQANOT*

Having their own judges and laws guaranteed the independence of the Jewries. This is repeatedly stressed by the civil laws:

> Lawsuits between Jews shall be judged by their administrators, and the party who files a suit shall file it with the *rab* and *oydor* responsible for hearing the lawsuits of the Jews of Molina, according to the custom of the *rab* of the court of the king of Castile, in both criminal and civil matters, and they shall confirm the *azquama,* which means the statutes, which were drawn up in Seville and used by the Jews of Castile hitherto.[12]

However, from the thirteenth century onwards, anti-Semitic groups not only attempted to introduce veiled restrictive measures into the doctrine governing relations between Jews and Christians; they also sought to put an end to the internal privileges of the *aljama,* which enjoyed jurisdiction over matters concerning Jews. At the end of the fourteenth century, the Jews' enemies grew even more radical and attempted to deprive them of their most legitimate rights. The bull issued by pope Benedict XIII (1415) criticizes the privileges granted to the Jews by kings and princes and calls for their abolishment:

> In the olden days Jews were granted jurisdiction in civil matters, although contrary to our wishes; but it became known that very often in certain Catholic regions governed by the princes, the Jews were not afraid to act among themselves as judges, with rash boldness, claiming to be authorized to do so by the privileges granted by the kings or by other secular lords.[13]

[10] Several notebooks recording the annual distribution of the tax burden still survive. Some scholars have attempted to conduct demographic studies on the basis of this information (Ladero Quesada, 1971). The so-called Padrón de Huete, dated 1290–91, shows the distribution for raising that year's royal taxes and provides information on the Jewries that existed at the time (though some are missing) and their importance.

[11] Lacave, 1998, p. 33.

[12] "Que los pleitos que hoviere judio con judio que sean juzgados por sus adelantados, e la parte que se apellare que sea el apellación ante el rab e oydor de los pleitos de los judíos de Molina, segund que usaba el rab de la corte del rey de Castilla, assy en pleito criminal como en cevill, et que les confirmedes la azquama, que quiere decir ordenación, la qual fue feyta en Sevilla, e usavam por ella hastaqui los judios Castiella." Llama, 1932, p. 276.

[13] "Fue lícita de antiguo á los judíos la ley civil de juzgar, aún cuando á despecho de nuestros deseos; pero súpose muchas veces que en ciertas regiones católicas, sujetas á los príncipes, los judíos no temieron en constituirse entre sí en jueces, con temerario atrevimiento, pretendiendo estar autorizados para ello, ya por privilegios de los reyes, ya de otros señores seglares."

Despite all these attempts at persecution, the Valladolid *taqqanot*, enacted twenty years after the papal bull, show that the king of Castile continued to support his Jews' right to possess their own judges and laws:

> For it is the wish of his majesty the king, may God protect him and grant him a long reign, that our lawsuits, both civil and criminal, be judged by the laws of the Jews; and he ordered, by means of a charter of privileges, that the honorable Rab Don Abraham, may God protect him, shall judge them together with the judges he may appoint.[14]

### THE COURT OF LAW: *BET-DIN*

Justice was administered by a court, the *bet-din*. It had three judges, the *dayyanim*, also commonly known as *betdines*. Jewish laws established the right to elect judges, of whom an irreproachable moral conduct and proven competence were required:

> Finally, we enact and agree that each *qahal* elect judges to hear their lawsuits in the aforesaid manner and grant them leave, but they must elect the most worthy and the most honorable men available and to be found in that place.[15]

The election of these judges by the *ma'amad* was a painstaking process. The members of the *ma'amad* had to reach a decision within three days, otherwise they would meet day and night for a further eight days. If, after all this deliberation, their choice was still not unanimous, the chief *rab* appointed the judge. The *salíah bet-din*, a sort of bailiff of the *bet-din*, was in charge of maintaining order in the court and on occasions intervened as an arbiter.

The judgments passed by the courts were recorded in writing; these records were displayed during the trial. Let us now examine one of these records written in Hebrew reporting on the session of the Tudela *bet-din* on the second day of *Sebat* 5228 (27 December 1467). In this document Fatbuena claims payment of her *ketubah* (marriage contract). Fatbuena, the daughter of Yehuda ben Daud, was a widow whose husband Solomon Abenabez, also called Solomon Malaj, had died the previous year; she had five sons and four daughters, all minors. The claimant demanded payment of her marriage contract, her dowry, and the gift from her husband.[16] The evidence supplied includes the marriage contract between Fatbuena and Solomon, the latter's will, the inventory of real property and personal property bequeathed by the deceased, and the experts' appraisal. The report begins by mentioning the composition of the court and the names of the judges and goes on to sum up the suit in question:

[14] "Porquanto [es] merced del dicho señor rey, *Dios le guarde, prolongue los días de su reinado*, que nuestros pleitos, asi civiles como criminales, sean librados por las ley[e]s de los judios; e mandó por su carta de probilejo que el *honrado* Rab don Abraham, *Dios le guarde*, los judge e los juezes que el pusiere por sí." As we shall see, judges were appointed by the *ma'amad* and ratified by the *rab*; if no agreement was reached they were chosen by the *rab*. Moreno Koch, 1987, pp. 49–51.

[15] "Porende, promulgamos y acordamos que en cada *qahal* e *qahal* sean *electores de jueces* que libren sus pleitos como dicho es, e los *admitan en el qahal*, pero deben seer *elegidos* los más dignos y los más honrados que se pudieren aber e se fallaren en el lugar." Moreno Koch, 1987, p. 37.

[16] For women's dowries and *ketubot* see the section on the status of women further on in this catalogue.

At this session we three judges were present, the undersigned, Abraham Ha-Leví (Abraham Leví), Isaac ben Menir (Azac Evenminir) and Judá, son of the noble Don Abraham, blessed be his memory, de la Rebiça (Judah de la Rebiça), *betdines* of the *aljama* of Tudela, may God protect it, in the year 5227 of the Creation of the world according to our calendar *(1466–67)*. Appearing before us was Fatbuena, daughter of the illustrious *Don* Judá, may he rest in peace, ben Daud (Judas Evendeut) and widow of the esteemed *Don* Salomón, son of the distinguished *Don* Yoná, blessed be his memory, ben Abu-al-Abasi (Salomón Abenabez), known as Malaj, and she showed us the document of her *ketubah* (marriage contract), her *nedunya* (dowry), her *tosefar* (addition) and her *mattanah lehud* (separate gift).[17]

The court ruled in favor of the widow.

Records of the bet-din. Tudela, 1467. Manuscript on parchment, Tudela (Navarre), M. I. Ayuntamiento de Tudela (Navarre)-Archivo Municipal (DH no. 2)

## THE LAWS: THE *TAQQANOT*

The *taqqanot* (statutes) are the laws drawn up by the *aljamas* themselves. These laws were often adopted by other communities. We know of the details of the Saragossa *taqqanot* of 1264 and those of Tudela of 1287–1305, 1300, and 1391.[18] The famous Valladolid statutes of 1435[19] are very different, as they apply to all the *aljamas* of the kingdom of Castile.

The laws of Tudela give us a fairly good insight into how the *taqqanot* were drawn up, disseminated, and enforced. They were kept in a chest in the synagogue. The 1287 laws constitute a significant corpus of law which preserves regulations already in force and adds new provisions. The chapter cited below shows how this corpus adopted existing laws and prevented people from resorting to other earlier laws not referred to in this book:

16. The *aljama*, may it be protected by its Rock and Redeemer, agreed to adopt and confirm all the written and signed statutes recorded in the book of parchment sheets in the possession of R. Moses bar Yoel ben [...]; any other statutes which are not recorded in the aforesaid book are hereby invalidated and held to be non-existent. And anyone who has seized or taken from the book of statutes kept in the chest of the *aljama* the statute which the *aljama* has drawn up and is to be signed by seven men from the seven families of this city, whosoever has taken the aforesaid statute shall inform the *aljama* and return it by next Sunday.[20]

[17] Lacave, 1998, p. 416.
[18] Published by Baer, among others; however here we are quoting from the Hebrew edition translated by Lacave, 1998, docs. 1, 3 and 42.
[19] Magnificently edited and translated by Moreno Koch, 1987.
[20] Lacave, 1998, p. 42.

At times justice was difficult to administer, since the legal system was largely based on rabbinic tradition and could be interpreted differently by different schools. In the preamble to the code, the lawmakers of Tudela inform us of the legal basis for these laws and their interpretation:

> A verdict shall not be issued in any trial, whatever the subject, unless it is based on the opinion of our master Moses [Maimonides], blessed be his memory, in all matters in which his opinion may be adduced, except for these two, which the *aljama* agreed shall not be settled in accordance with his opinion, namely: respite from debts during the sabbatical year and the reduction of debts in respect of houses that are pledged by means of transfer of their usufruct from debtor to creditor.

Such was the concern about interpretation of the law that the dissemination of any other type of doctrine within the *aljama* was banned:

> The *aljama*, may it be protected by its Rock and Redeemer, agreed that nobody residing in this city shall be authorized to preach in public at the synagogues or teach in them publicly any interpretation of the rabbinic law that goes against what was taught by our master Moses, blessed be his memory, ben Maimon, about what is forbidden and what is permitted.[21]

Statutes recorded in the book were housed in the synagogue, where they were available to all. The *kazan* (cantor) was made to read them in public once a year:

> And the *aljama* threatened with expulsion all the servants of the synagogues in order that all of them always had in their possession a copy of this statute to give

21 Lacave, 1998, p. 40.

to each cantor of their synagogue to read on the feast of Yom Kippur. And the cantors were to be expelled from the synagogue if they failed to read it every year on the day of Yom Kippur, when the servants handed it to them to read.[22]

New statutes could be drawn up at any time. Once they had been passed, they were recorded in the register. Such is the case of the *taqqanot* of 1303 and 1305. In other instances, numbers and periods of time were modified, which called for additions between lines or simply deletion. When a statute displayed many deletions and corrections and was generally in a poor state of conservation, it was rewritten, like the following *taqqanot* of about 1390.

> And since we have an [*between the lines:* old] bylaw on this, and in addition we need to renew it owing to wear and tear and to confirm the things it states, and to please the lordship and all the aforesaid protecting the laws of our lord the king, his majesty be praised, and everything decreed and ruled by the twenty aforesaid men or [part of them *deleted* and most of them *inserted between the lines*] on what they consider should be decreed and decided with respect to each of the aforementioned matters except for a statute on taxes, let it so be done and accepted by the whole *aljama*, may God protect it.[23]

The diverse nature of the statutes passed by the various *aljamas* hindered the operation of law among the Jews of the kingdom. The Jews pursued the same aim as the Christians, who had been attempting for nearly a hundred years to replace their local law codes with kingdom-wide legislation. The general statues, the Valladolid *taqqanot*, thus emerged. With the consent of King John II (1406–1454), the *rab de la Corte*, Don Abraham Benveniste, assembled the delegates of the *aljamas*, the rabbis, "and some good men there are at the court of our lord the king" in order to draw up a set of laws for the whole of Castile. The result was a law code divided into the following sections:

> Chapter one concerning the study of the Torah. This is the gate of Adonai and [the] righteous enter through it.
> Chapter two concerning the election of judges and other authorities.
> Chapter three concerning complaints.
> Chapter four concerning taxes and *servicios*.
> Chapter five concerning dress.

## LOANS AND USURY

As we shall see later on, much of the legislation governing relations between Christians and Jews focused on loans and usury. The numerous surviving documents — receipts and registers — speak for themselves about the importance of this activity among the Jewish communities.

[22] Lacave, 1998, p. 49.
[23] Lacave, 1998, p. 367.

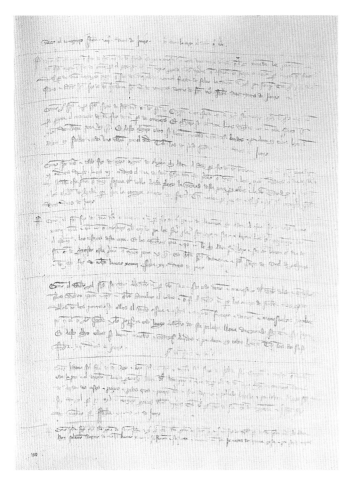

Not only were the most powerful members of society moneylenders; so were most of the people from the lower-middle class, who made small-scale loans that nicely supplemented the income from their professional activities. We possess fairly detailed knowledge of the loans granted by a textile merchant from the town of Ágreda in Soria.[24] He would lend his customers money to enable them to purchase clothing. These were small sums of money, and the receipt, which was issued in the presence of the public scribe and witnesses, stated the amount, the garment purchased, and the date payment was due:

> Domingo Gil [...] to give XXVI *maravedís* to Abraham [...] for a purple cape from Narbonne which he purchased from him and received in the presence of the scribe and witnesses, by Michaelmas, plus two *maravedís*.[25]

As this was a small sum, and because Abraham was financing his own business, the commission was minimal: two *maravedís*. However, he also loaned money for other ends; one of his customers was even a priest:

**Loan agreement: Gil Ferrans and Martín Peres are to pay Osua the thirty–three *maravedíes* he lent them and Gil Ferrans undertakes to pay Martín Peres any damages he may incur as guarantor of the loan. Ágreda (Soria), 12 June 1339. From the Ayuntamiento de Ágreda (Soria): Registro del Escribano del Concejo de Ágreda. Ágreda (Soria), Archivo Municipal (Códice no. 3)**

> Pero Sanches, clergyman of San Miguel, and Doña Romea, his sister, shall pay Abraham one hundred and fifty *maravedís* [...] which he lent them at a rate of three to four, in cash, as established by the king; and they received them, having been counted in the presence of the scribe and witnesses, and shall repay them by Michaelmas, plus two *maravedís*.[26]

The commission is the same but the interest rate is higher — the borrower must pay back four *maravedís* for every three he borrows. As the document explains, this is the rate established in the king's laws.

These receipts were entered in a register in which the family accounts were kept. The following excerpt is taken from one of the many surviving books of this kind, which belonged to three orphaned girls who inherited their father's capital along with his debts and loans. The document is very interesting as it provides an insight into the harsh reality of these moneylenders and their world. The document dates from around 1325 and hails from the Navarrese town of Puente la Reina. On the back is the following title in Hebrew: "This is the register of the three orphaned daughters of Moses bar Samuel ben Yahyón."[27] The book is

[24] There are several studies on Jewish moneylenders but in relation to the activities of a whole family who engaged in these minor loans. Of particular interest is the article by Hurtado Quero, 1987.
[25] Rubio Semper, 2001, doc. 173, p. 152.
[26] Ibid., doc. 176, p. 52.
[27] Lacave, 1998, p. 61.

written in the hand of the brother of the late Moses, who had been robbed and murdered by a Christian, and contains a list of the deceased's debtors (stating their name and place of residence, amount owed, date the debt falls due, and in some cases the guarantor). Half are very doubtful debts. The book also records the deceased's own debts and, at the end, provides interesting details of the robbery and murder, and the execution of the Christian murderer.

[column A]

[1] Johan de la Ferrera and his wife: 51 *sueldos* and 5 *robos* of corn; corn, due next St. Mary's day, and moneys due next Michaelmas; inhabitants of Mendigorria.

[2] Don Lop Capellan and Doña Teresa, inhabitants of Puente la Reina: 30 *sueldos*; due next feast day of St. Martin.

[3] Sancho Ximeniz and his wife, inhabitants of Villanueva: 20 *sueldos* and 4 *robos* of corn; due next feast day of St. Mary and next Michaelmas.

[4] Andreu Ferrero *(or ferrero)* and his wife, inhabitants of Çirauqui: 30 *sueldos*; [due], next feast day of St. Mary.

[5] Garcia Galar and his wife Françesa and Miguel Periz, son of the aforesaid Garcia Galar, inhabitants of Berbinçana;... 43 *sueldos*; due in 3 years, plus... [15] *(5 or 50) sueldos* due next Michaelmas and the... *(hole) (remaining? 20?)* in 3 years, without profit.

[6] Johan Lopiz, son of Don Lop, abbot of Mendilivarri, inhabitant of Eneriz: 40 *sueldos*; guarantor, Doña Juliana, inhabitant of La Puente *(de la Reina)*.

All the promissory notes recorded in the book from this point onwards refer to bad debts, as some of the debtors have fled, and other debts cannot be collected as the debtors are in dire poverty; and I am prepared to hand them over to the *aljama*, and if the time comes when I am able to collect something, I would pay the tax on them, depending on the sum I collect from them, without a doubt. They are as follows:

[7] Sancho, *abbot of* Villanueva: 40 *sueldos* and *robos* of corn; guarantor, Miguel de Esquiva, inhabitant of Villanueva.

[8] Pero Garcia de las Peñas and his wife, inhabitants of Sarria; and María Periz, daughter of both, and Miguel Periz de Larrea and his wife and Pascoal de Larrea and Garcia, son of Garcia Pastor, inhabitants of Sarria: 40 *sueldos* and 5 *robos* of corn, measure of Puente la Reina.

[9] Pero Garcia de las Peñas and his wife, inhabitants of Sarria: 30 *sueldos*.

[column B]

[10] Garcia Pastor, son of Garcia de Ahos, and Garcia, his son, and Pero Garcia de las Peñas and his wife, according to a promissory note, owe the sum of 75 *sueldos* and 11 *robos* of corn; reduced to 15 *sueldos* only; inhabitants of Sarria.

[11] Pero Garcés de Unçit (Unciti) and his wife, Doña Oria: 16 *cafices* of salt,

measure of Puente la Reina; inhabitants of Obanos; plus, 2 *sueldos*; this promissory note was acquired by my brother Moses *(Mosse)* from Isaac *(Azac)* Bonisac, with a deed and with my guarantee.

[12] Johan Sanz, *maestro*, inhabitant of Erneriz: 20 *sueldos*; guarantor, Ferran Martiniz, inhabitant of Eneriz.

[13] And [my brother] *(hole in document.)* Moses, who was murdered, [owed] 7 *libras*, by means of a promissory note and oath sworn on the Torah to Yosef *(deleted*: ha-Leví bar Abraham ha-Leví) bar Jacob, blessed be his memory, ben Yahyón *(Juce Evenayón)* to whom the murdered Moses was going to pay a sum of money *(seems to read: when he was murdered)*.

[14] In addition, [he owed] Reubén bar Isaac Mainos *(Rubén Mainos)* 40 *sueldos*, with a promissory note. And the orphans have not discounted anything from the amount recorded in this book for their bed.

When the murderer was hung, he confessed of his own accord that he had taken the bag from the murdered Moses, containing the promissory notes from Jews, and said that at the time he had not... *(illegible)* hand over the bag; and each day we were assured that they would give us ... from the Christian murderer. And in that bag there were other promissory notes signed by Christians and we do not know who they are... *(illegible)* and also promissory notes signed by Jews, but we do not know who they were or for how much. All the debts recorded herein, which are owed to me in Larraga and Miranda, are not worth taking into account for tax purposes, for all the debtors dispute them with me in the courts of justice, for some conceal their possessions and there are notes that are marked as being paid so that they do not pay what they owe.

As we can see, our unfortunate moneylender's debtors were blacksmiths, teachers, clergymen, etc., both Jews and Christians. He has many doubtful debtors and debts that are practically impossible to collect. And to make matters worse, the authorities have not returned the promissory notes Moses was carrying when he was murdered.

# Women and the Marriage Contract. *The Ketubah*

It was compulsory for Jews to comply with God's command: "Go forth and multiply" (Genesis, 1: 28). Failure to produce offspring amounted to a sin as serious as bloodshed; some saw it as the reason why God turned his back on Israel. Men were expected to marry upon turning eighteen, while women reached marriageable age at fifteen or sixteen.[1] Failure to comply with this mandate was a matter of reproach and evidence of serious personal shortcomings:

> He who has no wife, says Rabbi Jacob, subsists without good, without joy, without blessing, and without satisfaction. Others add: without peace and without life. (Yevamot, 62b)

Bachelorhood is even regarded as an imperfect state for a man:

> A single man is not a man in the full sense. (Yevamot, 63a).

Parents arranged marriage for their children far in advance, taking into account circumstances such as lineage, finances, and family relations. It was common to resort to the services of professional matchmakers, who helped arrange the marriage between families or, converserly, proved very useful in dissolving the tie. It might be said that only the poor got to marry the person of their choice, as they were not limited by background or social factors of any type. Some Jewries had charitable foundations that provided young women with dowries, enabling them to marry.

There were two distinct marriage ceremonies: betrothal *(kiddushin* or *erusin)* and the wedding proper *(nisuin),*[2] normally held no less than a year later.

At the *kiddushin* the groom gave the bride a valuable object, generally a ring, stating: "Look. You are betrothed to me by this ring, according to the law of Moses and of Israel." This was followed by the reading of the *ketubah*, which had previously been drawn up. From this moment onwards the bride was formally engaged and, as such, spoken for, though the groom could not consummate the marriage until the celebration of the *nisuin*.

This second ceremony was the wedding. It began in the morning, when the bride visited the *mikvah* and performed the purification ritual by immersing herself three times in water. Afterwards, dressed in white with a headdress of white flowers, she went to the place where the ceremony was held — this could be the synagogue, a house, or outside in the open air — and stood beneath a canopy

[1] Only scholars of the Torah could delay their weddings, provided they were able to control their appetites.

[2] Abraham M. Asan, 1990, pp. 408–409. Yosef Caro (1488–1575) is the author of the leading sixteenth-century legal work, whose summary, *Sulhan 'aruk,* is an extremely useful code of practice that is widely accepted.

*(huppa)* supported by relatives, flanked by her mother and mother-in-law. Although the ceremony of the *huppa* can be interpreted in several ways, it is widely seen as a symbol of the house where the groom brings his bride as a sign that she now belongs to him. The officiating rabbi pronounced the "seven blessings" over a glass of wine. Finally, according to the *Llibre dels costums* by Jacob Ben Mossé ha-Levi Molin (1360–1427),[3] the groom crushed the glass with his foot as a symbolic reminder of the fragility of earthly life and of painful events such as the destruction of the Temple of Jerusalem.

When things did not turn out well, the marriage could be dissolved if the man repudiated the woman. She could thus marry again, provided that a rabbinic tribunal ruled that her moral conduct had been irreproachable. Sometimes a woman's repudiation was not acknowledged and she was simply abandoned and unable to make a new life for herself. Bigamy was allowed, and it was not unusual for some men even to have concubines, despite the disapproval of the rabbis, who put this practice down to the "nefarious influence of the Muslims".

## THE *KETUBAH* AND ITS CLAUSES

The many surviving *ketubot* provide us with detailed knowledge of the contents of these contracts. They are very similar in form. The text is framed within a decorative border of geometric or vegetal motifs. The *ketubah* of Soli is the only Spanish Hebrew text decorated with two birds. If we compare it to that of Milagro,[4] dated 1309, we will see that the decorative scheme, except for the zoomorphic detail, was very typical. This border not only served a decorative purpose; it also ensured that the conditions set forth in the document could not be altered. Rabbi Simeon ben Zerah Durán of Majorca (1361–1444) recommended that all the blank spaces be decorated to prevent new clauses from being added.

The document generally began with a reference to how lucky the man was to have found the woman who was to be his wife: "He who finds a wife, finds a good thing, and obtains a favor from the Lord" (Proverbs, 18, 22).

For a better idea of the content and ideological context of one of these documents, with words and expressions of the period, let us examine José Luis Lacave's translation of the *ketubah* of Soli:

[3] This reference is taken from Blasco, 2002 (1), p. 134.

[4] The marriage contract between Samuel, son of Yom-Tob Surí, and Jámila, daughter of Isaac ben Bibach, dated the 5th of *Sivan* 5069 (15 May 1309). This is the only surviving Navarrese *ketubah* that does not relate to Jews of Tudela. The fact it was used as a cover for a notary's files no doubt saved it from destruction.

> On Thursday, two days from the month of *Edul* of the year 5060 of the Creation of the world according to our calendar (18 August 1300), in the town of Tudela, by the river Ebro, let it be known that the groom R. Salomon bar Yom Tob, may God protect him, Alparga, *(Salomón Alparga)* said to the maiden Soli, daughter of R. Hayyim, may God protect him, ben Galaf *(Vitas Galaf):* Be my wife according to the law of Moses and Israel and I shall serve, honor, maintain, and sustain you in the manner that the Jewish men serve, maintain, and sustain their wives loyally.

**Ketubah** (marriage contract). Tudela, 1300. Manuscript on parchment with decorative border. Pamplona, Archivo General de Navarra (Cámara de Comptos, Caja 192, no. 2)

**Ketubah** (marriage contract). Milagro, 1309. Manuscript on parchment with decorative border. Pamplona, Archivo General de Navarra (Cámara de Comptos, Caja 192, no. 54)

[5] This expression signifies that the husband enjoyed the usufruct of this property, which was owned by the wife.

I shall give you as a *mohar* for your virginity, guaranteed and certified with my belongings, 300 silver *zuzim* as established by the rabbi, as well as your maintenance, clothing, and other needs, I shall fulfill my marital duties towards you as is customary throughout the land. And Soli gave her consent and became his wife. And R. Salomon, the husband, has voluntarily brought her from his own estate, as an addition to her *ketubah*, 30 gold Alfonsine *maravedís*, of good gold and standard weight, not mixed with any other coins, which cannot be interpreted in practice as having a value other than their strict face value. And this groom, R. Salomon, has stated as follows: This is the dowry which Soli, this wife of mine, brings me, in clothing, jewelry and bed linen, which has been valued, and I have accepted, at 150 valid Alfonsine *maravedís* of good gold and exact weight; and henceforth I have voluntarily accepted these chattels as *tzon barzel*,[5] which, if they were to diminish, would diminish for me, and if they were to increase, would increase for me.

As a guarantee of this *ketubah*, addition *(tosefet)* and dowry *(nedunya),* I take payment upon myself, and upon my heirs after me, and upon all my property, both real and movable, from the most select chattels and property I possess on the face of the earth, that which I have acquired and that which I may acquire in future, including the cloak I am wearing, during my lifetime and after I die, from this day forth and ever after, with the validity of the guarantee of all the deeds of *ketubah*, addition *(tosefet)* and dowry *(nedunya)* that are customary practice with the daughters of Israel. By the four cubits of land, appropriately and in accordance with the rules of our sages whose memory is sacred, for this is not simply a theoretic promise or a mere formality. And we receive *kinyan*[6] from R. Salomon, this husband, for Soli, this wife of his, for everything that is written and specified above, full *kinyan* henceforth, with an object legally suited to the purpose. And everything is firm and binding.[7]

This document follows a standard formula: a token payment for the bride's virginity, the *mohar,*[8] the groom's commitment also extends to food, clothing and other needs, including marital relations; establishment of the real dowry, in figures, to which the groom commits himself, plus the value of the trousseau provided by the bride. And finally, the groom provides a guarantee of payment, if necessary. When drawn up between very important people of considerable wealth, the clauses were highly complex. One hundred and fifty years after these Navarrese *ketubot*, Bienvenida, a Jew of Arévalo, commited herself to Rabbi Moses Amigo. Her *ketubah* is similar in form and content, though the amounts of money are adapted to the legal tender of the kingdom. The girl was obviously not keen on the idea of sharing her husband with a second wife, as she made him sign the following clause:

> And the said Rabbi Moses, who is the husband, undertook and swore that he would not marry another woman during her lifetime and would not take her away from here to another place save on her wishes and orders, and if he disobeyed this oath and took another wife or took her away from this place, he would be severely punished.[9]

Unless it consisted of real property or exceptional objects, the bride's dowry was generally mentioned very briefly. Let us compare the terms of Jámila's and Bienvenida's contribution to the marriage:

> This is the dowry which Jámila, this wife of mine, brings me in clothing, jewels and bed linen, which has been valued, and I have accepted, at 3000 valid *sueldos* of Sancho.[10]
> And this is the dowry which she brought from the house of her father to the house of Rabbi Moses, the husband, including clothing and attire and household and bed linen, which he saw and received for fifty thousand *maravedís.*[11]

Documents of this kind were kept by the wife's family and were regularly used as evidence in lawsuits relating to repudiation, widowhood, etc. We have seen how

[6] In rabbinic law the *kinyan* is the act whereby the acquisition of a property or a commitment is validated. The pledgor and the acquirer exchange an object (nowadays a handkerchief) that symbolizes the property transfer or the commitment, which thus becomes irreversible.

[7] Lacave, 1988, pp. 44–45.

[8] The 300 silver *zuzim* were ancient Israeli coins.

[9] "E fizo obligación e juramento el dicho Rabi Mose que es el novio que no casaría con otra muger en su vida della, y no la sacaría deste lugar a otro lugar salvo por su voluntad y por su mandado, y sy pasare este juramento e tomare otra muger o la sacare deste lugar a otro lugar que yncurra en graves penas." As we mention further on, the document had to be translated in the sixteenth century in order to be used in a trial. We quote from the transcription by Emperador Ortega, 2002, pp. 95–96.

[10] Lacave, 1998, p. 51.

[11] "Y este es el dote que ella traxo de la casa de su padre a la casa de Rabi Mose que es el novio, entre vestidos e atavíos e serviçios de casa e de la cama de lo que él vio e rescibió por sy cinquenta mil maravedís de la dicha moneda." Emperador Ortega, 2002, pp. 95–96.

Contract of dowry and marriage (ketubah) between Rabbi Moses Amigo and Bienvenida, Jews of Arévalo (Ávila). Torrelobatón (Valladolid), 7 March 1479. Manuscript on parchment with Hebrew writing, sepia and red ink and border decorated with geometric motifs

Fabuena, on becoming widowed, presented her *ketubah* to the *bet-din* as evidence in order to reclaim her dowry to help bring up her nine children, all minors. But these documents were not only recognized by Jewish courts, as one might expect — they were also acknowledged by the Christians, even after the expulsion. In 1515, the aforementioned Bienvenida, now converted to Christianity with the name Mencía Velásquez, presented her *ketubah* as evidence to ask the prosecutor to return her dowry, which had been confiscated from her in the sodomy lawsuit she brought against her husband, the aforementioned Rabbi Moses Amigo, now a Christian called Nuño de la Torre and an apothecary by profession.

In all these documents the public nature of the commitment, which was to be made known to all, was very important. Most employ the same expression to stress this public knowledge:

> Let this pledge which I make be written in the street and signed in the plaza, in order that it not be a secret pledge or a pledge made by one who is sick in bed.

## THE STATUS OF WOMEN

Not only did a husband purchase his wife's "virginity"; she was also obliged to state contractually that she was a virgin. A husband was also entitled to repudiate his wife. If he did not formally repudiate her she was left utterly defenseless. And the husband's promise to fulfill his conjugal duties is a rather sexist one, to say the least.[12]

Medieval Jewish society was a male-dominated community in which women occupied a very secondary role. Girls did not receive the same education as boys and were commonly confined to the home. This extract from the book of proverbs of Samuel ha-Nagid (993–1056) is highly illustrative:

> Provide for your wives a bedchamber and a lock
> ..................
> Walls and palaces were created for women:
> Their glory consists of winding wool and weaving.[13]

There were even considerable restrictions on their participation in the synagogue, where they were made to sit apart from the men, in a gallery. Although some

[12] Just as the biblical sources establish a slave's rights to food, clothing and fulfillment of marital duties, it is logical that husbands should have granted at least the same to their wives in the *ketubot*.

[13] These lines are quoted in the Tova Rosen's article, "Representaciones de mujeres en la poesía hispano-hebrea," in Izquierdo Benito and Sáenz-Badillos, 1998, pp. 123–138, p. 137.

*Responsa* explain that the reason for keeping men and women apart is to prevent distraction during the ceremonies, this practice was obviously based on a concern for purity.

Although life was hard for women of all three religions during the Middle Ages, the status of Jewish women was closer to that of Muslim than Christian women. Even though we may find the following words by Tova Rosen on Sephardic women shocking, the fact is that they reflect the harsh reality of the time: "they cannot have feelings, opinions, appetites, wishes, tastes or aversions of their own."[14] Women's submission to men was ingrained into boys and girls alike during their upbringing. Men asserted their own status by putting women in their place; failure to do so damaged male prestige. The following lines by Samuel ha-Nagid give us an idea of a father's recommendations to his son:

> Beat your wife each day, so that she
> may not govern you like a man and hold her head high.
> Son, do not become the wife of your wife, and
> do not allow her to become the husband of her husband

Rosen wonders how a man who wrote such beautiful love poems idealizing the loved one could echo teachings of this kind. But ha-Nagid was simply behaving like any man raised in a patriarchal society where women were not equals but merely references in love poems or submissive creatures who looked after the home.

But whereas we might find ha-Nagid's words understandable in the context of a conversation between men, it is harder to comprehend the following recommendations on marriage made by a mother to her daughter:

> Take care not to do anything to irritate your husband. Do not express your annoyance when he makes love to you or when he is resting. Speak to him softly to calm his anger. Cook for him everything he desires, and pretend that you like his favorite dishes, even if this is not so. When he is sober do not remind him of the foolish remarks he made when drunk. Drink when he orders you to, but never become inebriated. Save his money, because it is good for a man to be generous and for a woman to be thrifty. Do not disclose his secrets. Do not take a dislike to the servants he loves. Do not disobey his orders, even though your opinion may be better than his. Do not be jealous. Do not ask him to do things for you that he will find it difficult to fulfil.[15]

The Jewish girl, familiar with the passive and humble role played by her mother, would gradually come to terms with her inferior position with respect to her future husband, whom she will depend on and obey. The considerable misogyny already rooted in Jewish religious tradition was further reinforced during the period of Muslim rule in Spain between the eighth and the eleventh centuries.

[14] Idem, p. 138.

[15] The text is by an author called Isaac, whose *Mislec 'Arab* was written in the late twelfth or early thirteenth century (Quoted by Rosen, pp. 137–138).

# Religion and its Manifestations

Visiting the synagogue and celebrating the feasts of the liturgical calendar with the family played an important role in the life of such a deeply religious people as the Jews.

## THE HOUSE OF YAHWEH: THE SYNAGOGUE

The *Partidas*, the law codes drawn up under King Alfonso X, express the Christian concept of the synagogue in the Middle Ages:

> Synagogue is the place where the Jews pray.[1]

This is how it was perceived by the inhabitants of Spain's Christian kingdoms. The people of Allariz, in Galicia, regarded it as the Jews' place of liturgical pomp:

> In the prayers and feasts which the aforesaid Jews hold in the district of the town below the castle.[2]

While the Christian community was undoubtedly aware of the most obvious significance of the synagogue, for the Jews it was much more than a place of worship, as the inscriptions on the walls of many synagogues indicate.

> I wish to dwell in the house of Yahweh every day of my life, to delight in Yahweh's grace and visit his temple in the morning.[3]

The quote above conveys the idea of the celestial abode represented on Earth by the Temple of Jerusalem and, in turn, by the synagogue, the house of Yahweh, which gives shelter to His people. An inscription in monumental lettering above the doors of Cordoba's synagogue reads:

> Open the gates, that the righteous nation which keeps faith may enter in. (Isaiah, 26: 2)[4]

A sign on the synagogue of Samuel Halevi in Toledo states that this building, which the "righteous nation" shall enter, is the temple, the house of God:

[1] "Synoga es el lugar do los judíos fazen oración."
[2] "Nas rogas é festas, que os ditos xudeus fan nos suburbios da vila por vaixo do noso castelo." Letter of agreement dating from 1289 reported by Fita and reproduced by Cantera Burgos, 1983, p. 164.
[3] Epigraph, Cordoba synagogue (Cantera Burgos, 1983, p. 14).
[4] Cantera Burgos, 1963, p. 13.

The design of this [temple] / is like the design of the work executed by Besalel / Go forth, peoples! And enter through its gates / and seek God, for this is the house of God, like BET-EL![5]

But this house is not only a place of prayer; like the paternal home, it welcomes all its children whenever community life so requires. It was the place where the *qahal* or community assembly met; the repository of the communal laws, which were available to all; and the place where the Law was zealously read out. The inscription telling of the establishment of the synagogue of Samuel Halevi reminds us of all these functions:

> Gaze upon the sanctuary which has been consecrated in Israel/ and the house Samuel has built /and the tower of wood for reading the Law in its center, / and the scrolls and crowns of the [sanctuary] devoted to His worship, / and its paterae and lamps for illumination, and its windows, which are like the windows of ARIEL [...] and its atriums for those who observe the perfect Law, / and its abode for those who dwell under His wing.[6]

## THE SYNAGOGUE COMPLEX

A number of Christian sources, mainly inventories taken of synagogues following the expulsion of the Jews from Spain, provide an insight into some of the characteristic areas of the synagogue complex. The compound was surrounded by a wall and, in addition to the prayer room — the core area — there were several courtyards that were used by either men or women. The synagogue of Ciudad Rodrigo (province of Salamanca) is described as follows:

> The synagogue with its wall and courtyards for the Jews and Jewesses of the aforesaid Ciudad Rodrigo and their Jewry...[7]

While the above source informs us that the synagogue in Ciudad Rodrigo had a courtyard for women and one for men, a similar record of 1492 referring to Gerona's synagogue tells us of other annexes and women's quarters:

> The schools of the Jewry, the house of the "donas judearum", the hospital, and the baths.[8]

A royal letter addressed to the council of Palencia gives further details of a specific area (other than the gallery above the prayer room) used by women for ritual ceremonies:

> And, in addition, another house and courtyard for women's use where the Jewish women usually pray and now pray in their own area according to their law.[9]

[5] Cantera Burgos, 1984, p. 98.

[6] Idem.

[7] "La synoga con su çerco e corrales que los judíos e judías de la dicha Çibdad Rodrigo e aljama dellos..." Letter from the Catholic Monarchs dated 1492. (Text by Millares Carlo quoted by Cantera, 1984, p. 200.)

[8] "Las escuelas de la aljama, la casa de las 'donas judearum,' el hospital y los baños," according to a document recording the purchase made by Jorge Rafart, presbyter, of a number of houses which were not subject to any charges (Mirambell, 1988, p. 657).

[9] Suárez Fernández, 1962.

A contract for building works carried out on the small synagogue in Huesca draws a clear distinction between the women's gallery and the women's room that gives onto a courtyard.[10] In addition to the baths, schools, and hospitals that were part of the synagogue complex, sources generally refer also to a courtyard for women and a room where they performed rituals "according to their law." Although frequently described in Christian medieval records as a "Jewish women's synagogue," "house of Jewesses," or "women's synagogue," this is in fact the room where women took ritual baths and engaged in other practices; it should not be confused with the gallery.

## THE PRAYER ROOM

Everything revolved around two focal points in the main hall: the *aron ha-quodesh* and the *bimah*.

The *aron ha-quodesh* or *hekhal* is the Holy Ark that houses the Torah,[11] according to the instructions given in Exodus (25: 16):

> And you shall put into the Ark the testimony which I shall give you.

In the *Sarajevo Haggadah* this ark is shown open, displaying the scrolls of the Torah inside. The triple row of arches at the Samuel Halevi synagogue gives an idea of what these wall niches must have been like. However, except for the *Sarajevo Haggadah*, which shows it as a recess, miniatures such as the illustrations in the *Sister Haggadah* and a Sephardic manuscript in Jerusalem depict the *aron ha-quodesh* as a large cupboard placed against the wall. The representation of the ark as a separate architectural element, as in the *Sister Haggadah*, is not an artist's whim; rather, it is a real depiction of this part of the synagogue. The word *hekhal* literally means "pavilion" or "palace" in Hebrew — that is, the repository and abode (palace, pavilion, or mansion) of the Law and, by extension, the sanctuary par excellence. Conventional iconography depicts the Holy of Holies in Jerusalem's Temple as a *martyrium*.[12] One of these conventional images closely matches a illustration in the *Sister Haggadah*. An inscription by the recess for the *hekhal* in Cordoba's synagogue alludes to this idea of a sanctuary:

> Sanctuary in miniature and abode of the Testimony, which was completed by / Isaac Moheb, son of Afraim / Wadawa (?) in the seventy-fifth year. Return, o God! And hasten to rebuild Jerusalem![13]

A feature commonly found in European illustrations but missing from the aforementioned images is the *parokhet*. This curtain, which is reminiscent of the veil that separated the sanctuary from other areas of the Temple, was placed over the door

[10] The whole document is reproduced in the section on benches.

[11] Originally an ark strictly speaking, it later came to be deposited inside a cabinet, which acquired the name of its contents.

[12] A small and central plan building, in origin containing relics. Despite belonging to Christian tradition, this architectural icon is perfectly consonant with the image of the Temple in Jewish culture.

[13] Cantera Burgos, 1983, p. 21. This inscription, like others found on European synagogues, is traditionally held to be a reference to the synagogue as a "small-scale" copy of the Temple.

of the *aron ha-qodesh*. Since there is documentary evidence of these curtains, they may have been concealed behind the architectural structure of these highly embellished sanctuaries, in direct contact with the Torah.[14]

The *bimah* is the platform on which people stand to read out the Torah. The chief reader was the *kazan*, or cantor, though various people took part in the reading[15]. The Torah must have been read from a stand, for comfort. It was removed from its cabinet and carried with utmost reverence to the *bimah* by the quickest route, so that the anxious congregation could derive comfort from its presence. The bearers' hands were wrapped in a shawl. The *Barcelona Haggadah* shows the *kazan*, his hands wrapped in a cloth in accordance with Christian practice,[16] lifting the Torah for veneration. After the service the Torah was carried back to its ark by the longest route as a sign of the community's sorrow at being deprived of the sight of the sacred book.

Scholars disagree on the *bimah's* location inside the synagogue. The epigraph on the Samuel Halevi synagogue, in addition to informing us of the material from which the *bimah* was fashioned, describes its location: "and the wooden tower for the reading of the Law in the center." This central arrangement is consistent with the recommendations of Maimonides, who considered that the congregation could hear better and gather around it. According to Josef Caro, it was typical for Sephardic Jews to place the *bimah* by the western wall opposite the *aron ha-qodesh*. The recess in the western wall of Cordoba synagogue seems to support this theory. The "sacred way" leading from one to the other was laid with special paving stones, such as those unearthed during the excavations at the Samuel Halevi synagogue, or simply covered with rugs like the one in the Berlin museum.

Judging by the images, the faithful did not position themselves in an organized fashion; it seems that the idea was to "stand, group together around…", as Maimonides states.

[14] Although a curtain of this kind was suitable for a simple village synagogue, splendid buildings such as the Samuel Halevi synagogue called for monumental structures of polylobed arches and columns.

[15] There are several records of these platforms breaking owing to poor state of conservation and overcrowding.

[16] This practice was common to both Jews and Christians.

The illustrations in the codices do not indicate the shape of the *bimah*. Those depicted in the *Sister Haggadah* and the *Oxford Siddur* appear to be made of wood, whereas those of the *Barcelona Haggadah* are metal structures. Both types are similar to the pulpits of medieval Christian churches. An old historical anecdote recorded by Abraham ibn Daud tells of the fate of a wooden *bimah* during the caliphal period in the time of Muslim rule:

> This was the custom of R. Janoq, blessed be his memory: every year, on the last day of festivities, he would climb up to the pulpit to display the Torah, accompanied by three of the elders of his generation, with the eyes of the

community upon him. In the 4775th year he climbed up as usual, accompanied by the others, but the pulpit was old and cracked, and everyone who had climbed up fell down, and the master broke his bones.[17]

To some extent, this *bimah* must have resembled the minbars (domed pulpits) in Muslim mosques.

### THE WOMEN'S GALLERY

The Cordoba and the Samuel Halevi synagogues each had a gallery for women. There were several reasons for separating the sexes. Some were derived from the old custom of designating a certain area of the courtyard to be used by women during certain celebrations; others related to the rules on purity, which restricted women's access to the prayer room. Certainly, some of the rabbis' *Responsa* insist on the need for segregation to prevent the men from being distracted. The inscription that frames the entrance to the gallery in the Samuel Halevi synagogue is chosen with a view to its occupants:

> And all the women went out after her with timbrels and dancing. And Miriam sang to them: "Sing to the Lord, for he has triumphed gloriously." (Exodus, 15· 20)[18]

In many cases the women's gallery was simply a wooden structure. There was no access to it from the prayer room.

### FURNITURE AND OBJECTS

The exact significance and use of the various furnishings found in Spanish synagogues is uncertain.[19] On the one hand, literary sources have yet to be fully exploited; on the other, although few, iconographic sources contain very explicit descriptions of synagogue interiors.[20]

Sources generally describe the menorah, the seven-branched candelabrum that imitates that of the Temple, as a principal feature of synagogues. Medieval menorahs had an extra candle that was kept permanently alight. Although the extant images dating from the Middle Ages do not depict the menorah, an illustration from the *Sister Haggadah* shows seven oil lamps arranged symmetrically opposite the *aron ha-qodesh*. These votive lamps seem to be performing the function of the seven lights of the menorah. In other representations of synagogue interiors, hanging lamps, although not fully visible, appear to be arranged in a similar fashion. These oil-filled ceramic lamps suspended from chains were very

[17] Abraham Ibn Daud, 1990, p. 90.
[18] Cantera Burgos, 1983, p. 138.
[19] For an introduction to this subject, see Cantera 1995 (1); Levy, 1963; Peláez del Rosal, 1968; Moreno Koch, 1998, pp. 135–141.
[20] Illustration from the *Sister Haggadah*, ca. 1350; group of faithful coming out of a synagogue in the *Sarajevo Haggadah*, also from the mid-fourteenth century; interior of synagogue in the so-called *Barcelona Haggadah*, from the same period; interior of synagogue of the Pentateuch in Portugal (The British Library, 27167), mid-fourteenth century; Spanish manuscript, Jerusalem.

common in medieval Spain.[21] As with the menorah, one lamp had to be kept burning constantly.

It is not known whether or not synagogues had seating. It is believed that in some cases the congregation sat on the floor, perhaps on rugs like the Muslims in their mosques. The miniatures show people sitting, but not on the floor — their posture suggests they are sitting on small individual seats of some kind. A contract for the benches for Huesca's smaller synagogue gives an idea of what sort of seating the town's carpenter was commissioned to fashion:

> On the third day of April of the year M CCCC LXXX III in Huesca, we, Çabadias Alxeth and Solomon Cohen, Jews of Huesca, as priors of the smaller synagogue near the gate of San Ciprián in the city of Huesca and on our own behalf, hereby engage you, Jaime Dabello, carpenter of Huesca, to make for the aforesaid synagogue of this city seating, seat backs, and decorated canopies, to be placed around it, like those which have already been begun in the aforesaid synagogue, in order to continue with the previous work, and likewise two seats beneath the gallery of the aforesaid synagogue, according to the instructions of the aforesaid priors. And likewise, in a courtyard which is reached via the second synagogue entrance, by the women's room, you shall make seats from the old wood of the synagogue and place the screen made of wood that will be given to you where instructed to by the priors. And all the aforementioned things are to be made by the said Jaime at his own expense, from wood and nails, and from all the necessary things. However, the work to be done inside the aforesaid synagogue shall be wholly from new wood, and shall be completed by next Passover in May, and inspected by Samuel Abengaston, a Jew. And to guarantee payment of the aforesaid work, the aforesaid priors undertake, jointly and each on his own behalf, to pay him three hundred *sueldos* and all the old wood and nails that are left over, except for the remaining seat backs of the aforesaid synagogue; of the said three hundred *sueldos*, one hundred shall be paid immediately, a further hundred halfway through the work, and the remaining hundred when the work is complete. And we undertake personally and with our own property to fulfill this obligation. Witnesses Johan Cortes and Moses Alazar, Jew of Huesca.[22]

As in medieval Spanish Christian churches, the faithful had their own chairs in certain areas, a right inherited by members of the family. In some places the right to use these reserved areas could be negotiated.

We know from the famous *Responsa* that there were rugs in the synagogues; these were used as both wall and floor coverings. The well-known rug housed in the Berlin museum, which belongs to the "ancient Alcaraz" type, may have hung on one of the sides of the *aron ha-qodesh* or have covered the pathway leading from this spot to the *bimah*. Its inscription may clearly allude to this function: "There is no God but God" (*La ilah ila Allah*).[23]

[21] They were hung using the same system of a wooden structure with pulleys, and chains affixed to the side walls.

[22] "Die tercia Aprilis anno M CCCC LXXX III Osce, que nos Çabadias Alxeth e salamon Cohen, judios osce, así como priores de la sinoga pecheña cerqua la portata de sant Cibrian de la ciudat osce, et en nuestros nombres propios, damus a stallo a vos nomine Jayme dabella, fustero osce, a fazer en la dicha sinoga a la redonda de aquella, banquos o respaldos e guardapols berdugados, así e segunt de los que stan ya principiados de fazer en la dita sinoga, e de aquella manera que la obra sea toda siguient, e así mesmo dos bancos debaxo la trebuna de la dita sinoga, alli do los ditos priores le assignaran. E así mesmo en hun patio que esta de fuera a la puerta segunda de la sinoga, jus la canbra de las mulleres, haya a fazer banquos a la redonda, de la fusta viella de la sinoga, e sitiar así las rexas de fusta que le daran, endo los ditos priores queran. E todas las sobreditas cosas a de fazer e faga el dito maestro Jayme a sus spensas, de fusta e clavazon enviadas, e todas las cosas necesarias. Empero la obra que fara dentro la dita sinoga toda aya de seyer de fusta nueba, la qual a de dar acabada daqui a el dia de pasqua de mayo primero vanient, a conocimiento toda la dita obra de simuel abengaston, judio. E por satisfacion e pago de lo sobredito, los ditos priores prometentes e se obligan cada uno dellos por si e por el todo darle trescientos sueldos e toda la fusta viella e clavazon que sobrara, exceptado las cadieras que queden de la dita sinoga, pagaderos los ditos tresientos sueldos luego de present cient sueldos, e los otros cient a mitat de la obra, e los otros ciento acabada la obra. Et a esto tener e complir obligan nuestras personas e bienes. Testigos Johan Cortes e mosse Alazar judio osce." Arco, 1949, p. 371.

[23] Although the rug is commonly dated to earlier centuries, the workmanship is more characteristic of the fifteenth century.

## RITUAL OBJECTS

Little is known about the smaller liturgical objects and utensils, such as small oil lamps and spice holders, as they are found mostly in medieval documentary sources and more recent art. Two medieval ritual objects have survived, though not all specialists agree on their exact function.

London's Victoria and Albert Museum houses a spice holder used for the Havdala ceremony at the end of the Sabbath. As well as celebrating the start of the Sabbath (at sunset on Friday), Jewish families have preserved the tradition of a special ceremony through the ages: the Havdala (literally meaning "separation" or "division"), which marks the end of the Lord's day.

Spice holder used in the "Havdala" ceremony concluding the Sabbath, thirteenth century. Bronze. From al-Andalus. London, Victoria and Albert Museum

The Victoria and Albert spice holder resembles a three-story tower that is crowned with a pyramid and rests on a circular base. The three horseshoe-arch windows on each side of each story allowed the aroma of the spices (*besamin*) to be diffused into the air during the Havdala ceremony. This spice holder is possibly the oldest surviving object of its kind, not only from Spain but in the whole of Europe. Although it is traditionally attributed to a workshop in al-Andalus and dated to the thirteenth century, it could well have been made the previous century in Castile León.

Equally rare is a metal case from the sacristy of Toledo cathedral. It is believed to be a phylactery case, as it is the same shape as objects of this kind found in North Africa near the Strait of Gibraltar, although it has also been suggested that it could be an alms box. Phylactery cases (small boxes containing verses of scripture parchment, which devout Jewish men wear during their weekday prayers) were generally made of embroidered cloth over a rigid base and were larger than this piece; the surviving examples date from the modern age. This piece is decorated with vegetal motifs — stems with three-petaled flowers. The top bears an inscription with the name of its owner: "Isaac Caro." It has a lock in the center and a circular ring allowing it to be hung.

Phylactery case (?), thirteenth or fourteenth century. Toledo, Toledo Cathedral-Sacristy

24 A *Sefer Torah,* possibly from 1492, is housed in the Archivo Histórico Provincial in Huesca. This fragment of parchment contains the passage from the book of Numbers written in square lettering without vowel points.

## THE TORAH

Although no complete copies of medieval Spanish Torahs have survived, there are significant fragments: the *Calahorra Sefer Torah* and the *Ágreda Torah.*[24]

The *Calahorra Sefer Torah* is believed to be a fourteenth- or fifteenth-century work; specialists are unable to date it more accurately. Nor is it clear whether it was produced in Calahorra or Tudela.

This piece is made from superb quality tanned leather, probably goatskin, and displays writing on the smooth side only. The very elegant square lettering could

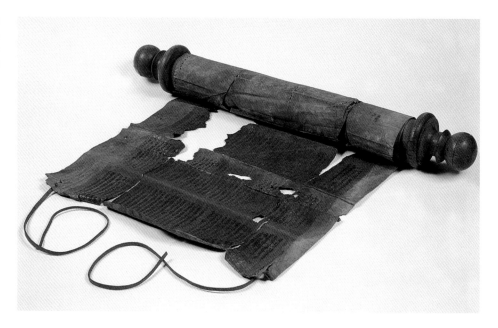

be the work of a Sephardic rabbi. The text is arranged in nine columns: the first five are written on the fragment that was later used to bind the minutes of the Cathedral Chapter and is in worse condition. Traces of another hand can be distinguished above and below the columns. This suggests that the parchment previously contained a different manuscript before the Torah. The extant passage is

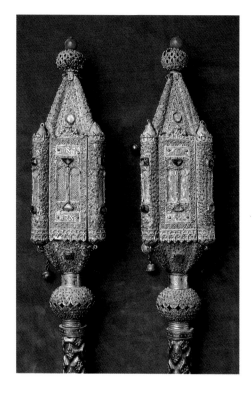

Fragment of leather scroll with Hebrew script; fragment of Torah from Ágreda synagogue (Soria), thirteenth or fourteenth century. From Ágreda synagogue (Soria). Ágreda (Soria), Archivo Municipal (Sección Histórica, Reg. 15/98; Exp. So–165)

Rimonim (finials for Torah scrolls), fourteenth century, Majorca cathedral

Maimonides, *Moré Nebujim (Guide for the Perplexed)*, Barcelona, 1347–1348, fol. 212r, detail. Copenhagen, Det Kogelinge Bibliotek (Cod. Hebr. XXXVII)

*Hebrew Bible,* Spain, ca. fourteenth century. Manuscript on parchment. Leiden (Netherlands), Leiden University Library (Ms. Or. 1197).

from the book of Exodus and goes from 4: 18 to 11: 10. The scroll probably measured forty meters (131 feet) when complete.

The surviving fragment of the Ágreda Torah is all that remains of the Pentateuch belonging to that town's synagogue, which is documented in late-fifteenth century records and was given by the "Catholic Monarchs", Ferdinand and Isabella, to the town council to be used as a town hall. The text covers Leviticus, 26: 43 to the end of the chapter and 1: 1–27. The manuscript is in poor condition and only the central column with the excerpt from Leviticus, 27: 10–34 is complete.

It is hard to gain from these poorly conserved fragments an exact idea of what the medieval Sefer Torahs we find in some miniatures actually looked like. Neither the mantle in which they were wrapped *(mapah)*, nor the breastplate *(tas)* placed on top, nor the crown *(keter)* has survived. The only extant medieval pieces are the so-called *rimonin* (literally "pomegranates"), or finials affixed to the scroll rods, that are housed in Palma de Mallorca cathedral. They are a superb example of fourteenth-century Sicilian workmanship.

> You shall not make yourself a graven image, or any likeness of anything that is in heaven above.

The above words, one of the commandments God gave His people, explain why there are no images of the divinity in the house of Yahweh. But this does

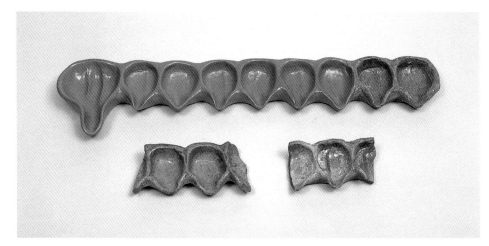

Hanukkah *lamp (hanukkiyah)*, fourteenth century. Honey glazed pottery. From Santa María la Blanca (Burgos). Burgos, Museo de Burgos (inv. no. 8.796/19.2 & 8.796/19.3)

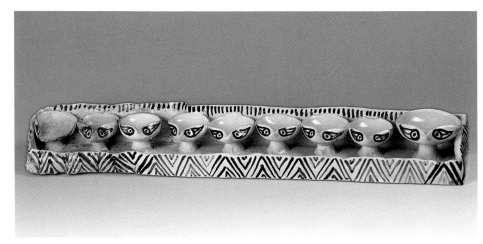

Hanukkah lamp *(hanukkiyah)*, fifteenth century. Teruel ceramic ware, green/purple series. From a site behind the Torreón de Ambeles, Plaza de la Judería, Teruel. Teruel, Museo de Teruel (inv. no. 7167)

not mean that synagogues lacked ornamentation. Brightly colored decorative schemes of abstract and vegetal motifs cover the walls of synagogues such as Samuel Halevi and Santa María la Blanca in Toledo, and that of Cordoba. We also find heraldic motifs such as royal coats of arms and symbols such as fleurs-de-lis.

Echoing a very ancient tradition which was also espoused — and raised to the highest status — by the Muslims, the most important ornamentation was words.

Most Jewish religious iconography would have been very familiar to Christians, as the two faiths share many images. In addition to what the Christians refer to as Old-Testament icons, the images of the unseen presence of God are also the same. The four symbols of ox, eagle, lion, and angel, depicted in an illustration from Maimonides's *Moré Nebujin*, are images that would have been understood by both Jews and Christians, as they derive from the vision of Ezequiel. The images in the manuscript were undoubtedly borrowed from Christian art. The symbol of a huge hand representing the divinity, as in the Masoretic illustration of the Song of Moses (Exodus 15, 1–18), is also highly characteristic of Christian art.

Book of Esther, fourteenth or fifteenth century. Manuscript on parchment scroll. From Toledo. Madrid, Archivo Histórico Nacional (Códice 1423B)

"A Passover seder scene," *Barcelona Haggadah,* fol. 19v, Barcelona, ca. 1350. London, The British Library (Ms. Add. 14761)

"Jews building the cities of Pitom and Ramses for the Pharaoh," *Barcelona Haggadah,* fol. 30r, Barcelona, ca. 1350. London, The British Library (Ms. Add. 14761)

## ARTS AND CRAFTS AT THE SERVICE OF RELIGION

The cycle of the Jewish religious year included a large number of celebrations, which could be solemn, major, or minor. Some events required particular objects and books, the quality of which depended on the family's purchasing power. A few of these are absolute masterpieces of medieval Hebrew culture.

The Feast of Lights or Hanukkah commemorates the purification of the Temple of Jerusalem in 165 B.C. Every Jewish home had a lamp with nine

Tesorillo de Briviesca. Five plates and two spoons, first half of fourteenth century. Silver. Burgos, Museo de Burgos (inv. nos. 745, 8782, 8783, 8784, 8785, 8787, 8790)

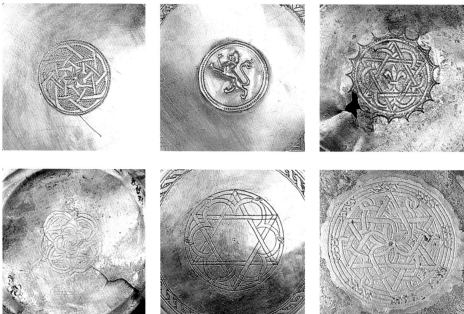

receptacles for oil (hanukkiyah), eight of equal size and one larger one. One was lit every day until, by the end of the eighth and last day of the feast, all were burning. The surviving fragments of lamps of this kind are made of a standard type of pottery. The fragments from Burgos's Jewry are very ordinary.[25] Although we might be inclined to regard the decorated lamp from Teruel with its expressive design as avant-garde, it is merely the product of popular wisdom.

The Feast of Lots or Purim commemorates the salvation of the Persian Jews by Queen Esther and her stepfather Mordecai. The scroll (Megilla) containing the story of Esther is read during the service at the synagogue.

Families did their utmost to create a sumptuous atmosphere for the Passover celebrations. The feast commemorated the deliverance of the Jews from Egyptian bondage. Families brought out their best dinner services and glassware on the solemn occasion of the Passover meal. The carefully prescribed ritual involved displaying the foodstuffs on a special plate, such as the superb mid-fifteenth-century ceramic plate from Valencia. There are many illustrations showing the whole family gathered around the lavishly decked-out table.

The archaeological finds known as "Tesorillos de Briviesca" include a set of plates and two silver spoons that may have belonged to a dinner service used on such solemn occasions. They are the most important surviving examples of Spanish medieval household silverware.[26] The medallions and borders are gilded and decorated with various themes such as ribbons, geometric shapes, and vegetal motifs, in addition to characteristic Jewish symbols such as stars, rampant lions, and fleurs-de-lis. One bears the mark of the earliest known Burgos silversmith.

The Haggadah, the book relating the story of the biblical Exodus, was of paramount importance in Passover ceremonies. Miniature illustrations show Haggadot laid out on tables to be read and commented on during the feast. Their quality varied from plain copies without illustrations to richly ornate books fit for princes, such as the Rylands Haggadah and the Golden Haggadah. The miniaturist who illustrated the Barcelona Haggadah included a shield for the coat of arms of the possible buyer. A Haggadah is among the earliest surviving books printed in Spain. As discussed in another chapter, illuminated manuscripts show a

25 See the ceramic ware from this Jewry in the section on household items.
26 Belén Castillo, 2002, pp. 181–185.

Copy of Pontateuch, Toledo, 1241. Manuscript on parchment. New York, The Library of The Jewish Theological Seminary of America (Ms. L 44a, vol. 2)

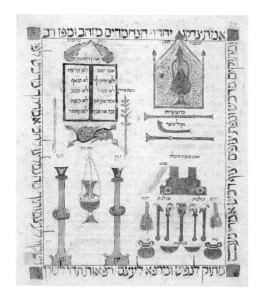

"Temple utensils," *King's Bible*, fol. 4r, Solsona, 1384, London, The British Library (Ms. King's I)

*Hebrew Bible,* Spain, second quarter of fifteenth century (?). Illuminated manuscript on parchment. Madrid, Biblioteca Nacional (Vit/26-6)

naturalistic type of illustration that verges on genre scenes: members of the family sitting around the table, bowing their heads as in the ritual toast, or washing their hands; or Jews under Pharaonic oppression making bricks and erecting a tower.

### THE BIBLE

The Bible is the cornerstone of Jewish liturgy and of individual conduct. During the Islamic rule, when Spanish Jews absorbed the influence of the dominant culture, one of the sciences in which they shone was language studies, which enabled them to gain a more exact knowledge of biblical texts. One of the fruits of this research was a paradigmatic text produced in León in the tenth century by Moses ben Hilel. The considerable number of copies of this Pentateuch (now missing), produced by scribes of Toledo, achieved great popularity during the whole of the Middle Ages.

The surviving Hebrew bibles are painstakingly decorated, though the themes illustrated in them, some of which are discussed in another chapter,[27] are very limited. Carpet pages were an effective non-iconic form of decoration, as a late-thirteenth-century bible completed in the fifteenth century shows. There are numerous references to the Temple, particularly plans or sacred utensils.[28] In some instances the symbolic message is more subtle, as in the illustration of the "Mount of Olives." Many ornamental elements are shared with Christian bibles of the period, particularly canon tables. Some bibles contain only floral or zoomorphic schemes that are highly characteristic of the late Gothic period and are no different from Christian ornamentation. Madrid's Biblioteca Nacional

[27] The section on art discusses micrography, calendars, carpet pages, and the "Mount of Olives" in greater detail.

[28] This theme emerged in the thirteenth century and became widely used in the following century, when it spread over two pages.

**Alba Bible, Maqueda, 1422. Madrid, Fundación Casa de Alba**

Translation of Books of the Old Testament ("Bible of Isabella 'the Catholic'"), Castile, thirteenth century; copy dating from the first half of the fifteenth century. Patrimonio Nacional, Biblioteca del Real Monasterio de San Lorenzo de El Escorial, Madrid (Ms. I–I–5)

[29] Found in many bibles from the fourteenth century onwards.
[30] Luis de Guzmán, Grand Master of the Order of Calatrava, commissioned Moses Arragel de Guadalajara, rabbi of the Jewry of Maqueda, a town near Toledo, to produce this Spanish translation under the supervision of Fray Arias de Enzinas, superior of the Franciscan monastery in Toledo. The translation was completed in 1430.

possesses a copy in which all the pages are illuminated in this fashion except for the episode of Jonah and the whale.[29]

Hebrew scholars and scribes also produced bibles for Christian customers. In Christian Europe, medieval Spanish bibles were famous for the quality of their texts, thanks largely to the Jews who translated them into the various Spanish vernacular languages. The so-called *Alba Bible*[30] is an exceptional example of a bible translated by a Jew for a Christian. The Christian customer wished to learn of the latest trends in Hebrew exegesis and commissioned the Jewish translator to add them to the translation. The 343 illustrations are one of the largest iconographic repertories of the time. Although executed by Christian illuminators, they display certain features that are somewhat out of place with Christian tradition. The scenes representing Abel bitten to death by Cain are rather naïve but highly expressive and explicit. The *Bible of Isabella "the Catholic"* belongs to a category known as "calques", biblical texts written in the Spanish vernacular language using a syntax and vocabulary that are grafted on to a Semitic structure.

### JEWISH BURIAL GROUNDS

Associations that organized burials sprang up towards the end of the thirteenth century. Their purpose was to help families cope with such a painful and costly affair. They took care of the burial preparations (purification rites,

"Cemetery," *Sister Haggadah*, fol. 11v
London, The British Library (Ms. Or. 2884)

"Jewish funeral procession," *Hispano-Moresque Haggadah,* fol. 84r, Castile, 1300. London, The British Library (Ms. Or. 2737)

making the shroud), the conveying of the corpse to the cemetery and burying it, and all the other funeral rites held at the synagogue and the family's home. Christians referred to these associations as "gravediggers" or "coffin bearers".

In some cases corpses were laid directly in the earth, shrouded in white linen, in accordance with Genesis, 3: 19: "you are dust and to dust you shall return." However, this was not the norm, as excavations attest to the existence of coffins. Preparation of the corpse involved both ritual purification and dressing. The grave goods unearthed at excavations of burial sites show that people were buried with the jewelry they wore when alive. Some were buried with rings on every finger, in keeping with the fashion of the time. Many women were buried wearing headdresses adorned with various accessories, including pins and even gold hairnets.

After mourning, which commonly involved tearing one's clothing, the funeral procession set off towards the cemetery. There are many Hebrew poems about death, such as the elegy composed by Judah Halevi (ca. 1070–1141) on the death of Moses ibn Ezra:

> Do not be afraid to weep and wail
> And mourn bitterly, rip your clothing
> May your tears not cease at such grief

Ibn Ezra portrays the cemetery as a place where the family was reunited to await the end of time:

> My thoughts spur me to pass by
> The resting place of my parents and relatives.
> I ask them, and nobody listens or replies,

**Fragment of epitaph, tenth-eleventh century. Brick. From Toledo. Toledo, Museo Sefardí (MS 2)**

**Epitaph of Abraham Salabi, fourteenth-fifteenth centuries. Sandstone. From the Jewish cemetery in Soria. Soria, Museo Numantino (inv. no. 75/17/1)**

Have even my father and mother betrayed me?
Silently they beckon me to them,
And show me my place by their side

To this day there are various place names, in all the Spanish vernacular languages, which denote sites where Jews were buried, such as "Fosar de los judíos" (Jews' burial ground), "Castro de los judíos" (Jews' hill), and "Montjuic" (Jews' mount), to name a few. Other place names are less obviously related to burial sites. In various Spanish towns we find a bridge known as the "puente de los judíos" (Jews' bridge), so called because funeral processions crossed it on their way to the cemetery.

We know of 118 Jewish burial sites in Spain.[31] Some of these cemeteries were located at a distance from the town, such as that of Barcelona. Most Jewries had their own cemetery, though in some cases not for long. In 1326 King James II granted the Jews of Burriana (in the province of Castellón) a plot of land within the town to be used as a cemetery, saving them the long and distressing journey to the neighboring town whenever they had to bury their dead.

Cemeteries were enclosed by walls and had one or more entrance gates.[32] Corpses were buried in rows. Sometimes, owing to special circumstances, a different arrangement was used. A pit with the remains of some forty people has been found in Valencia. This collective burial can be explained by the many deaths that resulted from the attacks on Valencia's Jewry in 1348 when townspeople blamed Jews for the Black Death. Corpses were generally buried with the head toward the west and the feet toward the east. This criterion seldom varied. It is believed that the north-south arrangement of the bodies buried in Valencia sprang from a wish to orient them to the city's main synagogue.

[31] Casanovas, 2002.
[32] Their area varied according to the Jewry's population; some Jewries had more than one cemetery.

**Tombstone of Mar Selomó ben Mar David b. Parnaj, 15 July 1097. From the "Castrum Iudeorum" (León). Museo de León (donated by the García de Arriba family, inv. no. 2000/26)**

The known graves date between the tenth and sixteenth centuries. Interestingly, there is evidence that some Jewish cemeteries continued to be used after the expulsion, until the sixteenth century. The different types of burial roughly correspond to the customs of the other religions practiced in Spain. The brick grave-marker now housed in the Museo Sefardí is typically Muslim.

Among the oldest tombs are the anthropomorphic type that are hewn out of rock; they resemble Christian graves in both form and date. We also find bathtub-shaped structures or brick-vaulted trapezoidal pits covered over with stone slabs and topped with a mound. The inscriptions bearing the name of the deceased sometimes included a eulogy or biblical reference, such as that of Mar Selomó ben Mar David b. Parnaj.

This is the tomb of Mar Selomó bar / Mar David ben Parnaj who died / at the age of forty on the fourth day / three days from the month of Av, year / four thousand eight hundred / and fifty-seventh year of the Creation / of the world according to the calendar of the city of León, may the Holy one, blessed be he / raise him and awaken he to the life of the world / to come and grant him a place with the righteous / and fulfill the Scripture, for it is written: / Your dead shall resurrect, my corpses shall rise from the dead, / awaken and rejoice, inhabitants of dust, for / the dew of light is your dew and the earth / shall emerge from the shadows, and you, look / and rest and you shall rise to your destiny / at the end of time.[33]

Not all tombstones were modestly sized; in fact, some were huge. When the Christians started to use large slabs arranged like gable roofs, so did the Jews, as the thirteenth-century tomb of Abraham Satibi shows.

[33] Avello *et alii*, 2002, p. 163.

# THE JEWS AND THE ARTS AND SCIENCES

# The Jews and the arts and sciences

E xcept for a few very specific genres and materials relating to their language or religion, which are dealt with in the relevant sections, it is not really possible to speak of Jewish science or Jewish art as such. Nevertheless, there were Jewish scientists (scholars) and artists who played an important role in Spain's arts and sciences in their day.

[1] As we explain in the section on "Jews, Moors, and Christians," this aspect appears to be inspired by the recommendations of the Prophet Jeremiah.

## THE JEWS AND THE PLASTIC ARTS

If we look at the Spanish synagogues that have survived, such as the synagogues of Samuel Levi and Santa María la Blanca in Toledo or the synagogue of Cordoba, we get the impression that the favorite Sephardic style of architecture was the Andalusian style. This, in addition to the decoration of some Hebrew codices with their richly ornate "carpet" pages, might appear to point to a Jewish taste for and assimilation of the Islamic aesthetic. Indeed, the Hispano–Jewish style is sometimes seen as another facet of the Eastern exoticism that inspired the imagination of the Romantic European historians who wrote of medieval Spain. This is not, however, entirely true.

No doubt owing to social considerations and religious reasons, the Jews voluntarily integrated fully into the society they lived in, whether Christian or Muslim.[1]

HCH Model
Model of Samuel Halevi synagogue, 2002, SEACEX

### Architecture

As with other aspects of Spanish Jewish culture, their architecture followed the same trends as those of the culture in which they lived. Just as Jews looked no different from the rest of the population (until required by both Christian and Muslim ecclesiastic authorities to wear distinctive signs), so too were their buildings outwardly indistinguishable from other buildings. The Besalú baths were built in the local Romanesque style of the period, and the Samuel Halevi synagogue at Toledo was built in the palatial style that was so popular in fourteenth-century Toledo. Even the Jewish homes in Muslim Granada were no different from Muslim homes. It could be said that, apart from strictly religious differences, the

Jews were like Muslims when they lived with Muslims and like Christians when they lived with Christians.

Examining the mansion of Samuel ibn Nagrella ha-Nagid (993–1056) in Granada, with its Byzantine-style domes and Oriental use of gardens and water, it is not possible to speak of a decisive Jewish influence on palatial architecture in eleventh-century Granada as some scholars have done. It is fascinating to read the description in the poems of Solomon ibn Gabirol (ca. 1022–ca. 1057) of some of these handsome palaces. The lion fountain reminds him of the sea of Solomon: "There is a copious pool which resembles/ the sea of Solomon/ but it does not rest on bulls/ such is the poise of the lions." The dome of one of the pavilions also has biblical echoes: "The vault resembles Solomon's palanquin/ suspended above the glories of the rooms.[2] There is nothing to suggest a Jewish tradition, either in the

[2] See the section on "Houses and Palaces" in the chapter on "The *Judería*".

View of the interior of Híjar synagogue, Zaragoza

type of construction or even in the concept of a palatial architectural style. What occurred was that the lifestyle of the prominent Jews was very similar to that of Islamic aristocrats, and the poet merely described his impressions using the imagery of his own religious culture.

A panel from the famous altarpiece by Jaime Serra showing St. Stephen preaching in the synagogue shows a typical Mediterranean Gothic building with ribbed vaults, small, high rose windows, and skeletal structure. The artist purposely avoided the use of imagery on the walls. Clearly, he was familiar with the interior of synagogues and the Jewish prohibition against icons. It could be argued that since the painting was painted by a Christian for Christian viewers, the depiction of the synagogue is no more than a conventional architectural setting. But pictures of synagogues painted by Jews are similar. The *Sister Haggadah*, an illuminated manuscript made in Barcelona in 1350, shows the interior of an equally Gothic building with a wooden ceiling supported by typical pointed arches and spiral columns. Not only is the architecture Gothic — so is the color of the walls and even the slightest detail of the furnishings. Nothing in the picture is even vaguely Moorish in style. The platform in the center of the painting is identical to pulpits in churches of the day and is clearly derived from old Romanesque designs. The same can be said about the synagogue and its furnishings portrayed in the *Sarajevo Haggadah*. The architecture of Híjar synagogue in Aragon, with its wooden roof supported by pointed diaphragm arches, is no different from that of Christian Gothic churches, which had the same wall and support structure.

Fragments of stuccowork with Hebrew inscription, fourteenth century. From the synagogue in Cuenca that became the church of Santa María la Nueva and, subsequentaly, that of Santa María de Gracia, and was finally demolished in 1912. There are archaeological remains beneath the current Torre Mangana. Cuenca, Archivo Diocesano de Cuenca

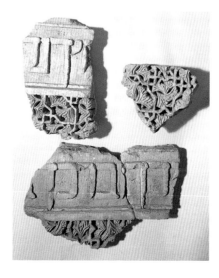

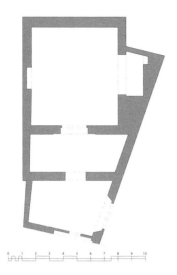

HCH Model.
Model of Cordoba synagogue, 2002,
SEACEX

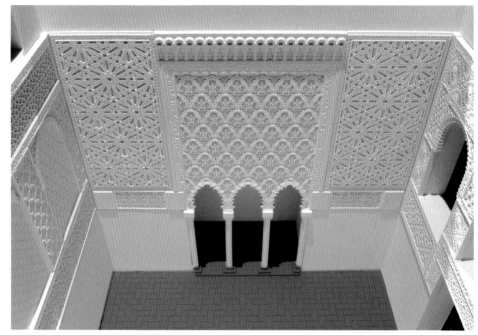

Going from religious architecture to private dwellings, whether sumptuous palaces or humble houses, both the illustrations in codices and archaeological evidence show that these buildings had a design similar to others of their kind.

## The Great Spanish Synagogues

Although we have old descriptions of synagogues,[3] and even some fragments of their decoration,[4] only four standing synagogues give us an idea what the original buildings looked like: the Samuel Halevi and Santa María la Blanca synagogues in Toledo, that of Tomar in Portugal, and that of Híjar in Aragon.

The synagogue of Cordoba is a small building with balanced proportions and magnificent decoration. A courtyard leads to a rectangular portico adjacent to the prayer room, which is a nearly square room of just under seven meters (25 feet) on each side. Above the portico is the women's gallery. In the east wall is the *hekhal* niche (the ark containing the Torah scrolls). Although the arch that framed it has been lost, it might have been similar to the one that is found in the Samuel Halevi synagogue. In the wall across from this is a niche with a multilobed arch which, as we have already mentioned,[5] was the place for the *bimah*. Although extensively restored, the stuccowork of the walls is beautifully decorated with geometrical designs and interlacing motifs. A frieze of windows runs along the top of the walls.

The style and decoration of the Samuel Halevi synagogue is typical of fourteenth-century Toledo, particularly as regards its monumentally. It consists of a large rectangular sanctuary measuring 9.5 x 23 metres (31 x 75 feet) with a height

[3] Cantera, 1955 y 1984.
[4] We have fragments of masonry of great beauty from the Synagogue of Cuenca, intricate Islamic vegetal motifs.
[5] See the section on the functions of places and furnishings in synagogues ("Religion and its Manifestations").

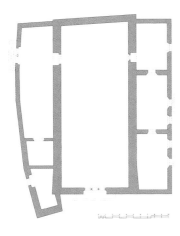

**HCH Model.**
**Model of Samuel Halevi synagogue,**
**2002, SEACEX**

of 17 meters (55 feet). There are a number of adjacent rooms along its long sides, and above the southern rooms is the women's gallery with large balconies overlooking the sanctuary. This prayer hall had a handsome coffered ceiling with chamfered corners. The eastern wall has a multilobed triple arcade, behind which is the *hekhal* or the *aron-ha godesh*. A frieze of arches runs along the top of the walls, some with plaster lattices that allow light to shine through.

There is a feeling of palatial architecture in the rich decoration of the walls and ceiling, and this is further emphasized by the brilliance of the colors. The stuccowork includes very lifelike oak and vine leaf motifs set inside conventional, non-naturalistic scrolls and interlacing. Juan Carlos Ruíz Souza has linked the style of this ornamentation to the workshops whose production is found at Santa Clara de Tordesillas, and dates it to between 1359/60 and 1361.[6] There is also a royal crest and inscription. The use of the Castilian king's coat of arms is explained by the fact that Samuel Halevi was Peter I's[7] treasurer.

Owing to lack of documentation and to the fact that the architectural style and decoration of the Santa María la Blanca synagogue were used over a long time period, there is much debate over the exact date it was built. It is a trapezoidal structure divided into five aisles of different sizes by four rows of horseshoe arches. The piers are octagonal with plaster capitals, and decorated by interlaced bands of scrolls and protruding pinecones. The arches and the spaces above them are decorated with scrolls and curious discs. Adorning the upper walls of the arcades is a frieze of blind arches. The stuccowork is a nineteenth-century restoration. Since the east end was altered when the synagogue was

[6] Ruiz Souza, 2002, pp. 235–236.
[7] We must remember that this is how the Jews expressed their submission to the king (see the chapter on "Jews, Moors, and Christians under the King's Authority").

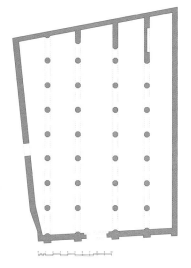

**HCH Model.**
**Model of Santa María la Blanca**
**synagogue, 2002, SEACEX**

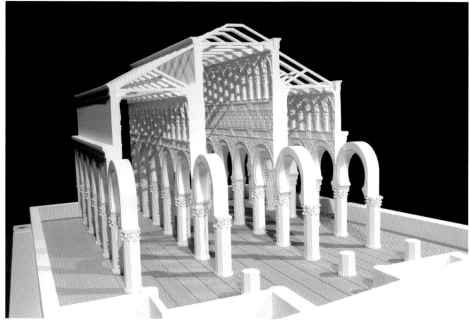

converted into a church, we know nothing about the placement of the *hekhal.*
All of its features, both structural and decorative, indicate that it was built in the
Islamic style during the thirteenth or fourteenth centuries.[8] The synagogue of
Segovia, which was converted into a church in 1419, appears to be a replica of
the Toledo structure, with three aisles, as we can see in the photographs taken
before it burned down.

### PAINTING AND BOOK ILLUMINATION

An important chapter in Jewish art is painting and, because of the type of works that
have survived, the illumination of books in particular. However, although we do not
have a sufficient number of codices to draw any precise conclusions about the evolution
of this art form, we can nonetheless put forward some general views on the subject.

No pictorial techniques can be considered exclusively Jewish from the
standpoint of materials, colors, or supports. As far as painters are concerned, we
do not have sufficient evidence either. However, the nature of the actual writing
conditioned the illumination of books to an extent.

As we know, Hebrew writing is read from right to left, that is, the opposite of
Roman writing, although both are read from top to bottom. Logically, the pictures
must be viewed in the same direction. The absence of capital letters — richly
decorative elements in Christian manuscripts — called for a special treatment. The
epigraphs were written in larger letters, highlighted in gold in some cases, and
were set within a frame against a monochrome background. At times the artists

[8] Contrary to the traditional chronology,
Ruiz Souza recently attributed it to the
fourteenth century (2002, p. 232).

Hamilton Siddur, late thirteenth century,
Spain or Languedoc (France).
Manuscript on parchment.
Berlin, Staatsbibliothek zu Berlin-
Preussische Kulturbesitz,
Orientabteilung (Ms. Hamilton 288)

used anthropomorphic lettering, a technique which was extremely popular among Christian miniaturists. The *Hamilton Siddur* includes a rich variety of this lettering,[9] which is probably based on much earlier models used over a long period of time, as shown by the colophon of the *Cervera Bible* and its copy, the *First Kennicott Bible*, published in La Coruña in 1476.

Micrography, the use of words and letters to define images, was one of the most interesting ornamental devices in Jewish illustration, and some very

[9] A piece done at the end of the thirteenth century, in either Spain or the Languedoc.

impressive results were produced.[10] It was used in the Masorah,[11] and although
the intricacy of the composition makes the text extremely difficult to read, if in
fact it makes any sense at all, the pictures formed by the letters are very clear.
The *Pamplona Bible*, published around 1400, reproduces a variety of real and
imaginary animals which closely coincide with some very popular Christian
models.[12] The centaur seems particularly typical of this. The fourteenth-century
*Hebrew Bible of Leiden* includes a Masorah with a micrographic illustration of the
parting of the Red Sea, and a reference to the Song of Moses (Exodus, 15: 1–18):
the enormous hand representing God who delivered Israel from Egypt.
Micrography is used in a fantastic combination with a carpet page in the *Hebrew
Bible of Copenhagen.*

[10] Ulrich, 1991, pp. 602–614.
[11] The Masorah is the body of notes on
the textual traditions of the Old
Testament compiled for memorization.
[12] Silva Verástegui believes that this
entire iconographic repertory is related
to the imagery in Pamplona Cathedral
(1988, p. 187).

"Micrographic Masorah with the figure
of a centaur," Bible (1400). Pamplona,
Archivo catedralicio

But what do we know about the history of these styles and illustrations? Our view is limited by the scarcity of surviving examples, and this makes it impossible to trace a stylistic evolution of Jewish painting during the fifteen hundred years that the Jews lived in Spain — or even a complete artistic period. Then again, some examples of sacred art appear very conservative in their treatment of iconography. This conservatism must also have influenced the use of color and painting style as well. The surviving works would appear to represent almost all of the various trends in painting and drawing in medieval Spain.

One of the masterpieces of Spanish Jewish painting is the picture of the Mount of Olives in the 1404 *Zaragoza Bible.* A full-page illustration on page 4 shows a small hill with coloured rocks — red, light blue, and brown — and two greyish-

וַעֲמָדוּ רַגְלָיו בַּיּוֹם הַהוּא עַל־הַר הַזֵּיתִים אֲשֶׁר עַל־פְּנֵי יְרוּשָׁלַ͏ִם

**Zaragoza Bible, Saragossa, 1404.**
**Paris, Bibliothèque nationale de France**
**(Ms. Heb. 31)**

green trees with intertwined trunks and two birds on either side. According to Jewish tradition, the theme of the Mount of Olives alludes to the place where the Messiah was to appear to announce the redemption. There is a touch of melancholic expressionism in the artist's treatment. In my opinion, no other Jewish illustration captures so well the spirit of this nation of landless people who wandered the wilderness waiting for the fulfillment of God's promises to them.

**Abraham Kalif, Bible. Toledo, 1492; Constantinople, 1497. New York, The Library of the Jewish Theological Seminary of America (Ms. L.6)**

**Leaf from the *Damascus Keter*, 1260. Manuscript on parchment, from Burgos. Toledo, Museo Sefardí (Inv. 230)**

[13] The compilation of this bible was affected considerably by the expulsion of the Jews in 1492. Copied in Toledo by the scribe Abraham Kalif a few months before the decree of expulsion, it was finished five years later in Constantinople, when Hayyim ibn Hayim added the Masorah.

[14] Each of the sections into which Pentateuch is divided for reading over the course of the year.

Although the most powerful elements of the illustration are the two colored bands in the background, which are very ancient devices, the illustration looks surprisingly modern. These colored bands were used frequently by Spanish miniaturists following late Roman patterns throughout the pre-Romanesque to the Romanesque periods, and their influence can be seen in works such as the *Blessed Saint-Sever*. Perhaps our artist had access to ancient images of this type which he used for reference, but it was his glorious idea to place them in this illustration — an illustration that has survived, albeit in rather poor condition, to our day.

Ancient sources are also suggested by the illustration in the bible of Abraham Kalif, a curious creation from Toledo around the time of the expulsion.[13] The table of correspondences on leaf 2 recto follows the characteristic pattern of biblical canons and Christian gospels, which in turn owed much to late Romanesque models. Below the green and yellow arcade is a list of the books of the bible and their corresponding *parasiyyot*.[14]

The decorative schemes found in Jewish bibles produced under Muslim rule were still employed in Castile in the thirteenth and fourteenth centuries. The famous Damascus Keter, a bible published in Burgos in 1260, with patterned

Joshua Ibn Gaon, Bible with Masora,
fols. 2v and 4v. Soria (?), 1300-1312.
Paris, Bibliothèque nationale de France
(Ms. Heb. 21)

decoration of vegetal motifs framed by a geometrical composition consisting of a micrographic Masorah, illustrates this stylistic dependence. Andalusian influence is more apparent in the architecture of the arcaded portico in the bible of Joshua ibn Gaon, although his calendar is structurally reminiscent of late ancient patterns, even though the vegetal decoration also uses Moorish shapes.

The most famous illustrated codices follow the various pictorial trends of the fourteenth-century Gothic style as regards both decoration and overelaborate iconography. There is an abundance of sinuous stalks with fantastic animals, like true *drôleries*, in works such as the *Barcelona Haggadah* or the British *Haggadah in the British Museum*. The *Golden Haggadah*, so called because of its richly decorated golden backgrounds, uses the elegant stylized forms of a pictorial trend that was highly influenced by the Italian school of the first half of the fourteenth century. This same refined influence, although in another artist's hand, can also be found in the copy of Maimonides's *Moré Nebujim*, which was illuminated in Barcelona in 1347–48. These pieces were obviously created for the aristocratic elite, such as the Jewish falconers reproduced here.

Other more popular forms of Gothic painting display a more original and spontaneous iconography. Whereas the imagery of the bibles usually remains very true to ancient prototypes, no doubt out of respect for tradition and religious values, other images, such as the illustrations in the *Haggadot,* pursue an

*Barcelona Haggadah*, Barcelona, ca. 1350-1360. London. The British Libray (Ms. Add. 14761)

"Passover seder, slaughtering and roasting the lamb," *Haggadah*. London, The British Library (Ms. Or. 1404, fol. 8r)

"Astronomers' discussion," Maimonides, *Moré Nebujim*, Barcelona, 1347–1348. Copenhagen, Det Kogelinge Bibliotek (Cod. Heb. XXXVII, fol. 114r)

Maimonides, *Compendium of the books of Galen*, Catalonia, fourteenth century, Paris, Bibliothèque nationale de France (Ms. Heb. 1203, fol. 45v)

unbridled creativity. The illustrations depicting family Passover[15] scenes appear to have been the most appropriate framework for artists who wanted to paint without religious restrictions. The artists appear to have been unrestricted in their creative freedom in these illuminations. However, this freedom was expressed in very different ways, and, of course, the technical skills of each artist varied. If we compare the images of the *Golden Haggadah* to those of the *Barcelona Haggadah* or the so-called *Hispano-Moresque Haggadah*, we can clearly perceive distinct

[15] We briefly dealt with iconographic repertories in the section on "Religiona and its Manifestations".

**"Preparations for Passover,"** *Golden*
*Haggadah*, fol. 15r, Barcelona, 1320.
London, The British Library
(Ms. Add. 27210)

criteria. In all three examples the artist
followed his own personal creative design
without predetermined patterns. However,
the first is very conventional in its
treatment, whereas the other two depict a
Jewish society which the artists actually
experienced. The architecture, people, and
objects in the *Golden Haggadah* would not
be out of place in any Christian, secular, or
Jewish illustration; the artist simply added
figurative elements until the scene was
complete. Using a more colloquial language,
the artist who illustrated the *Barcelona*
*Haggadah* portrays the Passover *seder* scenes
as genre pictures that could easily represent
life in a house in the Call de Barcelona. The
family sitting at the table taking part in the
various *seder* ceremonies looks perfectly true
to life. Unlike other illustrations, the dining
room with its green silk and gold decorated
curtains and the table, despite the
somewhat coarse workmanship, do not look
stiff and unnatural. The *Hispano-Moresque*
*Haggadah*, which was painted by a Castilian
Jewish painter around 1300, is another
example of popular art. Despite his technical limitations, the artist
enthusiastically depicts his surroundings. The women kneading bread look like
typical Castilian women. The oven scene, the immersion in the *mikvah,* the
preparation of the *kharoset,* etc., all show a creative spontaneity and an attempt to
reflect real life.

Surviving Jewish miniatures include several scenes from the interiors of
synagogues which also display a concern to reproduce real environments,
furniture, and objects.

Late-Gothic style, with its intricate floral ornamentation found in fifteenth-
century books of hours and bibles, is found in a bible housed in Madrid's Palacio
Real. The Renaissance style is not represented in Hispano–Jewish works.
The Portuguese Bible[16] which was created in Lisbon follows fifteenth-century
Gothic patterns; its Renaissance illustrations were not painted on the Iberian
peninsula and date from a different period. Nor is the Renaissance style found in
the first Hebrew works to be printed in Spain; these early editions continued to
use the same woodblock techniques.

[16] National Library, Paris, Ms Heb. 15.

הַזֶּה כָּל יָמֵי חַיֶּיךָ לְהָבִיא לִימוֹת הַמָּשִׁיחַ
בָּרוּךְ הַמָּקוֹם שֶׁנָּתַן תּוֹרָה לְיִשְׂרָאֵל
בָּרוּךְ הוּא כְּנֶגֶד אַרְבָּעָה בָנִים
דִּבְּרָה תוֹרָה אֶחָד חָכָם וְאֶחָד רָשָׁע וְאֶחָד
תָּם וְאֶחָד שֶׁאֵינוֹ יוֹדֵעַ לִשְׁאוֹל ׃

חָכָם מָה הוּא אוֹמֵר מָה הָעֵדֹת וְהַחֻקִּים
וְהַמִּשְׁפָּטִים אֲשֶׁר צִוָּה
אֱלֹהֵינוּ אֶתְכֶם אַף ׃

*Haggadah*, Spain or Portugal, late
fifteenth century. New York, The Library
of the Jewish Theological Seminary of
America (Very rare Collections, 5637)

**ARTISTS**

What do we know about the artists who created these
works? Virtually nothing. Some colophons provide names,
but, as in the case of the Christian works, it is not known
whether they refer to the scribe or the illuminator. In the
aforementioned 1404 *Zaragoza Bible*, the colophon tells us:
Hayim b. Saul, known as Vidal Satorre, completed the copy
of this bible at the age of 60, with the aid of eyeglasses,
under commission by R. Izhaqb. R. Judá Abendiná, in
Zaragoza in the month of *Sevat*, of the 5164th year of
Creation (January/February 1404).[17] We know that Vidal
Satorre produced another bible in Cervera in 1383. The styles
of the two works are so different that we may conclude that
they were produced by two different illuminators. We are
luckier in other cases where the colophons specifically
mention the illuminators. For example, the *First Kennicott
Bible* includes an inscription in anthropomorphic letters:

I, Joseph ben Hayim, illuminated this book and
completed it.

Joseph based his work on the *Cervera Bible*, in which the
author's name was also inscribed in zoomorphic letters: "I,
Joseph Hasarfarí, illuminated this book and completed it."
These colophons demonstrate the importance of the artist's contribution to these
works, not only by the fact that they signed their names, but also because their
signatures occupy so large and prominent a space for posterity. This feeling of
artistic pride in their work is a well-known tradition among the late-medieval
Spanish miniaturists, and had no match within European tradition. We also know
about contractual agreements for the illumination of books: a Jew from Mallorca,
Aser Bonnin Maymó, accepted a commission in 1335 to copy a bible and two
books by Maimonides for David Isaac Cohén.[18]

The aforementioned Joshua ibn Gaon included the following information in
his bible: "I, Joshua b... Abraham ibn Gaon, have completed the first copy of this
book for the venerable doctor R. Abraham de Leiria, son of..."[19] He proves to be a
good Masorete and illuminator, and a specialist in calendars.

Through the many references to easel paintings, we know that many Jewish artists
made altarpieces for Christian customers, such as Abraham de Salinas.[20] Although we
have no specific supporting or contradicting documentary evidence, it seems likely
that the opposite was true as well: that Christian artists worked for Jewish clients.

[17] Blasco and Romano, 1991, pp. 3–11.
[18] Hilgarth and Narkis, 1961, pp.
297–320.
[19] Leiria is a town near Soria where our
scribe/illuminator probably composed
most of his work.
[20] Blasco Martínez, 1988.

## Sciences

Attached as they were to their profound religious beliefs, the Jews regarded Solomon as the father of science. A fictional character created by Judah Halevi (ca. 1070–1141) asserted other nations' debt to Jewish science as follows:

> Nowadays, he complains, it has been forgotten that sciences originated from the Hebrew people, and they are attributed to Greeks and Romans.[1]

Although the concept of science going hand-in-hand with Jewish religious tradition was eventually superseded, it is obvious that the medieval concept of science differed from that of today. Felipe Maíllo Delgado describes these differences shrewdly:

> We should bear in mind that medieval science bore very little resemblance to the science developed in Western Europe following the Renaissance. Whereas Western science applies mathematical hypotheses to nature, [medieval science] uses the experimental method, distinguishes between primary and secondary qualities, geometrizes space, accepts the mechanical model of reality, and tends towards universalization[2] because of its capacity for making generalizations.

Just as medieval science differs from today's, so are medieval scientists rather sui generis. The following text written by Sa'id al-Andalusí (d. 1070) gives an idea of what they were like. In his *Kitab Tabaqat al-umam,* this cadi (Islamic judge) and scientific historian living in Toledo paints a varied picture of a group of Jewish scientists with whom he was personally acquainted:

> Later, during the civil war period, lived Menahim b. al-Fawwal, an inhabitant of Saragossa. He was an expert in the art of medicine and was also well-versed in the art of logic and the other philosophical sciences. He has a treatise which provides an introduction to the philosophical sciences, entitled *Kanz al-muqill* ("The Poor Man's Treasure"). He wrote it as a set of questions and answers, and included all the laws of physics in it.
>
> In Saragossa, during the same period, lived Marwan b. Yanah, a person interested in the art of medicine and with a vast knowledge of the Arabic and

[1] Quoted by Alfonso, 2002, p. 68.
[2] Maíllo, 2002, p. 280.

Hebrew languages. He has written a treatise on the interpretation of simple medicines, and on determining the dosage of these medicines used in the art of medicine using weights and measures.

Among them also is Ishaq b. Qustar, who was in the service of al-Muwaffaq Muyahid al-Amiri and his son Iqbal ad-Dawla Ali.[3] He was versed in the fundamentals of medicine, was familiar with the science of logic, and had studied the opinions of the philosophers. He was a man of laudable conduct and excellent morals. I have frequented his company and have not seen a Jew like him as regards equanimity, sincerity, and well-roundedness. He possessed an admirable knowledge of the Hebrew language and excelled in the law of the Jews, being one of their rabbis. He died in Toledo in 1056, at the age of seventy-five. He never married.

Among the Jews were some who were interested in certain branches of philosophy. Sulayman b. Yahya, known as Ibn Gabirol, an inhabitant of the city of Saragossa, was an enthusiast of the art of logic and a man of keen intelligence and excellent judgment. Death befell him when he had scarcely turned thirty, in the year 1058.

Among the young scholars of our day is Abu l-Fadl Hasday b. Yusuf b. Hasday, an inhabitant of the city of Saragossa, who belongs to a noble family of Jews residing in al-Andalus who descend from the Prophet Moses, peace be to him. He developed an interest in the rational sciences and has acquired the knowledge of their branches after his own methods. He has an excellent command of the Arabic language and has mastered a considerable part of the arts of poetry and rhetoric. He is outstanding in the science of numbers, in geometry and astronomy. He has mastered the art of music and has attempted to put it into practice. He has studied the science of logic and has practiced the method of observation. Then he progressed to the study of natural sciences, beginning with the study of the Aristotle's *Physics (al-Kiyan),* and acquiring a splendid mastery. He then took up the treatise *On the Heavens.* He gave it up in 1065 when he had penetrated its secrets. If he lives to an old age and maintains his zeal, he will become an eminent philosopher and will grasp the different branches of knowledge. He is still a young man who has not yet reached maturity, but God in his greatness endows whomever he wishes with his grace.[4]

It is clear from this long list of Jewish scientists that they all embraced a variety of disciplines. Medieval Jewish sages, like those of other religions, did not specialize in a particular science: they all excelled in several.

An important task in which these intellectuals engaged was translation. Their translations into Latin and into the Spanish vernacular languages

[3] Sovereigns of Denia and the Balearic Islands from 1012 to 1075.

[4] I quote Maíllo, 2002, pp. 284–285.

facilitated the dissemination of Oriental culture throughout Western Europe. The Muslims had misgivings about this activity, which the twelfth-century jurist Ibn Abdun regarded as usurpation:

> Science books shall not be sold to Jews or Christians, except for those dealing with their law, because they then translate science books and attribute them to their own people and bishops, even though they are the works of Muslims.[5]

## POETRY

Carrying on with their most characteristic tradition, the Hispano-Jewish poets continued to write religious poetry (liturgies, invocations, and laudatory and penitential prayers). As in so many other aspects of culture, their contact with Muslims deeply changed these tastes and led to the emergence of a secular poetry imbued with a sensuousness that far exceeds that of works produced by other communities of Jews in exile. This poetry enjoyed a heyday in the eleventh and part of the twelfth centuries. The list of poets of this golden age includes names as prominent as Samuel ibn Nagrella (993–1055), Solomon ibn Gabirol (ca. 1020–ca. 1057), Moses ibn Ezra (ca. 1055–1135), and Judah Halevi (ca. 1070–1141).

The following short poem by Moses ibn Ezra, the third of the great poets of that period, illustrates well this Jewish love poetry:

> My heart, my heart yeans for the gazelle
> it loved even before she existed;
> since the day she left, there is no sleep for
> its eyes, which shepherd the stars above.

Don Santo de Carrión (thirteenth-fourteenth century) is one of the Jewish poets who also wrote in the Romance vernacular, infusing Castilian poetry with a lyricism of marked Muslim origin:

> When the rose is dry
> as its ripeness departs
> the fragrant rose-scented water remains
> which is more valuable.

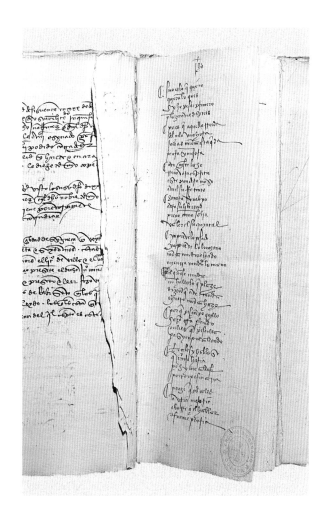

*Coplas del rabino Don Sento* (Verses of Rabbi Don Sento), Castile, 1355–1360, copy Sigüenza, 1492. Manuscript on paper. Cuenca, Archivo Diocesano (Inquisición 6/125).

[5] Quoted by Alfonso, 2002, p. 65.

His best known work is the *Proverbios morales*, a compendium of some six hundred verses in Castilian dealing with virtues and faults according to Arab and Jewish moralistic tradition.

## GRAMMAR

Despite earlier, minor attempts, Hebrew grammar as a science emerged in the tenth century owing to the influence of important studies on Arab linguistics. The first Jewish grammarians were Seadya Gaón in the East, Yehuda ibn Curays in North Africa, and Menajem ben Saruc and Dunás ben Labrat in al-Andalus. Since understanding the Bible was one of the chief concerns of the Jewish sages, it is hardly surprising that biblical exegesis should have been one of the earliest preoccupations of philology: an attempt to find explanations for some biblical terms.

According to Menajem ben Saruc, born in Tortosa around 910, the essence of philological studies was the following:

Jonah ibn Janah (ca. 985, Cordoba?), *Sefer ha-hahasvaá*. Zaragoza, eleventh century, thirteenth-fourteenth century copy. Manuscript on parchment. Madrid, Biblioteca Nacional (Ms. 5460)

To express the Hebrew language with clarity in accordance with the essential content of its fundamentals and the essence of its roots.[6]

The poets were also interested in learning the rules that govern and organize language. Some of the great philologists were Judah Hayyuj (ca. 940–ca. 1000) and Jonah ibn Janah (ca. 985, Cordoba?–?). The latter, a physician by profession, was the author of the *Sefer hahasvaá* (the Hebrew version of the *Book of Reprobation),* originally written in Arabic. This book may be considered the first complete and systematic grammatical work on the language of the Bible.

The Kimhi family settled in Provence and several of its members wrote books on grammar. One of them was David, the author of a Grammar or *Mijlol* (Generalities), which includes a full description of the Hebrew bible and a vocabulary or dictionary, the *Sefer hasorasim* (Book of Roots). This grammar book, together with that of Abraham ibn Ezrá, may be regarded as the basis of all subsequent works of this kind.

[6] According to a translation by Sáez Badillos, 1986.

المواضع العلة من الأعضاء المجاوره لذا ذنا لا اكثر مما خلا ...

Moses ben Maimon (Maimonides)
(Cordoba, 1138–Cairo, 1204), *Medical Aphorisms*. Fostat, 1187–1190,
undated copy. Patrimonio Nacional,
Biblioteca del Real Monasterio de San
Lorenzo de El Escorial, Madrid
(Ms. Árabe, 869)

## MEDICINE

The list of Jewish physicians in the service of the Muslim princes of medieval Spain is endless: Hasdai ben Shaprut (ca. 910–970), who also cured King Sancho I of León of dropsy; Menajem ibn al-Fawwal, at the court of the Saragossa *taifa* king; Yisjac ibn Qustar, at the court of the Denia *taifa*; Abraham ibn Zarzal, physician first to King Muhammad V and subsequently, from 1359, to King Peter I, the Cruel, of Castile. Equal in number and fame were the Jewish physicians of the Christian monarchs: Pedro Alfonso (Moses Sefardí) (b. 1062), physician to King Alfonso I of Aragon and of King Henry I of England; Seset ben Yisjac Benveniste (1131–1209), physician to King Alfonso II and King Peter II of Aragon and the author of some as-yet-unpublished medical treatises.

However, none attained the fame of the great philosopher Maimonides (1138–1204), who was born in Cordoba but forced to flee with his family following the arrival of the Almohads. After visiting different parts of Spain and Africa, he eventually settled in Cairo, where he practiced medicine, first in the service of a cadi, the vizier of Saladin, and subsequently for Saladin's eldest son. His vast medical oeuvre, which embraces a variety of themes, was written in Arabic and then translated into Hebrew and Latin. Ten medical treatises survive. Of these, the *Medical Aphorisms* is the most voluminous, containing 1,500 aphorisms derived from the work of Greek physicians. The *Guide to Good Health* is his best-known and most widely translated work.

Arib b. Said translated Dioscorides's *De Materia Medica* into Arabic. He was particularly interested in pharmacology, and explained the secrets for concocting theriac, a miraculous remedy known since antiquity. This medicament, which contained opiates, could cure serious illnesses and even male impotence.[7]

## HISTORY AND TRAVELS

With the exception of cartography, Jewish authors did not produce significant works on geography, travels, and history.

Jewish histories show greater concern with transmitting oral laws — that is, rabbinic tradition — than narrating the events which shaped the history of the people of Israel over the ages. The title of the work by Abraham ibn Daud

[7] Barkai, 1994, pp. 17–18.

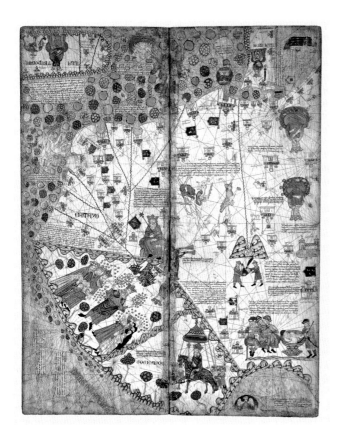

**Cresques Abraham, illuminated mappemonde, fourteenth century. Paris, Bibliothèque nationale de France (Ms. esp. 30, pl. 2–3)**

(ca. 1110–1180), *Sefer ha-qabbalah* (Book of Tradition), clearly shows the author's aims as a historian. Maimonides was scornful of historical works:

> The books we find among the Arabs, books on history, the customs of kings, the lineage of the Arab tribes, of poetry and similar things, are books lacking in wisdom and practical utility and are only a waste of time.

The fifteenth-and sixteenth-century chronicles come closest to our idea of history. The beginning of the *Compendio de la memoria*, by R Yosef ben Saddiq, points out the change in the concept of history: "It will recall the history of our forefathers." Abraham Zacut's *Book of Genealogies*, Solomon ibn Verga's *Scepter of Judah,* and Abraham ben Selomoh de Torrutiel's *Sefer ha-qabbalah* are other historical treatises dating from that period which focus on the events immediately after the expulsion.

Benjamin of Tudela, born around 1130, is the most famous of the medieval Jewish travelers. In his *Sefer Masaot* or "Book of Travels" he describes at great length the highlights of his travels from Tudela to Rome, Constantinople, and Jerusalem as far as Baghdad, and his return to Paris via Cairo and Alexandria. The richness of detail makes this work a prime source of information on the Mediterranean world in the twelfth century.

The most important fourteenth-century cartographic work was compiled by two Jews, father and son, Abraham Cresques and Yehuda, *magistri mapamudorum et buxolarum* (master map-makers).

### EXEGESIS, LAW CODES, AND CABBALA[8]

As pointed out earlier, the Spanish Jews placed their knowledge of grammar and philosophy at the service of biblical exegesis. The greatest exponent was Abraham ibn Ezra (1093–1167), whose work was widely disseminated among Jewish communities in France, Italy, and England.

Rabbinical exegesis was based mainly on the methods known as *pesat,* or literal meaning of the biblical text, and *derás,* which consisted in deriving rules of conduct and theological teachings from the text. Although he did not write any

[8] This brief summary follows that of Alba Cecilia, 2002, p. 320.

works dealing specifically with this theme, Maimonides is the most influential of the exegetes. Indeed, his entire oeuvre is full of exegetic material. One of his most outstanding followers was David Kimhi (1160–1235), who introduced philosophical exegesis into his commentaries.

Maimonides was also an eminent jurist: his *Misneh Torah* is the first great law code. Its fourteen books regulate all aspects of Jewish life clearly and systematically. The fact that he did not cite the opinions of the great Talmudic scholars who preceded him was highly criticized by his detractors. Another attempt at compiling a clear and practical law code was made by Jacob ben Aser (Toledo, 1270–1343). His *Arbaá Turim* (The Four Rows) seeks to regulate everyday life in the Jewish communities of the time. His code, structured into four areas, draws from Central European and Spanish legal traditions. He greatly influenced Joseph Caro (1488–1575), whose *Sulján Aruj* faithfully reflects his style and structure.

The Cabbala is the most significant form of Jewish medieval mysticism. It attained its height of development in Spain: first in Gerona, in the circle of Nahmanides, and later in Castile. Its theology is a speculation (theosophy) on the belief in a complex concept of the divinity consisting of a *deus absconditus* (hidden God), and ten *sefirot*, attributes or manifestations of divinity. This theosophy is accompanied by a theurgical (magical) component based on the belief that human activity can influence the world of divinity. Among the cabbalists of the Gerona group who spread knowledge of this system were Ezra and Azriel.

Various strands of Cabbalism sprang up in Castile, although the theosophical-theurgical current was the most widespread and produced the most important work of its kind of all time, the *Zohar*. The *Zohar* is a mystic commentary on the Torah written in Aramaic and attributed to a second-century rabbi, Simeon ben Yohai. Most of the book derives from Moses of León and cabbalists from his circle.

The diocesan archive in Cuenca houses a curious cabbalistic amulet from an inquisitorial trial. According to A. Alba Cecilia, it displays some very typical elements such as the invocation to the angels Temuniel, Yofiel, and Hasdiel in the central ring, and two verses from the Psalms around the square endosing the circles ("My refuge and my fortress; my God, in whom I trust." For he will deliver you from the snare of the fowler and from the deadly pestilence" [Psalms, 91: 2-3], and "[The Lord is] your keeper, the Lord is your shade on your right hand" [Psalms, 121: 5]). Psalm 91 was recited at night, before going to sleep, in order to keep demons at bay, and 121 appears in many spells against Lilit, the she-devil who causes evil to newborns and women in childbirth. The four circles at the corners contain the names of three planets — *Maadim* (Mars), *Nogah* (Venus), and *Tsedeq* (Jupiter) — and *Hamma* (the Sun). The two smaller circles contain "magical squares" in which letters of the Hebrew alphabet are written according to their numerical value.[9]

[9] Alba Cecilia, 2002, p. 323.

*Cabbalistic amulet,* Spain, fifteenth century. Manuscript on parchment. Cuenca, Archivo Diocesano

## PHILOSOPHY

The Hispano-Jewish philosophers absorbed the influence of the major Greek schools of philosophy, such as Neoplatonism and Aristotelianism, through the Arabic versions written by such thinkers and commentators as Alfarabi, Avicenna, and Averroes. The chief characteristic of medieval Jewish philosophy is its predominantly religious vein: it attempts to express and explain the main tenets of Judaism — a single God who created everything that exists and who reveals himself to man and communicates with him — in philosophical terms and concepts.

Solomon ibn Gabirol (ca. 1021–1058), who was born in Malaga and lived in Saragossa, was the first great Hispano-Jewish philosopher. His *Fountain of Life,* which displays a clear Neoplatonic influence, sets out to shape a universal metaphysic that shies away from the specificity of the Judaic religion. *Hobot ha-Lebabot* (Duties of the Hearts) written by Bahya ibn Paquda (Saragossa

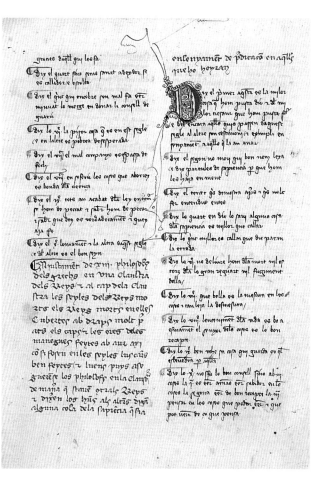

*Moses ben Maimon* (Maimonides) (Cordoba, 1138–Cairo, 1204). *Moré Nebujim
(Guide for the Perplexed)*, Fostat, 1190. Manuscript on paper. New York, The
Library of The Jewish Theological Seminary of America (Ms. 8254.5)

Yehuda ben Astruc de Bonsenyor (?–ca. 1331), *Llivre de Paraules e dits da
savis e filosofs* (Book of the words and sayings of sages and philosophers),
Catalonia, 1298, copy dated 1385. Manuscript on paper. Madrid,
Biblioteca Nacional (Ms/921)

ca. 1040–ca. 1110) displays an original combination of Neoplatonic ideas, Jewish
tradition, and Sufic mysticism.

One of the themes that attracted the interest of the Hispano-Jewish
philosophers was religious dogma. The great rationalist philosopher Maimonides
(Moses ben Maimon, Cordoba 1138–1204) was the first to establish the dogmas
that Jews were required to believe. In *Moré Nebujim* (Guide for the Perplexed), he
attempted to reconcile Aristotelianism and faith, making a decisive contribution to
the understanding of the created universe. In his opinion, understanding reality
should help man fulfill his duties.

However, the excessive rationalization of faith and religion, by reducing it to
pure reason and Aristotelian categories, triggered reactions against philosophy, and
the works of Maimonides sparked a major controversy among Jewish thinkers.

Another writer on philosophy was Yehudah ben Astruc de Bonsenyor (?–ca.
1331), a physician and interpreter of Arabic, who lived at the court of King James II
of Aragon. The monarch commissioned him to write the *Llivre de Paraules e dits
da savis e filosofs*. This didactic work, written in Catalan, is a compendium of
Middle-Eastern-style ethical maxims.

# JEWS, MOORS, AND CHRISTIANS
# UNDER THE KING'S AUTHORITY

# Jews, Moors, and Christians under the King's Authority

As with so many other aspects of Spanish history, interpreting the coexistence of Jews, Moors, and Christians in a particular time and space has given rise to heated debate. According to some, the concept of "three cultures, three religions," a sort of slogan that conveys an idyllic situation, is in fact a euphemism, a politically correct expression that is a far cry from the raw sociological reality of medieval Spain. Those who hold this view reject the idea of interrelation and will only accept the term "coexistence." Others do not hesitate to use terms such as "tolerance."

There is no doubt that the religious communities which each exercised power at some point, the Christians and the Muslims, imposed their ideas on the rest with varying degrees of coercion. These attitudes obviously varied substantially, depending on the period, from the most indulgence tolerance to the most intransigent lack of understanding and resulting repression. Although there is currently a certain tendency to understand the attitude of the Spanish Muslims and harshly criticize that of the Christians, it is clear that both communities held very similar attitudes towards the Jews as regards both understanding and repression. The same could be said of the Jewish community's attitude towards Christians and Muslims: they adapted to both. The Jewish minorities to whom the king or caliph delegated power yielded to the sovereigns and exercised their authority harshly, even with their own people — a fairly common occurrence in the history of ethnic group behaviour.

As an ethnic and religious minority, the Jews were constantly obliged to seek the support of the person who governed the community — the king, the prince or simply the lord. In these relationships the Jews, owing no doubt to their weak position in a convulsive and aggressive society, invariably proved to be naively tolerant of the attitude of some monarchs. Solomon ibn Verga (1460–1554) refers gratefully to the behaviour of Manuel I of Portugal (1495–1521) after the 1506 massacre of Jews in Lisbon, failing to realize that it had in fact been this Portuguese monarch who had ordered the compulsory conversion of the Portuguese Jews in 1497:

> The King of Portugal, who was a pious monarch, was not in the city at the time, but when he learned of it [the calamity] he wept and deplored the misfortune; he at once came to the city, made inquiries, and discovered the lies of the friars. He gave orders for the church from which the evil had sprung to be demolished, but his princes did not give their consent.

Coat of arms, synagogue of Samuel Halevi, Toledo

This unconditional submission to the king's authority stemmed from religious tradition. When the Hispano-Jewish rabbis were asked to reply to certain questions on this matter, they based their arguments on passages from Jeremiah and Nehemiah. The Jews of the Diaspora always cited Jeremiah to justify their commitment and loyalty to the kingdom where they resided:

> But seek the welfare of the city where I have sent you into exile, and pray to the Lord on its behalf, for in its welfare you will find your welfare. (Jeremiah, 29: 7)

And according to Nehemiah, royal taxes were justified as a divine imposition:

> And its rich yield goes to the kings whom thou hast set over us because of our sins; they have power also over our bodies and over our cattle at their pleasure, and we are in great distress. (Nehemiah, 9: 37)

In this connection Maimonides did not hesitate to state that "the inhabitants of the country accepted the king and take for granted that he is their lord and they his servants." However, this servitude had a limit — the spiritual realm, as we may infer from the words which, according to the chronicler Solomon ibn Verga, the Jewish community addressed to the Almohad monarch who obliged them to convert to Islam:

> You shall be the lord of our bodies and the owner of our farms; but of our souls the only king and lord is He who sent them to our bodies and shall summon them to Him to judge them and you, our lord, on your throne, are free of this.[1]

There were two very distinct stages in the relationship between the Sephardim and the monarchs: the king as the main enemy of the Jewish community, and the Jews as the king's property. Generally speaking, in both cases the Church attempted to prevent the monarchs from becoming the protectors of the Jewish communities and, at times, energetically promoted a climate of opinion that facilitated a belligerently anti-Jewish policy.

As the chapter on the historical background illustrates, relations between the monarchy and the Jewish community got off to a bad start during Spain's Gothic age (551-711). Although the Arab invasion (711) brought about a significant change in relations with the dominant power, the Jews ended up being cruelly persecuted. The situation then changed radically as Christians began to reconquer Spain from the Moors. The population was made up of three communities that were clearly differentiated by their religion: Jews, Moors and Christians. All three were the kingdom's subjects and, in principle, enjoyed full rights. The oldest law codes and

[1] Cantera Burgos, 1927, p. 48.

charters allocating lands to the new settlers draw no distinctions between Christians and Jews. The monarchs address the municipalities referring very specifically to the heterogeneous nature of their inhabitants:

> To our beloved and faithful vassals, to the mayor and to the law officer and to the municipal officials and to all the council of the Christians and of the Jews and of the Moors of Tudela, health and love.[2]

This expression, used by King Henry I of Navarre in an act granting a privilege to the council of Tudela in 1271, is also found in royal documents issued by the Crown of Aragon and the kingdoms of Castile and León from the twelfth century onwards. It is therefore not surprising that Alfonso VI should have been known as the "king of the three religions."

Not only were the monarchs who ruled the kingdoms of the peninsula the effective guarantors of the coexistence of the three religions; they also gave rise to stories, objects, and monuments which testify delightfully to this close and direct relationship between the prince and his subjects. During the thirteenth century the court of Castile made a point of proclaiming to all and sundry, as a basic principal of the royal ideology, that the king's subjects practiced all of the three major religions. Accordingly, any kind of statement made by the monarch was readily used for propagandistic purposes. In this regard some works linked to Ferdinand III (1201–52) are very enlightening.

A tradition, reported by the historians Gonzalo Argote de Molina, Luis de Peraza, and Diego Ortiz de Zúñiga, has it that when Ferdinand III made his triumphal entry into the recently conquered city of Seville, the Muslim king Axataf knelt before the Christian monarch to hand over the keys to the city. The Jewish community joined in this solemn ceremony by also presenting the king with the key to the Jewish quarter. From a strictly historical point of view, it is very doubtful that conquered Seville had a Jewish community at that time.[3] This curious story grew into an evocative legend and eventually materialized as two keys, tied together with a red silk cord, which were first recorded in the inventory of Seville cathedral in the sixteenth century.[4] The larger key, made of gilded silver, has a head decorated with an eight-pointed star, a cube with a ship and a galley engraved on each side, and a knob decorated with castles and lions. The wards at the end of the bit form a pierced-work inscription in Spanish:

DIOS ABRIRÁ. REY ENTRARÁ (God shall open. King shall enter)

On the border, a second inscription in Hebrew reads:

THE KING OF KINGS SHALL OPEN. THE KING OF THE EARTH SHALL ENTER[5]

[2] "A nuestros amados et fideles vassaillos, al alcalde et a la justicia et a los jurados et a todo el conceio de los cristianos et de los judios et de los moros de Tudela, salus et amor," Carrasco *et alii*, 1994, doc. no. 89, p. 92.

[3] That there was no Jewish quarter at the time of the conquest of Seville is argued by Montes Romero-Camacho, 1995.

[4] Laguna, 2000.

[5] According to the sixteenth-century cathedral inventories, this key had been a gift from the electors of the Empire to Alfonso X, who gave it to the cathedral.

Keys of the city of Seville. Mid-thirteenth
century. Iron and gilded silver.
Seville, Cathedral (inv. nos. 112/68
and 112/69)

The other key is made of iron and the workmanship is much simpler. The wards
bear the following words in Arabic characters, also in pierced work:

GRANT US, ALLAH, THE BENEFIT OF PRESERVING THE CITY[6]

Ferdinand's son, Alfonso X, prepared a spectacular scenographic arrangement for his
parents' mausoleum in Seville cathedral:[7] the metalwork images of the king and
queen, sheathed in silver and covered in jewels, were shown seated in silver-plated
chairs beneath gilded silver baldachins. The sarcophagi at their feet were emblazoned
with castles, lions, eagles, and crosses, as if in a tapestry. According to some
specialists, the king himself chose the wording of the epitaphs. They were written in
four languages: Spanish, Latin, Arabic and Hebrew.[8] Although the monument was
largely remodeled at the end of the sixteenth century, the epitaphs were preserved.[9]
Their content was similar, as is only logical, though adapted to the idiosyncrasies of
each culture. The Hebrew translation reads as follows:

> On this spot lies the tomb of the Great King, Don Ferdinand, lord of Castile,
> and of Toledo, and of León, and of Galicia, and of Seville and of Cordoba and
> of Murcia, and of Jaén. May his soul rest in the Garden of Eden. He who

[6] This key was owned by Don Antonio
López de Mesa, *caballero Veinticuatro* of
Seville, who donated it to the cathedral.
[7] Arco, 1954, pp. 229 *et seq.*
[8] Spanish, Arabic and Hebrew depending
on the language of the subjects and Latin
as the scholarly and ceremonial language
of the period.
[9] The inscriptions are carved out of two
pieces of marble (0.57 x 1.42 m) and
must have originally been displayed on
the long sides of the urn or platform
on which it stood. They currently form
the base of a silver urn crafted by
Juan Laureano de Pina (Laguna, 2000,
p. 245).

**Hebrew inscription on the mausoleum of Ferdinand III, Seville, Chapel Royal of the Cathedral**

conquered the whole of Sepharad, the Upright, the Just, the Prudent, the Magnificent, the Strong, the Pious, the Humble, he who feared God and served him every day of his life, he who beat and destroyed all his enemies and exalted and honoured all his friends, and conquered the city of Seville, which is the Cradle of the whole of Sepharad, and died there on the night of the sixth, twenty-second day of the month of *Sivan*, in the five thousand and twelfth year of the Creation of the World.[10]

## "THREE LANGUAGES, THREE RELIGIONS" AND THE REALITY OF DAILY LIFE

[10] From an eighteenth-century translation published by Ricardo del Arco (1954, p. 231).

[11] According to early Christian tradition, the king was received as God's envoy; accordingly, in very early times, the monarch was considered to be the angel of God, and the people recited the psalm *"Benedictus qui venit in nomine Domini..."*

What was day-to-day life like in a society whose members practiced three religions and had three different languages? The people of Israel adapted so well to the established power that they adopted the public behaviour of the majority unless there were serious religious impediments. Just as the Christian population took to the streets to welcome the king with the raised cross,[11] the Jews performed a similar ceremony, bearing the Torah from their main synagogue. Only when constraints on the Jews became widespread were certain restrictions placed on the luxury of these celebrations and solemnities:

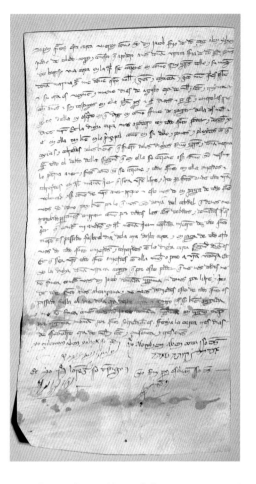

We order, rule, and uphold that from now on, when the Jews go out to receive us, they not wear linen vestments over their robes, except he who bears the Torah.[12]

Language remained a problem for some time, though it was not long before the minority groups underwent a linguistic inversion. Over time these people's mother tongue became a relic that was only used by sages.

For a time public documents still reflected the linguistic variety of the signatories and provide an insight into how people assimilated each other's languages. A record of the transfer of a debt dated 1315 and housed in the Toledo cathedral archive illustrates this situation in practice. The subject of the document, a complex chain of debt transfers, is basically as follows: Don Jacob, son of Don Çag Yahión, a Jew of Toledo, presents Doña Urraca, daughter of Don Pedro Gómez de Barroso, with a letter stating that Ruy Gutiérrez Tello and his wife, Doña Marina, owe this Jew the sum of 4,185 *maravedís* which he had lent them on 29 August 1300, and of which 2,100 *maravedís* are outstanding. This is in payment of what Don Jacob in turn owes Doña Urraca of the sum she lent him to buy cloth. By means of the letter, the part of the debt that Ruy Gutiérrez and his wife still owe Don Jacob is transferred to Doña Urraca. Doña Urraca agrees to the operation at her own risk. Ramón Gonzálvez, Toledo cathedral's current archivist, rightly notes that this document illustrates the cultural reality of Spain around 1300, when, despite political interests and sectarianism, there the cultures are clearly interacting:

This document is notable on many accounts. First, for originality of content. Also for the close relationship between Toledo's Christians and Jews. But, above all, the manner and system of validating the document is striking. It involves three witnesses and a scribe. In the first column the witness Çulemán Aben Yahex signs in his own hand, in both Castilian Spanish and Arabic. Beneath it is the signature of Pedro López, also in Spanish and Arabic. In the second column

[12] "Ordenamos mandamos defendemos que de aquí adelante quando los judios ovieren de salir a nuestro recibimiento non lieven vestiduras de lienço sobre las rropas salvo el que llevare la tora."

Abraham Aben Cota signs in Spanish and Hebrew. Beneath it is the signature of the scribe, Ruy Pérez, in Spanish and Arabic. The two witnesses who sign at the top of the columns are Jews. The other two are Mozarab Christians of Toledo. The signatures in Arabic, particularly that of the scribe, indicate that the document fell under the jurisdiction of Toledo's Mozarab mayor. The well-known Toledan Gómez Barroso family belonged to this Christian minority.

The people who signed their names at the end show that they are deeply imbued with the dominant culture. In the early fourteenth century Castilian Spanish became a literary as opposed to simply a documentary language. All those involved in the document express themselves very well in writing. The Jews are very familiar with the Spanish language and also with Arabic and Hebrew. Toledo's Mozarab minority are fluent in Arabic, their mother tongue, and Spanish; their rulers are also familiar with Latin. Many Jews and Mozarabs came from families that lived under Islamic rule in al-Andalus for centuries and were subsequently forced to emigrate to Toledo, a city where tolerance was practiced.[13]

## THE KING: "THE JEWS ARE MINE"

The fact that the Jews formed a religious minority caused a certain amount of friction with the rest of the community. This tension was fueled by the Church, which initially endeavored to conduct missionary proselytizing but ended up trying to impose unity of worship by force.[14] For these reasons, as well for as other more complex sociological motives, the kings came to regard the Jews as their own affair; this gave rise to such personal expressions as "my Jews" and "the Jews are mine."

The Jews thus became the "king's men" or "king's servants" *(homines regis* or *servii regis).* We should seek no further significance for this expression than a form of vassalage with a remote theological origin, the doctrine of Augustine of Hippo. The 1176 Teruel law code conveys this formula using an expression of the time: "The Jews are slaves — *servi* — of the Crown and belong exclusively to the royal treasury." This sense of protection, though lukewarm at times, was always expressed by the monarchs, as the following document issued by John II in 1443 shows:

> The Jews and Moors are mine and pertain to me and my chamber, for I take and receive them under my custody, and under my safety and protection, and Royal defence.[15]

The king's interest in the Jewish community basically lay in two aspects: in the group as a whole and in the prominence of some of its members. The Jews were

[13] Gozálvez Ruiz, 2002, p. 267.

[14] This is analyzed in the section entitled "History of a Conflict."

[15] "Los judíos et moros son propios et cosa mía et de mi cámara, ca Yo los tomo, et rescibo en mi guarda, et so mi seguro et amparo, et defendimiento Real," *Pragmática* (type of law) issued in Arévalo whereby the king placed the Jews under his protection (Amador de los Ríos, 1875–76, pp. 992–993).

[16] The Jews always showed themselves to be united vis-à-vis the oppression to which they were subjected by the Christians, as the law of survival dictated. However, their internal differences were very great. The interests of farmers clashed considerably with those of the urban craftsmen, not only in economic matters but also in religious practice. These differences were even greater with the wealthy classes of merchants, bankers, and officials, among others, whose lack of religious zeal was harshly criticised by their fellow Jews. The king himself had to step in on several occasions to mediate in quarrels strictly related to doctrine. Alfonso VII (1126–1157) was obliged to intervene in matters of orthodoxy, with the help of Yehudah ben Ezra, to crack down harshly on the Caraites, a sect who rejected the Talmud.

[17] The list of Jewish physicians is very long. Here we will merely cite Abraham Alfaquim, in the service of Ramón Berenguer IV, and Isaac and Abraham ben Warkar at the court of Sancho IV.

[18] Many Jews featured among James I's closest advisers: Benvenise de Porta, Jefudá de la Caballería, and the Vives family in the kingdom of Valencia.

[19] One of the most famous was Samuel Halevi, Peter I's treasurer.

[20] Prominent names during the reign of Peter III (1276–1285) were Astrug and Yosef Ravaya, father and son, bankers and lenders of taxes.

[21] "En los Reynos de Castilla, se fortificaron los Judíos en la parte que les tocaba en la Ciudad de Burgos, contra el Rey Don Enrique, que haviendo muerto el Rey Don Pedro su hermano, y señoreándose de todos sus Reynos, aclamado de los Grandes, y Pueblos de España, pidió a los Judíos que se les entregasen, alo qual respondieron que ellos no conocían otro Señor, que el Rey Don Pedro, o al que legítimamente le sucediese; y que por defender esta causa todos perderían resueltamente la vida." Quoted by Bunes, 1988, p. 84.

[22] Chapter 50 of the *Compendio Memoria del Justo* by R. Yosef ben Saddiq (Moreno Koch, 1992, pp. 58–59).

a unitary social group[16] that was loyal to the crown and ever willing, though sometimes reluctantly, to defray the monarch's many financial needs. Jewish influence on the sovereign was basically exercised through his closest associates: personal physicians;[17] council members;[18] high-ranking officials;[19] and bankers,[20] among others. Their close contact with the king's private life led the monarch to understand and facilitate many of the wishes of the people of Israel. However, on many occasions, these officials were entrusted with implementing measures that were most unpopular with the people, both Jews and Christians, who reacted very differently. In the view of the Jews, their brothers were acting like "Christian dogs," while the Christians blamed the Jewish community for the voracity of the royal treasury. On many an occasion the Jewish official fell from royal favor and the people retaliated by committing some atrocity in the Jewish quarter.

The history of the Spanish kingdoms is full of examples of Jews' loyalty to their king. During the civil war that erupted between Peter I and his half-brother, Henry of Trastámara, the Jews supported the legitimate king, Peter (Don Pedro). Trastámara's supporters made them pay a high price for backing the legitimate ruler: in 1355 Toledo's Jewish quarter was sacked; in 1360 the Jewish populations in Nájera and Miranda de Ebro suffered the consequences; French soldiers devastated Barcelona's Jewish quarter in 1366; and England's Black Prince punished the Jewish districts in Aguilar and Villadiego. A historical anecdote, converted into a popular fable, provides an insight into the noble attitude of the Jews during this civil strife:

> In the kingdoms of Castile, the Jews fortified the part of the City of Burgos that was assigned to them against King Henry, who, after the death of King Peter his brother and seizing all his kingdoms, acclaimed by the Grandees and Peoples of Spain, asked the Jews to surrender, to which they replied that they knew no other Lord than King Peter, or his legitimate successor; and that they would all resolvedly defend this cause with their lives.[21]

Although the significance of this anecdote can be played down, the price the Jewish community paid for their legitimism became engraved on their historical memory, as the Hebrew chronicles narrate with expressive realism:

> King Henry, son of the king, Don Alonso, killed the king his brother Don Pedro Manuel. It was a time of great bitterness for all the Jewish communities throughout the kingdom of Castile. And the holy Jewish community, the *qahal* of Toledo, suffered doubly to such an extent that they fed upon the flesh of their sons and daughters, and eight thousand Jews, adults and children, died in the siege. Few escaped death and the king forced them to pay such a tax that not as much as a scrap of bread remained for its inhabitants.[22]

"Arms of Aragon or four bars gules," *Sister Haggadah*, fol. 27v. London, The British Library (Ms. Or. 2884)

"Castle of Castile with three turrets," *Kennicott Bible*, fol. 15r. Oxford, Bodleian Library (Ms. Kennicott 2)

Not even at the most difficult times, such as the years when the expulsion was brewing, could the monarchs accuse "their Jews" of treason.[23]

The Jews, fully complying with Jeremiah's recommendations, showed their loyalty to the king by praying for him in their synagogues. Indeed, they did not hesitate to display proudly their lord's coat of arms on the walls of their place of worship. Royal lions and castles cover the walls of the synagogue of Samuel Halevi in Toledo, while the epigraph clearly proclaims King Peter as the savior of the people of Israel.

> KING DON PEDRO: may God help him and magnify his power and glory and protect him as a shepherd protects his flock! For the King has glorified and exalted him and has raised his throne above all the princes who are with him [and by dint of his mandate he rules over all his people] and has placed in his hand all that he wishes and, without his consent, nobody moves a hand or foot. The nobles [and grandees, for his lordship is acknowledged throughout the country and among the peoples] thus look up to him. Throughout all the kingdoms has his fame spread and he has become Israel's savior.[24]

[23] There is no reference to this in the document decreeing their expulsion.

[24] Cantera Burgos, 1973, pp. 107–108.

147

Compared to these monumental manifestations of compliance with the king's wishes, there are other, more private ones that may be considered more sincere. The pages of many holy books display the arms of the different monarchs of the Spanish kingdoms. The bars of the arms of Aragon decorate the pages of *Sister Haggadah* and the castles of the dynasty of Castile adorn those of the *Kennicott Bible.*

Then there are the praises by the palace-dwelling Jews. Todros ben Yehudah ha-Levi Abulafiah (1247–1306), a court poet given over to life's pleasures, provides different poetic portraits of Alfonso X. According to this poet, when he presented himself to the monarch to enter his service, he offered the king a cup engraved with the following poem:

> Never was such loyalty seen
> Since Don Alfonso was crowned king.
> On coming to serve you I bring your Majesty
> A cup engraved with a poem.
> May it never be raised empty
> Under the mandate of my Lord![25]

Todros's courtly flattery goes even further in another poem dedicated to the same monarch, which includes such lines as:

> What a delight it is to obey the orders of the king.
> Don Alfonso banishes all bitterness.
> His will is done when something he decrees.[26]

It took a combination of all the forces of the kingdom to break a relationship as close as the one the king enjoyed with "his Jews." Although throughout the long history of this relationship there were hard times when monarchs had serious problems avoiding falling into the traps set by the enemies of the Jews, they always managed to clear these hurdles until the "Catholic Monarchs" (Ferdinand and Isabella) eventually accepted what had become a popular clamor, no doubt well organized by a minority of radically anti-Semitic clergy in connivance with groups with ulterior motives.

The ecclesiastical authorities governed by the Roman pontiffs never approved of the Spanish kings' relationship with the Jews. Alfonso VI (1072–1109) was reprimanded by Pope Gregory VII for his tendency to favor the Jews. The Spanish kings opposed practically all the repressive measures drawn up by the popes during the thirteenth century. But the net progressively tightened around the Jews when the ecclesiastical authorities were joined by important social groups. During the first half of the fourteenth century, the church made every effort to do away with the privileges the Jews had been granted by the kings. Pope Clement V again stressed this matter at the Council of Vienne, and by this time his influence on the

[25] Quoted by Sáenz-Badillos, 1991. pp. 202–203.
[26] Ibid., p. 203.

Spanish church was considerable, as illustrated by this canon of synod of Zamora in 1313, presided over by the archbishop of Santiago de Compostela:

> That the Jews may not enjoy the privileges granted to them by Kings or by lay Princes, according to which they cannot be defeated in trials at any time by testimonies of Christians, and warn both King and lay princes from now on not to grant such privileges or to respect those already granted.[27]

The monarchs received similar demands from another source, namely the Cortes or parliament. Precisely that same year, Queen María and the Infante Don Pedro, Alfonso XI's tutors, found themselves obliged to accept the demand that "no Jew should hold office in the royal household."[28] This was followed by more demands, and the freedoms and rights of the Jews were progressively constrained. Even so, during that century, the monarchs nonetheless restored many of the Jews' prerogatives and did not hesitate to criticize harshly the town councils, nobles, middle clergy, and even the pope himself. In 1307, Don Gonzalo, archbishop of Toledo, reminded the cathedral chapter of the instructions of Ferdinand IV:

> That they knew well how our Lord the King had ordered them twice to order and firmly uphold in his letters that none of them should dare to use the letters of Our Lord the Pope, which some clergy and laymen obtained for themselves against any Jews of the archbishopric of Toledo, on the grounds of usury.[29]

A century later, John II retaliated harshly to a chain reaction sparked by a papal bull, which had resulted in the abolishment of Jews' rights, by suspending or softening these measures. As regards the papal bull, he announced that he intended shortly to send "my petition to our Holy Father for [the measures] to be declared and limited to the purpose of serving God and myself and for the good of my Kingdoms and for the protection of my rights."[30] The monarch is obviously reminding the pope that since the Jews are his affair, all matters relating to them should take into consideration not only God but also the king, the kingdom, and the rights of the sovereign.

These words may be among the last manifestations of a medieval king who still saw himself as duty-bound to protect his subjects' freedom to practice all three religions. Although there are some later manifestations of this kind, they undoubtedly cannot be regarded as sincere. To cite Queen Isabella's address to the council of Trujillo in July 1477:

> All the Jews of my kingdoms are mine and are under my protection and shelter and to me it falls to defend and protect them and maintain justice.[31]

Given the mood of the time, this royal concern was obviously a question of habit and expressed a royal privilege rather than a real worry about the quality of life of the Jewish community.

[27] "Que los judios no usassen de privillejos que toviesen ganados de Reyes nin de Príncipes seglares, sobre que non pudiesen ser vençidos en juiçios en ningunt tiempo por testimonios de cristianos, et amonesta á los dhos, Reyes et Príncipes seglares que daquí adelant non otorguen tales previllejos, nin guarden los otorgados." On this synod see the section on the dispute with the Christian church.
[28] "Judío ninguno non aya offiçio en casa del Rey nin en la nuestra."
[29] "Que bien sabien ellos cómo nuestro Señor el Rey les avia enviado dos veces mandar é defender firmemente por sus cartas que ninguno dellos non fuese osado de usar de las cartas de Nuestro Sennor el Papa, que algunos omes clérigos é legos ganaron para ellos contra algunos judíos del arzobispado de Toledo, en rassón de las usuras." Amador de los Ríos, 1875–76, p. 932.
[30] "Mi suplicaçion ser, ello á nro. Santo Padre, por que aquellas sean declaradas, et limitadas, segunt cumple á serviço de Dios et mio et á bien de mis Regnos et á guarda de mi dro." Ibid., pp. 992–995.
[31] Azcona, 1964, p. 629.

## ALFONSO X'S *SCRIPTORIUM,*
## THE SYNTHESIS OF THE EFFORTS OF THE PEOPLE OF ALL THREE RELIGIONS

One of the most attractive and important manifestations of the activities of the people of three religions working under a king's authority may well be Alfonso X's *scriptorium* and the works that emerged from it.[32]

Although the Mudejar uprising, unrest among of the nobles and civil war cast a shadow over the last years of the reign of Alfonso X of Castile (1252–1284), it is obvious, as M. González has pointed out, that he was one of the most universal men of the Middle Ages, and that he steered Castile onto the path of what is known as a "modern state."[33] Rather than dealing with his role as a statesman, we will focus on his intellectual activities. He was the first to put into practice his own recommendations for educating princes:

> And the sages of old not only considered that kings should know how to read; but that they should learn from all spheres of knowledge so as to make use of them; and for this reason King David advised the kings to be learned and knowledgeable, for they must judge the earth: and King Solomon his son also said this, that kings should learn the disciplines and forget them.[34]

Such was Alfonso's effort to acquire and disseminate knowledge that his subjects christened him with the epithet "the Wise." Hebrew sources bear this out categorically: "This king with his great wisdom — he was the greatest sage in every science."[35] His enthusiasm and sponsorship gave rise to huge scientific and cultural endeavors that not only reflected and reinterpreted Western and Eastern tradition but also encouraged new ideas and experimentation. A huge variety of

[32] The related bibliography, particularly works analyzing particular areas, is very large and well known. Here I will simply refer to a recent publication, the work coordinated by Montoya Martínez and Domínguez Rodríguez, 1999.

[33] González Jiménez, 1999, p. 15.

[34] "Et non solamiente tovieron por bien los sabios antiguos que los reyes sopiesen leer, mas aun que aprendiesen de todos los saberes para poderse aprovechar dellos: et en esta razon dixo el rey David consejando a los reyes que fuesen entendidos et sabidores, pues que ellos han de juzgar la tierra: et eso mesmo dixo el rey Salomón su fijo, que los reyes aprendiesen los saberes et los olvidasen" *(Partida Segunda,* tit. V, ley XVI).

[35] As described by R. Yosef ben Saddiq in his *Compendio de la memoria del justo,* written between 1467 and 1487 (Moreno Koch, 1992, p. 52).

subjects was addressed: history, the translation of Arabic authors, jurisprudence, agriculture, alchemy, and astronomy, to name a few.

This large and diverse oeuvre was produced by highly specialized teams. Jews, Moors, and Christians contributed to the dissemination of the great scientific treatises in Castilian. Some of the most prominent contributors whose names have gone down in history are: the Jews Isaac ben Sid, Yehudah ben Mosé, Rabí Çag, Mosé ha Cohen, Yehudah Mosca, and Abraham Alfaquin;[36] the Arabs (converted Muslims or Arabic-speaking Christian Mozarabs) Bernardo el Arábigo and Guillén Arremón;[37] and Christians such as Juan Daspa and Garcí Pérez. Translation was entrusted to a pair of scholars familiar with the particular discipline: one would be an expert in the original language and the other in the language into which the work was to be translated, and both had Spanish in common. The work of the scriptorium helped to establish Spanish as a scientific and "modern" language. The translations ultimately sprang from the king's wishes, but, as Américo Castro has pointed out, it is also obvious that the Jewish translators were the means of creation. Hebrew sources reflect this:

> In the fourth year of his reign [Alfonso X] ordered the scholar Gudsal ben Monse al-Kohen, of the council of the city of Toledo, to translate from Arabic language to ordinary language the honorable book written by the scholar 'Albuhatani-al-Rahman ben 'Umar Asufí which speaks of matters of the stars and the zodiac and its figures according to drawings of the sky. The planetary tables this king composed were also copied, and my eyes saw this honorable book, and it was all written in pure gold, and I stress that anyone who has not seen this book has not seen a magnificent and beautiful object [ever].[38]

Not only was the monarch the authority and patron who allowed Jews, Moors and Christians to contribute to works of such significance; he also participated in these endeavors more actively than other medieval patrons.[39] No doubt, as R. Yosef ben Saddiq states, he was not the author of the "Alfonsine Tables;" yet his role as coordinator and director of this scientific activity was decisive:

> The King makes a book, not because he writes with his own hand, but because he provides the reasons for it, and modifies, and corrects and rectifies, and shows the manner in which should be done, and they are written by the person whom he orders, but for this reason we say: the King makes the book. For when we say that the king builds a palace or some other work, we are not saying that he made it with his hands, but rather that he gave orders for it to be built and provided the things that were necessary to do so.[40]

Although some specialists in Hebrew culture, among others, dispute Alfonso's role in the production of the works of the scriptorium, Don Juan Manuel, the

[36] An essential reference for the Jewish specialists at Alfonso's scriptorium continues to be David Romano's work of 1971. This same author provides us with an updated view and new bibliographic references in Romano, 1994.

[37] Alfonso had established an Estudio General (University) in Seville and a School of Latin and Arabic, where Christian and Muslim masters taught medicine and sciences.

[38] R. Yosef ben Saddiq in his *Compendio* (Moreno Koch, 1992, pp. 51–52). According to this chronicler, apart from the king's prominent role in astronomical matters and the role played by the Jews in translating them, the royal activity of his scriptorium achieved fame in jurisprudence: "he ordered and laid down precepts and laws in his religious affairs to judge all the *goyyim* in his kingdom and called them *Las Siete Partidas* because altogether there are seven... Since these books appeared and their precepts and laws the whole of the kingdom was to be judged in accordance with them. All the sages and kings and princes and all the people after him resolved to continue using them until the present today."

[39] In this respect there is no comparison been Alfonso and Peter the Ceremonious, king of Aragon, or Frederick II of Stauffen.

[40] "El Rey faze un libro, non porque él escriba con sus manos, más porque compone las razones dél, e las enmiendas, et yegua, e indereça, e muestra la manera de cómo se deben fazer, desí escribelas qui el manda, pero dezimos por esta razón: el Rey faze el libro. Otrosí quando dezimos: el rey faze un palacio e alguna obra, non es dicho por que lo él fiziere con sus manos, más por quél mandó fazer e dio las cosas que fueren menester para ello." (*General Estoria*, Lib. XVI, cap. XIII.)

Alfonso X (1224–1284), *Libro de las formas et de las imágenes que están en los cielos*, 1276–1279. Manuscript on parchment. Patrimonio Nacional. Biblioteca del Real Monasterio de San Lorenzo de El Escorial, Madrid (Ms. h–I–16)

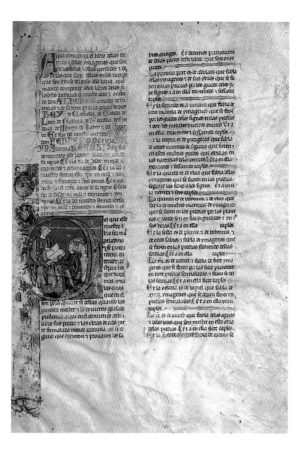

monarch's nephew, leaves no room for doubt. The king is the intellectual driving force who monitors the progress of the work very closely, discussing it with his scholars and expressing his opinions:

> And even, according to those who lived in his house, those who wished could speak to him whenever he wished, and there was a place to study the things he wanted to do himself, and even to see and complete the scholarly things he ordered the masters and the scholars he brought to his court.[41]

Of all the fields of knowledge transmitted by Alfonso's *scriptorium*, astronomy and astrology had the most far-reaching significance for Christian Europe. Presided over by the king, there was a centre for studies and astronomical observatory at the Casas de la Galiana del Alficén in Toledo. Various works on the science of the stars[42] were compiled in three large encyclopaedias: *Libros del saber de astrología*, *Libro de astromagia* and *Libro de las formas e imágenes que son en los cielos*.

The *Libros del saber de astrología* came to be entitled *Libros del saber de astronomía*. Part of one of these manuscripts survives in the library of the Universidad Complutense. Philip II commissioned a copy of this work for Prince Carlos in 1562. It has been said that the drawings it contains were done by the architect Juan de Herrera. It consists of a catalogue of stars derived from Al-Sufi's work, in addition to a series of technical treatises on the construction and use of tools for solving problems of spherical astronomy.

The little that survives of the *Libro de astromagia* is very fragmented.[43] Only Alfonso's manuscript of the *Lapidario* preserves its original format and arrangement.[44] This richly illustrated manuscript is a study of the properties of precious stones in relation to the astrological signs. The illustrations instruct the reader where to find them and show the astrological representation of each one.[45]

[41] "E avn, segunt dicen los que uiuían a la su merced, que faulauan con él los que querían e quando él quería, en ansi auia espacio de estudiar en lo quél quería fazer para sí mismo, e avn para veer e exterminar las cosas de los saberes quel mandaua ordenar a los maestros e a los sabios que traya para esto en su corte." (*Crónica abreviada*, Preface.)

[42] The main works of this kind were *El lapidario*, the *Libro complido en los ludicios de las estrellas*, the *Libro de las cruces*, the *Libro del quadrante sennero*, the *Tablas de Azarquiel* and the *Picatrix*.

[43] García Avilés, 1996.

[44] Alfonso X commissioned the translation from Garci Pérez and Yehudah ben Mosca.

[45] Domínguez Rodríguez, 1982; and Chico Picaza, 2002.

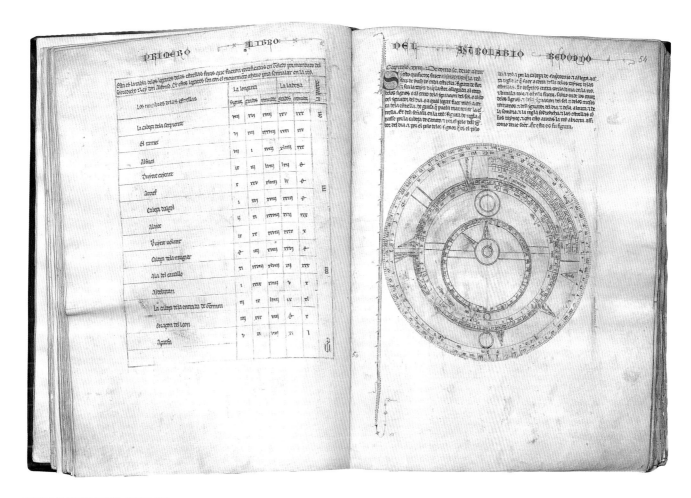

Alfonso X (1224–1284), *Libros del saber de astronomía,* ca. 1276–1277. Manuscript on vellum. Madrid, Biblioteca de la Universidad Complutense (MS. 156)

The *Libro de las formas e imágenes que son en los cielos* was a summary listing the uses of talismans. All that remains of it is a detailed index of the great astromagical encyclopaedia that was compiled by the monarch between 1276 and 1279 with that title. It includes fragments of earlier translations sponsored by Alfonso, such as the *Lapidario* and the *Liber Razielis.* Although it must have been very richly illustrated, it now only contains the very conventional image showing the presentation of the manuscript to the king. Nothing is known — not even descriptions — of the astrological figures to which it refers.[46]

All these works and treatises provided the Christian West with a body of knowledge that was not superseded until centuries later. These accomplishments are described below:

Alhazen's treatise on astronomy, *On the Configuration of the World,* translated by Abraham Hebreo,[47] was the leading book on the subject until the Renaissance theoreticians passed the knowledge down to Copernicus and Reinhold.

The *Tablas alfonsíes* (Alfonsine Tables) were a set of planetary tables drawn up by Isaac ben Sayyid (Don Zag)[48] in 1272, with the collaboration of Yehudah ben

[46] García Avilés, 1996.
[47] Two versions were produced: one in Latin *(Liber de mundo et coelo)* and the other in Hebrew.
[48] Commonly known as Ben Sid, whereas in Spanish he was known as Don Zag. The original version is no longer extant, though there are some indications as to how it was illustrated.

Mosé. Don Zag, who was the astronomer on the team, based the work on various observations of the skies using instruments crafted by his own hand or under his supervision. Yehudah was entrusted with the task of what we might call bibliographical documentation. The fact that the tables were not designed for a particular calendar and could be adapted to the Muslim or Christian calendars by means of a simple mathematical operation made them universally accepted by astronomers and ships' navigators.[49] The values of the tables were calculated on the basis of the radix year, 1252, when Alfonso X came to the throne, and the Toledo meridian. The tables were widely used and esteemed up to the seventeenth century: Juan de Lignieres (†1355) adapted them to the Paris meridian; and in the mid-fourteenth century they were adapted for Oxford. John of Saxony's adaptation continued to be used until they were replaced by Kepler's *Tabulae Rudolphinae* (1627).

The Arab world's profound knowledge of the stars was disseminated among Christians by the translation of al-Sufi's *Book of the Fixed Stars*, which became the basis of the *Los cuatro libros de la octava esfera* and *Libros del Saber de astronomía*.

Not only were the theoretic aspects of astrology of interest — so were the mechanical experiments enabling them to be applied to daily practice. Yehudah ha-Cohen and Juan Daspa translated the Arabic work by Qusta ben Lupa into Spanish. The monarch himself commissioned Yehudah ben Mosé to complete this treatise with a chapter devoted to armillary spheres. The tables of Ibn al-Samh and Azarquiel are described in the *Libros del Saber de astronomía* under the title *Libro de las láminas de los siete planetas*.

Alí Abenragel's astrology book, translated by Yehudah ben Mosé as *El libro complido en los iudizios de las estrellas,*[50] and al-Istikiyi's *Libro de las Cruces* became basic reference works on this subject during the Late Middle Ages.

The role played by the Jews in all aspects of astral magic and the significance of magical images in medieval society was no less important than their contribution to knowledge of astronomy as a science strictly speaking. The following brief text by García Avilés gives us an idea of this:

> The contribution of the Jews to the Alfonsine science of the stars was not limited to their role as interpreters and, later, observers of the sky. Alfonso sought in Hebrew wisdom that which had constituted the Jews' chief contribution to astral magic: an angelology that used the names of these intermediaries between heaven and earth as magical instruments. According to a Jewish legend, Adam in paradise had received from Raziel the *Book of the Secrets of God (Sefer Raziel),* which he passed on to his descendants in a chain of knowledge that extends as far as Solomon . . .
>
> The visual representation of what is explained in the text plays a major role in the Alfonsine concept of knowledge of the stars. In the case of talismanic art,

[49] It is significant, when establishing for whom works of this kind were designed, that the Jewish calendar was not envisaged.

[50] Yehudah himself had collaborated on a Latin translation around 1233.

*El Libro de Ajedrez, Dados y Tablas,*
Seville, 1283. Manuscript on
parchment. Patrimonio Nacional,
Biblioteca del Real Monasterio de San
Lorenzo de El Escorial, Madrid (T.I.6)

astral magic becomes a visual art: it is essential to know what the figure looks like that needs to be recorded at a given time to attract the influence of a certain star. So much so that this art was often called "the science of images."[51]

The translators of the *Libro de ajedrez, dados y tablas* were also Jews, though the book comprises three independent treatises on aristocratic board games of Eastern origin that arrived in al-Andalus during the Abbasid caliphate. The work was written in 1283, a year before the monarch's death. Both the games and the repertory of images are perfectly in keeping with the melancholic spirit of the king's last days, as illustrated in Omar Khayyam's poem:

> The world is a board of black nights and white days in which Destiny plays with men as if they were chess pieces: it moves them from here to there, it checkmates them and tosses them one by one into the drawer of Nothingness.

More than in any other work, the series of images that unfold before our eyes ofter the best picture of the people of the three religions, king's subjects all of them, who make up thirteenth-century Spain. Jews, Moors, and Christians placidly converse over board games in a setting that is truly a synthesis of East and West.

[51] García Avilés, 2002, p. 336.

# HISTORY OF A CONFLICT

# History of a Conflict

If we look back over the almost fifteen hundred years the Jews lived in Spain, we realize that a conflict — or rather *the* conflict — arose on many occasions, creating tensions that invariably resulted in restrictions on the rights of the smaller community, that is, the Jews. This section briefly analyzes the conflict and its effects on the legal situation of the Jews in Christian Spain, the image the Christians had of the Jews, and, lastly, the settlement of the conflict: expulsion.

The conflict had a traumatic outcome, the expulsion edict of 1492. For years afterwards, the banished Sephardic Jews continued to ponder over what had led to such a situation. After much reflection, one of them, Solomon ibn Verga, failed to find any answers. His interpretation of events springs from the traditional deterministic view of the history of the exiled Jews found in theological sources. The following passage quoted from his work, *La vara de Judá*, leaves no room for doubt:

> Violence and persecutions which the Israelites suffered in the land of the infidel and which I have translated so that they be known to the children of Israel and they may beg for pity from the Lord of mercy in order that He, showing mercy for those who suffered, may forgive their sins and put an end to their afflictions.

In the view of most Christians — and certainly the view of those mainly responsible for their expulsion, the "Catholic Monarchs", Ferdinand and Isabella — there was no other cause than religion[1]. The decree states very explicitly:

> To fully remedy the crimes and offenses against our holy Catholic faith it is not sufficient for such great dishonor and offense to the Christian faith and religion to cease, for every day we find and see that the said Jews increasingly persist in their evil and harmful ways wherever they live and lead their lives, and because it is time they cease offending our holy faith [...] Consequently we order all the Jews and Jewesses to depart from our kingdoms and never again return to them.[2]

Both sides, Jews and Christians, based their arguments on religion. They clung zealously and stubbornly to everything that linked them to their God. Throughout the conflict, both sides used whatever arguments they could come up with. In this

[1] Ever since the expulsion took place it has been considered by some to be a political and economic instrument cleverly designed by Ferdinand the Catholic. Machiavelli regarded the expulsion as a *pietosa crudeltá* devised by Ferdinand to obtain the property of the exiles to use it in his political program.

[2] "Crimines e delitos contra nuestra santa fe catolica no basta para entero remedio para obviar e remediar como çese tan gran oprobio e ofensa de la fe y religión cristiana, porque cada dia se halla e pareçe que los dichos judios creçen en continuar su malo y dañado propósito donde biven e conversan, y porque no aya lugar de más ofender anuestra santa fe... Por ende acordamos de mandar salir todos los dichos judios e judias de nuestros reynos e que jamas tornen ni vuelvan a ellos."

[3] Only on very few occasions were the Jews in a position to use force as an aid in the doctrinal debates, but when they were they had no qualms about using it or at least attempting to do so.

respect, the doctrinal disputes were continuous and date back to the earliest times, though the most famous occurred from the thirteenth century onwards. Nonetheless, the human condition of the disputants led the most powerful side to resort to other arguments, such as the use of force.[3] As the conflict intensified, the Jews were progressively stripped of their legal rights and ended up totally defenceless. Relations between Christians and Jews no doubt influenced a host of social, economic, and political issues, either directly or indirectly. Although these are analyzed in the different chapters of this catalogue, the main reason for the conflict was strictly religious.

**Fernando Gallego, *Christ Blessing (Maiestas)*, details: Church and Synagogue. Madrid, Museo Nacional del Prado (Inv. 2647)**

# Church versus Synagogue

Given Christianity's origins as a movement within Judaism, there was always debate and confrontation between Jews and Christians. At certain times in the Late Middle Ages, the quarrel developed into a violent and dramatic dispute in which the more powerful side ended up attempting to impose its ideas by force. This dispute[4] has come to be embodied in the theme of Church *versus* Synagogue, which possesses a very rich historiography and extremely beautiful iconography, as we may appreciate in Fernando Gallego's famous panel of the *Maiestas* or in some of the works shown in the catalogue.[5] One of the most dramatic and intense depictions of the Synagogue is Felipe Vigarny's sculpture for the chapel of the Constables of Castile. Gazing at this early sixteenth-century work, one feels the pain of the people it personifies following the terrible edict of 1492.[6]

## FROM ROMAN SPAIN TO VISIGOTHIC SPAIN: THE EMERGENCE OF THE *CONVERSO*

The Spanish church's earliest references to the Jews are found in four canons adopted by the Council of Elvira (300–306):[7]

16 – Maidens shall not be wedded to infidels
49 – The Jews shall not bless the fruits of the Christians
50 – Concerning Christians who eat with Jews
78 – Concerning married faithful who commit adultery with a Jewess or Gentile

The fact that the synod devoted so many lines to it has been interpreted as an indication that by then the Jewish community in Spain had grown to a considerable size. At the time the Christians had not become integrated into the imperial Roman power structure. Jews were treated as infidels, either heretics or simply "gentiles", and contact with them was considered unadvisable as they could induce believers to evil. However, the punishments are not at all severe: exclusion from Holy Communion for a time. Only re-offenders guilty of blessing the fruits were expelled from the Church.

Although the aforementioned Council of Elvira has been held to be the earliest manifestation of the controversy between Christians and Jews in Spain,

[4] For the latest views of Spanish historians on this subject, a work of great interest is *Homenaje a Domingo Muñoz León*, 1998.

[5] On the iconography of the synagogue, see the section entitled "The image of the other" further on in this catalogue.

[6] Although we should bear in mind that this type of iconography is Christian, the pathos of the image and the effort that the artist put into it would seem to indicate it is a tribute paid by the artist. This is merely a conjecture as there is no evidence to support this.

[7] There is disagreement over the exact year of this council, the first of its kind organized by the Spanish church. Most specialists agree it took place before the Edict of Milan in 313 (Vives, 1953, pp. 1–15).

Felipe Vigarny, The Synagogue
(ca. 1522–1526). Burgos, Cathedral,
Capilla del Condestable

this is actually not the case. The doctrinal dispute did not arise until the appearance of the works of Aurelius Prudentius (348–405), who wrote the treatise *Adversus Iudaeos*, and Gregory of Elvira's *Tractatus Origenis*.[8] Both are strictly doctrinal works and base their arguments on the theology of Tertullian and Cyprian. Prudentius does not fear the Jews; he aims to convince them of their error.

The shift from simple doctrinal controversy to the obstinate and arrogant quarrel that was to lead to the compulsory conversion of the minority religious group occurred shortly afterwards, during the early fifth century, on the island of Minorca. Reports reveal to us the clash between Church and Synagogue in all its crudity and with all the elements that were to characterize the phenomenon throughout the thousand years that the Jews remained in Spain. The events are recounted in the encyclical letter of Severus, bishop of Ciudadela, which some historians date to 418.[9] We know from this document that there were two main towns in Minorca: Yamona (now called Ciudadela), and Magona, or Mahon. The Christians lived in Yamona, which was an episcopal see, and there were no Jews — not because they were banned but because a series of supernatural phenomena prevented them settling there. Magona was the home of the Jews, who, on account of their "ferocity" and "malice" are compared by Severus to wolves and foxes, which, like serpents and scorpions, "daily bite Christ's Church." Despite these harsh expressions, the idea is basically the same as the theological argument: Christians enjoy divine protection, whereas Jews are the irreconcilable enemies of the Church.

The two Minorcan communities, which until then had gotten along with each other, subsequently witnessed a breakdown of relations. The arrival of the relics of St. Stephen, the first Christian martyr executed by the Jews, led to the emergence of fanatics among the Christian community demanding vengeance be wreaked on the Jews. This was followed by a series of events: a doctrinal disputation with which the Christians attempted, unsuccessfully, to convert the Jews; and a violent attack that ended with the synagoge in flames. This violence prompted the Jewish population to convert en masse (the more powerful members of the community, out of economic interest and to gain social prestige; others impressed by the supernatural happenings; and others simply driven by fear).

Some specialists assume that the conversion of the Visigothic king Recared to Catholicism at the third Council of Toledo (589) led both the secular and the religious authorities to persecute the Jews, seeking the unity of worship of all the kingdom's inhabitants. Regardless of whether or not this interpretation is correct, the fact is that canon XIV adopted by this council not only reiterates some of the prescriptions of Elvira; it goes even further by banning the Jews from certain types of public office and from practicing the religion of Moses:

[8] Gregory was bishop of Elvira in the fourth century and his treatises, although not addressed to the Jews but to those of the Christian faith, may be placed in the context of the traditional polemic against the Jews. Whatever the case, some raise serious doubts about the dating of this work.

[9] For information on the dating and an analysis of the letter from the perspective of the controversy between Christians and Jews, see Valle, 1988, pp. 62–76.

It shall not be permitted for Jews to have Christian wives or concubines, nor for them to purchase Christian slaves for their own use, and if from such unions offspring should be born, they shall be baptized; they shall not be appointed to public office in which they may impose punishment on Christians, and if any Christians have been dishonored by them, by the Jewish rites, and circumcised, they shall return to the Christian religion and be granted freedom without paying the price.[10]

From this moment onwards, the council regulations lay down a series of provisions that display the same fanatical spirit which had incited the Minorcan Christians the previous century[11]. Although some reigns were more permissive, anti-Judaism thenceforth generally became more radical.

The forced conversions that had taken place covertly during Severus's day were revealed in all their brutality under the reign of King Sisebut, who, in 616, ordered that the Jews convert or abandon the kingdom; those who refused to do so would have their property confiscated. One can infer that the idea of forced conversion would have appealed to the most sectarian circles of the Church, while the confiscation of property would have benefited the royal treasury.

Indeed, the ecclesiastical authorities were in favor of converting the Jews, though their ideas as to how to go about it differed. Isidore of Seville advocated the most moderate position, that conversion should be carried out on the basis of persuasion; while Archbishop Aurasius, metropolitan of Toledo, may have been one of the instigators of Sisebut's laws against the Jews in 612.[12]

Isidore's attitude towards the Jews is a recurrent theme in his writings. In his analysis, Diez Merino states that "his attitude is pastoral, seeking their conversion; he does not adopt the bitter and disdainful language observed in other earlier authors, and above all that which other Christian theologians subsequently adopted in the medieval controversy over the Jews."[13] Although it has been said that Isidore promoted forced conversion — which does not seem in keeping with his writings — we know for sure is that he headed the fourth Council of Toledo (633), whose canons put an end to the forced conversions imposed by Sisebut and clearly condemn the use of violence:

Concerning the Jews, the holy council orders that henceforth nobody shall force them to believe, "for God is merciful with whom he wishes and harsh on whom he wishes" [...] Therefore they should be persuaded to convert not with violence but using their own judgment and it should not be attempted to force them.

However, the council took a very tough stance towards those who had been forcibly baptized during the rule of Sisebut. These converts were not allowed to

[10] Vives, 1963, p. 129.

[11] Most historians tend to hold either of two totally opposite positions: that the anti-Jewish measures of the councils sprang from the king's wishes and had the consent of the council members; or that the king was under pressure from the clergy. This is an old problem of interpretation of the legislation emanating from the councils of Toledo; however, as regards the Jews, except for very specific aspects, the anti-Judaic spirit of these councils reflects the opinion of the most radical sectors of the Christian church.

[12] The chief synagogue of Samuel Halevi brought a suit against this prelate with the court of Froga, *comes* of the city, for forcibly or deceitfully converting many important Jews, including Rabbi Isaac.

[13] *La controversia...*, 1998, p. 110.

renounce Christianity, as this would amount to an affront to the God of the Christians:

> It is advisable that those who were previously converted by force to Christianity, as occurred during the period of the most religious Prince Sisebut, for they are recorded as having received the holy sacraments and the grace of baptism, and who were anointed with chrism, and who participated in the body and blood of the Lord, should retain the faith which they forcedly and necessarily accepted in order that the name of the Lord may not be profaned and the faith that they accepted be held as vile and despicable.[14]

This same spirit is found in the Sevillian scholar's other works. In his *Historia gothorum*, which judges Sisebut's conduct, he readily criticizes the king:

> At the beginning of his reign, by forcing the Jews to adopt the Christian faith, he admittedly showed holy zeal, but not dictated by good judgment; for by exercising his royal power he obliged those whom he should by rights have attracted using the rational arguments of our faith.

Isidore collected all these arguments in his well-known work *Contra los judíos* (Against the Jews) which was widely disseminated throughout Christian Europe of the High Middle Ages. In the prologue, which is dedicated to his sister Florentina, he states that the purpose of his writings is twofold: to "corroborate faith by the authority of the prophets and to prove that it is a mistake not to know the truth about the Jews."

These two different attitudes shown by the Spanish Gothic Church — Isidoro's scholarly and conciliatory stance and Aurasius's radically aggressive position — are both very hard on possibly insincere *conversos* (converted Jews) and those who openly return to Judaism. They are to be deprived of legal authority over their children and obliged to continue to uphold the Christian faith, if necessary by force.[15] Despite the toughness of these attitudes, this doctrinal stance cannot have been very much in keeping with the violence used in other European countries. This is mentioned in the letter from Pope Honorius I, dated 638, which severely criticises certain "Spanish bishops who are like dogs unable to bark at the danger that Jews pose to faith."

Despite certain periods in which the rules were eased somewhat, Christian intransigence towards the Jews reached a new height under the reign of King Euric. It has been argued that the new laws expressed the monarch's will and therefore sprang from the secular power. However, when analyzing them, we will see that they are mainly based on the doctrinal principles of the Spanish Gothic ecclesiastics and, in particular, on the harshest attitudes of the most radical sector of the Church. Euric's laws were greeted with utmost enthusiasm by the members of the twelfth Council of Toledo (681). Canon IX is directed "against the malice

[14] Canon LVII (Vives, 1963, pp. 210–211). The following canons up to LXVI also deal with restrictions on the behaviour of Jews and *conversos*.

[15] In this connection see the following canons of the fourth Council of Toledo: "On classes of Jews [...] Those who shall be obliged to believe by force and those who shall not"(c. LVII); "Concerning Jews who were Christians and later converted back to their original faith" (c. LIX); "The children of Jews shall be separated from their parents and given to Christians" (c. LX); some complementary aspects of canons LXI to LXVI.

Isidore of Seville, *Contra Judaeos* (France?). Paris, Bibliothèque Nationale de France

of the Jews" and concerned with "the execrable infidelity of the Jews." Not only were all the previous anti-Semitic laws and the many civil rules renewed; many new ones were also drawn up designed to please the Christian side in the religious quarrel. The Jews were accused of blaspheming against the Holy Trinity. *Conversos* were banned from renouncing their new faith: "the Jews shall not withdraw from the grace of the baptism nor shall their children or servants". Not only were Jews banned from practicing the principles of their religion: "they shall not celebrate Easter according to their rite, nor the circumcision of the flesh [...] they shall not celebrate the Sabbath nor the other feast days of their religion"; they were also made to respect and comply with the precepts of the Christian faith, namely "to cease from toil on Sundays and other feast days [...] and they shall not dare marry without the blessing of their bishop."

The close relationship between Church and king in shaping an anti-Jewish policy during Gothic Spain prompted the Jews, whenever possible, to take sides against both institutions, either together or separately. During the revolt of the Visigothic noble Paul against King Wamba, the Jews sided with the former in the hope of securing the favour of a new secular power. However, after Paul was overthrown, St. Julian stated that "a whorehouse of blasphemous Jews" had formed in Gaul.

Given these circumstances, it is hardly surprising that in 711 the Jews welcomed the Muslim invaders as liberators.

### THE DISPUTE BETWEEN JEWS AND CHRISTIANS UNDER ARAB RULE

The Muslin invasion and the new rulers brought about a radical change. As for religious affairs, under the new authorities the Jews upheld the anti-Christian doctrine they had previously lacked the freedom to develop. However, they were not equally critical of the doctrine of the Muslims; nor would the latter have permitted it. Specialists reckon that Jewish criticism of Christianity in al-Andalus was the basis of Hebrew anti-Christian literature in Europe: "Both Jacob ben Rubén and Yosef Kimhi, authors of the first specifically anti-Christian treatises in Christendom, *Las guerras del Señor* and *El libro de la Alianza*, respectively (both dated 1170), were highly familiar with the Andalusian tradition."[16]

16 Lasker, 1998, p. 170.

**St. Martin of León (León, 1120/30-1203),** *Obras de Santo Martino* **(detail). León, Archivo de la Real Colegiata de San Isidoro**

[17] This Eleazar was the deacon Bodón, a member of the chaplaincy of Louis the Pious, king of France and Germany; he fled to al-Andalus in 839 and converted to Judaism.

[18] There are few records of converts to Judaism: those of this period could be counted on the fingers of one hand. Whatever the case, the history of the "victors" made sure of their *damnatio memoriae*. The concern that comes across in several council canons of the Spanish Gothic period is a good indication that this phenomenon was fairly constant; indeed, it is still found in thirteenth-century law.

[19] See the chapter on "Jews, Moors, and Christians under the King's Authority."

[20] Martin's work covers a total of 701 folios arranged into two volumes. As the author explains in the prologue, he called it *Concordia* "because the Old and New Testaments mutually agree in it." The codex was produced around 1200 with the help of seven scribes paid by Queen Berenguela. As for the painted illustrations, the depictions of St. Isidore and Martin himself are particularly notable.

The situation of the Christians was very precarious under Muslim rule and, naturally, the clergy lacked the support of the civil authorities to impose conversion when doctrinal arguments failed to convince. The most important known dispute of this kind was between the Mozarab (Arabic-speaking Christian) Alvaro de Córdoba and the Jew Eleazar.[17] This dispute is very curious since Eleazar was a Christian who had recently converted to Judaism and, like all new converts, a great zealot.[18] His reasoning lacks power, as he resorts to the traditional arguments (the Messiah, the Incarnation and the Trinity, etc.). The most significant aspect of this dispute is how it ended, for now Eleazar was closer to the power and did not hesitate to resort to his influence with the Muslim authorities to force Christians to convert to Islam or Judaism.

## FROM POCKETS OF CHRISTIAN RESISTANCE TO 1200

Throughout the period of Muslum rule in Spain, small Christian kingdoms stood their ground. As heirs of the Visigoth kings, these Christians espoused their ideas, but they were in no position to put them into practice for a long time. By this time a large Jewish community had built up, and the Christian rulers changed their attitude towards the people of Israel, whom they came to regard as important vassals,[19] and the Church shunned its missionary activities in favor of an older type of doctrinal argumentation. It should also be borne in mind in this connection that the Jews had long lost all interest in proselytizing.

The most significant work during this long period was produced by St. Martin of León (ca. 1125–1202). During his later years he wrote an important commentary which paid particular attention to the Jews.[20] According to A. Viñayo, Martin's interest in the Jews sprang from his concern about the burgeoning Jewish community in León and the possible link between the Jews and heretical movements in the south of France.[21] The themes of Martin's polemic were by no means original: the Messiah, Trinitarian theology and the errors of the Jews, drawing from the arguments of Isidore, Augustine, and Gregory the Great for his exegesis of the Scripture, and from Peter Lombard for Trinitarian doctrine.

Although Martin's work did not enjoy any influence beyond his own city during his lifetime, it echoed the new wave of anti-Semitism that was spreading through Europe in ecclesiastic circles. I agree with Adeline Rucqui that the spirit of Martin's *Concordia* heralds a shift from an interpretation of the Jewish phenomenon based solely on theology to one that also reflects an emerging negative reality, anti-Semitism.[22]

Nor do we find anything similar to the Gothic councils in the ecclesiastical legislation of the period. The references I am familiar with deal more with aspects of civil legislation. Ferdinand I (1016-1065) had considerably diminished the anti-Judaism of these councils.

## FROM INTENSIFIED DISPUTE TO DOGMATIC INTOLERANCE: THE THIRTEENTH TO THE FIFTEENTH CENTURIES

From the thirteenth century onwards, heretical movements such the Albigensians among others, brought home to the popes the need to defend the unity of their faith not only by persecuting heretics but also by making the Jews their targets. This more radical position unleashed all the demons of the past. The mendicant religious orders, particularly the Dominicans, contributed decisively to this new situation. Examples of this new attitude are the sermons which the Jews were obliged to attend, the public debates, and the considerable coercion exercised by the popes and transmitted through the diocesan clergy. The well-known image of St. Stephen preaching to the Jews at the synagogue became a popular symbol of these doctrinal clashes, reminding Christians that Stephen, despite his missionary efforts, was murdered by those he wished to save.

Jaume Serra (doc. 1358–1389), *Altarpiece of St. Stephen*, detail. Barcelona, Museu Nacional d'Art de Catalunya (Inv. 3947)

21 Viñayo, 1948. A broad view of St. Martin and his period can be found in *Santo Martino*, 1987.
22 Rucquoi, 1994.

At the end of the twelfth century, Pope Innocent III aimed to establish a tolerant climate of relations between Christianity and the Jews, hoping that one day the Jews, guardians of Scripture and in possession of the Promise, would become convinced of their error and eventually recognize Christ as the Messiah they were awaiting. Such is the spirit of St. Augustine and Isidore of Seville, which the pope conveyed in his *Constitutio iudaeis*, written in 1199. In a very short space of time, the Church adopted a more radical position. While not as extreme as the older Theodosian and Justinian law codes, the provisions of the fourth Lateran Council (1215) certainly discriminated against the Jewish community:[23]

> Ban on holding public office.
> Payment of tithes to the Church.
> Jews were not allowed to treat to Christians, since in improving or curing the body they could influence their souls.
> They could not have Christian slaves or servants.
> They could not show themselves in public on certain Christian feast days.
> The practice of usury was banned.
> Jews were to appear in public wearing distinctive clothing so as to distinguish them from Christians[24].

Fourth Lateran Council. Lateran (Rome), 1215; copy from the first half of the sixteenth century. Toledo, Toledo Cathedral, Archivo Capitular (Ms. 15–26)

[23] Canons 67–70 regulate the behavior of the Jews.

[24] The Council of Arles (1235) later stressed this by ordering that "Jews shall wear over their clothing, by the heart, a round yellow badge with a diameter of four fingers."

These rules, which some historians have regarded as conciliatory and by no means anti-Semitic, failed to satisfy the Church hardliners and were particularly criticized by some *conversos*, who argued against the Church's traditional confidence in the effectiveness of conversion. They convinced the pope that there was no hope, since the rabbis had created a tradition, the Talmud, which distorted the scriptures. This new claim, together with a Curia (papal court) convulsed by a spirit of crusade against the enemies of the church, led to a harsher treatment of the Jews, who thenceforward were regarded as traitors and heretics.

Pope Gregory IX's cruel *Decretals* (1234) are a response to this new policy of harassment and isolation. The pope commissioned scholars from the University of Paris to study rabbinic tradition in relation to the Holy Scriptures. The result was a trial with a huge public impact, a solemn condemnation, and the cremation of the book of the Talmud.

This was followed immediately by a series of measures obviously designed to achieve conversion, either voluntarily or by force. To perform this evangelizing and coercive task, the Roman Curia and the bishops relied on the help of the Dominicans. As well as being compelled to listen to the missionaries, it was recommended that Jews be confined to enclosed spaces, and that unsuitable books be weeded out and burned.

During the second half of the thirteenth century all these coercive measures, which had been applied for some time in Europe, emerged with greater force in the Kingdom of Aragon. On 28 August 1263, James I ordered his officials to compel the Jews to hand over all their copies of Book XI of Maimonides's *Mishneh Torah* (Book of Judges) as it was thought to blaspheme against Christ. Four years later, the restrictive measures on books were tightened: Pope Clement IV ordered the archbishop of Tarragona to persuade the king to make the Jews in his kingdom surrender the Talmud and all their books. Only those containing no "slanderous" allegations against the Christian faith would be returned to them, whereas the rest were to be stored in a safe place. This operation was performed in the presence of Dominican and Franciscan friars.

But the most terrible aspect of this was that by then physical violence had become an instrument of "persuasion". Clement IV himself asked James I to punish severely Moses ben Nahman (Nahmanides) "who in your presence debated Paulus Christiani, and has now written a book with many lies." The only types of violence excluded from the punishment — and what makes this particularly spine chilling is that other cases he no doubt considered the possibility — were death and amputation of a limb. Given this state of affairs, it is not surprising that Nahmanides fled Catalonia and settled in Jerusalem on 23 August 1267.

The Castilian monarchs were reluctant to put the harsher measures into practice, particular those that were anti-Semitic in nature. Numerous testimonies

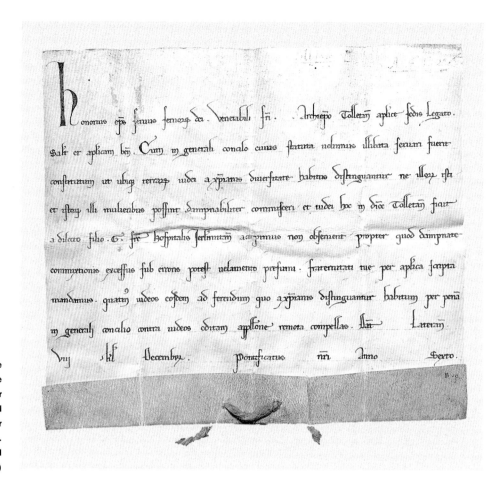

speak of the many anti-Semitic rules that were not applied in Castile. In 1219
Ferdinand III asked Pope Honorius to waive the rule that Jews should wear
distinctive clothing. The friars of the order of St. John of Jerusalem informed
Honorius that the Lateran rules on the Jews were not being observed in the city
of Toledo. The pope hastily replied, dispatching a bull in 1221 to the Toledan
archbishop demanding he abide by the rules "in order that the Jews may not mix
with Christian women and a strict separation be established between the two
communities."

But the relaxation of the observance of the papal rules not only affected the
distinctive clothing Jews were supposed to wear; the bans on certain books also
failed to be enforced. In 1239, Gregory IX sent a bull to Ferdinand III, king of
Castile and León, stating that rumors had reached Rome that the Jews in his
kingdoms used the Talmud, "which contains so many abuses and harmful
things that they cannot be heard or told without horror and shame." Therefore,
bearing in mind the ecclesiastical rules, the pope found himself obliged to ask
the king that "on the first Sabbath of the next Lenten period [1240], when the
Jews go to the synagogue, all the books of the Jews in the Kingdom be

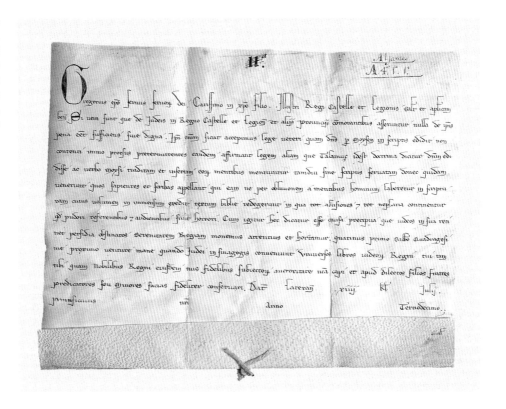

confiscated and handed over to the Dominicans and Franciscans in order that they may keep them."

Both Ferdinand III and his son, Alfonso X, were reluctant to implement such measures. As we shall see in other sections of this book, at the beginning of the fourteenth century some Church representatives demanded that king observe them.

The restrictions imposed by the popes on certain Jewish reading material are also found in the law codes of Alfonso X,[25] though, as we shall see, he also protected Jewish orthodoxy:

> We forbid the Jews to dare to read any books that speak of and violate their law or keep them hidden; and anyone who should have or find them shall dutifully burn them at the door of the synagogue. Furthermore we forbid them either to read or possess books known to speak of and violate our law; but we grant that they may read and have all the books of their law as it was handed down to them by Moses and by the other prophets.[26]

Alfonso's same lawmakers, while allowing the use of distinctive clothing for the Jews (though this was not practiced in the thirteenth century), were aware that the pope was raising serious objections to Jewish religious practices. Therefore they clearly state that such bans are not allowed in the kingdom of Castile and León:

[25] We will refer to this further on in the section on the "The Law of the Kingdom."

[26] "Defendemos que ningún judío non sea osado de leer ningunos que fablen en su ley e que sean contra ella por desfazerla nin de los tener escondidos; e si alguno ouiere o los fallare, quémelos a la puerta de la sinagoga concergeramient. Otrossí defendemos que non lean nin tengan libros a sabiendas que fablen en nuestra ley et que sean contra ella por desfazerla, mas otorgamos que puedan leer e tener todos los libros de su ley assí como les fue dado por Moysén e por los otros prophetas" (Fuero Real, Libro IV, tit. 2, ley 1ª), *Fuero Real del Rey Don Alonso el Sabio. Copiado del Código del Escorial señalado ij. z–8*, Madrid, 1836.

We do not forbid the Jews to observe their Sabbaths and other feast days established by their law and to use all others granted by the Holy Church and other kings, and nobody shall dare change the law.[27]

This benevolence and respect for the Jews' religious practice began to change from the fifteenth century onwards. A provincial synod presided over by Rodrigo, archbishop of Santiago, was held in Zamora (ca. 1312). The preamble to the acts indicates the spirit of this encounter:

> Against the stubborn Jews, in the name of the Christian and Catholic faith and of law […] constrain and stem their malice and the presumptuousness with which they turn against the Christians and against the observance of the name of God.[28]

As the members of the synod explain, what they aim to do is enforce not only what Clement V had laid down at the Council of Vienne (1311) but also the 1215 rules, which had been approved on two earlier occasions but not yet entered into force.

A century later, following the dispute of Tortosa, Pope Benedict XIII enacted a bull against the Spanish Jews (1415). Its thirteen precepts set forth all kinds of prohibitions and constraints on the practice of their religion.[29]

Although the action of the kings[30] and some prelates managed to ease these coercive measures somewhat, the fact is that part of the clergy felt entitled to rouse the hostility of the masses against the Jews from the pulpit[31]. By then it was common practice to mock the Jews by parading them in Christian ceremonies:

> In this city of Avila we have seen an abuse that we have seen in no other Christian place. The Jews and Moors are obliged to walk in a procession and perform dances and other rejoicing on the day of the Corpus of our Lord and in other religious and Christian feast-day processions.[32]

The synod of Avila denounced these events and banned them in 1481. This provincial council drew up seven chapters that sum up the whole ecclesiastical theory on the Jews shortly before their expulsion:

1 No Christian man or woman shall dwell in a house with a Jew or Moor, either paid or free, or give milk to their children.

2 No Christian shall attend weddings or funerals of the Jews to honor them, and particularly, the aforesaid infidel shall not be invited by the faithful to their own ceremonies.

3 Christians shall not eat or drink the food of the Jews.

[27] "Non defendemos que los iudios non puedan guardar sus sábados e las otras fiestas que manda su ley e que usen todas las otras que an otorgadas por Sancta Eglesia et los otros reyes, e ninguno non sea osado de ge lo tollernin y de ge lo controllar." (Libro IV, tit. 2, ley VII.)

[28] "Contra los porfiosos judíos, en otorgamiento de la Fée Cristiana, é católica é del derecho.. ccostrennir é vedar sus malicias é las sus presunciones con que se avuelven contra los cristianos e contra la guarda del nombre de Dios," Amador de los Rios, 1875–76, pp. 935–938.

[29] Ibid., pp. 970–985.

[30] See the chapter on "Jews, Moors, and Christians under the King's Authority."

[31] See, in the chapter on "Historic Background," the serious events that occurred in Seville as a result of the sermons of canon Ferrand Martínez.

[32] "Una abusion avemos visto fazer en esta ciudad de Ávila, la qual en ningun lugar de cristianos vimos. Que los judios y moros son compelidos a andar en procesión y fazer danças y otras alegrías el día del Cuerpo de nuestro Señor y otras procesiones generales de religiosa y cristiana alegria," Council of Ávila, 1481 (Synodicon Hispano VI. Ávila y Segovia, 1993, p. 205).

4   When a Jew or Moor may remain in the church while mass and other holy offices are being said, and when not.

5   All the Jews and Moors shall wear their usual signs so that they may distinguished among the faithful Christians.

6   In councils or processions held in honor of God, Jews and Moors shall neither take part nor be present, nor called to attend.

7   Jews and Moors may not rent privileges or loans.[33]

As we can see, almost twelve hundred years after the Council of Elvira, the doctrine hardly varies.

## THE DOMINICANS AND THEIR "LANGUAGE SCHOOLS" (*STUDIA LINGUARUM*)

The mission of the Dominican order, approved by Pope Honorius III in 1216, essentially amounted to evangelization based on scholarship, and the spoken and written word were therefore the chief resources. The Dominicans soon realized that, in order to perform their missionary work among Muslims and Jews, they needed to learn their languages to make themselves understood[34] and to familiarize themselves with their religious sources to point out their errors on the basis of their own traditions.

The superiors of the order gave instructions for centers to be set up for learning these languages. The first of these were devoted to Arabic studies, and were followed by centers of Hebrew: the school in Murcia taught Arabic and Hebrew; the Barcelona *Studium hebraicum* had been running since well before 1281. The Dominicans' general chapter meeting of 1291 established in Játiva "a house where we wish and order that there always be a school of Hebrew and Arabic." This task was continued by others like Ramon Llull, who, in 1276, founded the School of Languages of Miramar, and the Council of Vienne (1311–1312), which established that at the leading ecclesiastical schools (Roman Curia, Paris, Oxford, Bologna, and Salamanca) "there be suitably paid teachers of Hebrew, Arabic, and Chaldean." From these schools emerged names as prominent as Raimundo Martí (1220–1285), who in 1278 completed his *Pugio fidei adversus Mauros et Iudaeos* (The dagger of faith against Moors and Jews) which was directed especially against the Jews according to its author, who displayed a thorough knowledge of rabbinic literature.

## COMPULSORY ATTENDANCE OF PREACHING AND THE GRAND DEBATES

Between the thirteenth and fifteenth centuries popular interest in the controversy between Jews and Christians reached its height, calling for a fitting public event to be staged. The aim was to impress both the Christian majority and the Jewish minority, as the authorities considered this was the best way of getting the lesson across: to the

[33] "1 Que ningun christiano ni cristiana more con judio nin con moro en una casa, ni a soldada ni de gracia, ni den leche a sus fijos. 2 Que ningun christiano vaya a bodas ni mortuorios de los judios por los honrar, ni menos los dichos infieles sean llamados por los fieles a las semejantes suyas. 3 Que los cristianos no coman nin bevan de los manjares de los judíos. 4 Quando el judio o moro puede estar en la iglesia al tiempo que se dize la missa y los otros divinales oficios, y quando no. 5 Que todos los judíos y moros traygan sus señales acostumbradas para que puedan ser conocidos entre los fieles cristianos. 6 Que en los ayuntamientos o procesiones que se fizieren a honor de Dios, no intervengan ni esten los judios y moros, ni para ellos sean llamados. 7 Que los judios ni moros puedan arrendar beneficio ni prestamo." Ibid., p. 203.

[34] This refers more to the African and Middle Eastern infidel, since those living on the Iberian Peninsula spoke Romance languages.

former, in order to prevent them falling into the error of heresy, and to the latter, to convince them to desist from it. The Christian clergy resorted chiefly to two means: zealous preaching to the infidels and doctrinal debates with them. The easiest part was the preaching. Not only did the Christian orators lack opponents to refute their arguments; as they enjoyed the backing of the secular authorities, their public was obliged to listen to them. As we have seen, the practice of disputation dated back many years and furthermore allowed both sides to present their arguments.

The mendicant orders' evangelizing zeal led them to undertake the task of preaching to the "infidels". Eager to achieve great things for their religion, they succeeded, with the help of the pope, in making it compulsory for Jews to listen to sermons. In the 1242 statute, James I the Conqueror (1208–1276) imposed this obligation upon non-Christians in his kingdom:

> Whenever the archbishop or the bishops or the preaching or lesser friars arrive at a town or place where there are Saracens and Jews and wish to explain the word of God to the Jews or to the Saracens, these must attend when called and listen patiently to the preaching; those who do not wish to come of their own accord shall be obliged to do so by our officials, ignoring any excuses.[35]

Together with other social factors discussed elsewhere in this catalogue, these missions, which continued for over two centuries, gradually stirred up the lower clergy and ordinary folk. On other occasions homilies about extraordinary events roused the masses, resulting in bloody crimes against members of the Jewish community. On the death of Charles IV the Fair,[36] Pedro de Ollagoyen of Estella, preaching at the Holy Week services of 1328, provoked the ire of the people, who reacted by massacring Jews in Estella, Viana, and Los Arcos. The Jewish chronicler relates this terrible incident:

> On Friday afternoon of the month of *Adar* in 5088 [1328], God unleashed his anger on his people, and the king of France, who ruled over Navarre, died, and the natives of the country rose up to destroy and kill all the Jews in his kingdom and killed nine thousand Jews in Esbilía in Navarre and in other places.[37]

The most famous missionary endeavor was carried out by Vicente Ferrer between 1411 and 1412. Instructed by Pablo de Santa María, the famous *converso* bishop, he toured the diocese of Cartagena preaching in the towns of Alicante, Orihuela, Elche, Murcia, and Lorca. From there, surrounded by a company of flagellants, he continued to the towns of Castile, amid popular fervor. His sermons were quite a spectacle, in which a frenzied public witnessed the most extraordinary events. González Dávila reports the legendary tale of Ferrer's performance at the synagogue of Salamanca, after which the number of practising Jews in the city was practically reduced to zero:

[35] The contemporary Jewish reaction to being forced to listen to preaching is especially reflected in *Milhemet miswa* (1240–1270) by R. Meir ben Simeón (Chazan, 1989).

[36] The sobriquet with which Charles IV of France is known in French history; in Navarre he was known as Charles the Bald. Although he effectively reigned Navarre until his death on 1 February 1328, his legitimacy was contested by all the Navarrese.

[37] Chapter 50 of the *Compendio Memoria del Justo* by R. Yosef ben Saddiq (Moreno Koch, 1992, p. 56 and note 207).

The glorious Saint held a crucifix in his hand; he entered the Synagogue when none of those inside were expecting him; they became agitated, and he calmed them with kindly reasons, begging them to listen to what he had to say and […] began to preach. And by the grace of God, while he was preaching, some white Crosses appeared upon the clothing and head garments of all those in the Synagogue. And […] at the sight of such a great wonder, the Jews […] asked for Baptism water; and said they wanted to be Christians, and became converted, many taking the name of Vicente in memory of the Saint […] The Synagogue where this miracle took place is now the College of the True Cross, of the Order of our Lady of Mercy, taking its name from the miracle, and what was the Synagogue is now a refectory and still standing is the door through which the Saint entered to preach, which had a sign in Hebrew stating: *Haec est porta Domini, Iusti intrabut per ea.*[38]

Although Vicente opposed bloodshed and forced conversion, his fervent sermons triggered considerable rioting that sometimes ended in violent incidents. The impression left by Vicente's preaching and the dramatic pressure exerted by the lower clergy and the zealous people led many Jews to convert. The Spanish-Hebrew chronicles are a bitter testimony to this:

> The tonsured Vicente, through Doña Catalina, the queen, and Don Fernando, king of Aragon, made over two hundred thousand Jews change their religion in 5172 [1412].

These happenings made such an impression on the Jewish community that the same chronicler related them to certain astonishing events that occurred that year. These dire occurrences were undoubtedly interpreted by the people of Israel as clear signs of God's displeasure with his people and instilled in them an apocalyptic sense of the times in which it had fallen to them to live:

> God caused a hurricane that cleft mountains, shattered rocks and wrecked all the ships in the sea and felled all the trees in the countryside.[39]

In his chronicle, Abraham bar de Selomoh de Torrutiel dispenses with niceties and is categorical about these happenings, which he describes in a similar way but calls for Vicente Ferrer's "name and memory to be erased". As for the tonsured priest's action and the natural disasters, he explains that "the Saint, bless him, sent those two calamities against them on account of Israel's sin."[40]

The doctrinal debates had a great impact on the people. They were intended as public contests rather like tournaments between chivalric knights but using the instruments of theological learning and knowledge of the Holy Scriptures. As we have seen, this practice dated from the time of Severus on the island of Minorca,

[38] "Traia el glorioso Santo en la mano vna Cruz; entro en la Sinagoga quando ninguno de los de dentro pensaua en ello; alborotarose, sossegòles co amorosas razones, rogadoles le oyesse lo q. les queria decir y [...] començò à predicar. Y por la misericordia de Dios, estado predicado, apareciero sobre las ropas, y tocas de todos los que estauan en la Sinagoga vnas Cruces blacas. Y [...] vista por los Iudios vna tan gran marauilla [...] pidieron el agua de Baptismo; y q. queria ser Cristianos, conuirtiedose, tomado muchos el nobre de Vicetes, en memoria del Santo [...] Era la Sinagoga donde sucedió este milagro, adode aora es el Colegio de la Veracruz, del Orde de nuestra Señora de la Merced, q. del milagro tomò el nobre, y lo q. era Sinagoga es oy dia refitorio, y en el està viua la puerta por dode entrò el Santo à predicar, q. tenia vna letra Hebrea q. dezia: *Haec est porta Domini, Iusti intrabut per ea.*" González Dávila, 1606, pp. 348–350.

[39] Chapter 50 of the *Compendio Memoria del Justo* by R. Yosef ben Saddiq (Moreno Koch, 1992, p. 61).

[40] *Sefer ha-Qabbalah*, in *Dos crónicas hispanohebreas...*, (Ibid., p. 101).

Personal seal of Nahmanides, thirteenth century. Inscription: "Mosé ben Najmán Gerondí". Jerusalem, The Israel Museum

but developed considerably from the thirteenth century onwards. Although events of this kind were basically designed to convert scholarly debate into a dramatic event in which argumentation was the chief weapon, the fact is that desire for victory led to violently coercive actions on many an occasion.

Prompted by the Dominicans and moved by his concern for the Jews, James I, hoping to achieve their repentance and conversion, staged the Gerona debate and the famous Barcelona debate of 1263. The Dominican monk Paulus Christiani, a Jewish *converso*, who engaged in many missionary activities among the French and Aragonese Jews, was entrusted with the Christian side's strategy at the Barcelona event.[41] The Jewish representative was Moses ben Nahman[42] (Nahmanides), the most famous rabbi of the time. Israel's champion asked for guarantees of freedom of expression, which he was granted by the monarch himself.

We have a good idea of how the debate unfolded thanks to the two surviving versions: the Christian report, a summary of the minutes of the debate, bearing the seal of King James; and a Hebrew text attributed to Nahmanides. The Christians, basing their arguments on their knowledge of Jewish sources, set out to prove the mistakenness of Judaism; what is more, they intended to do so by defeating in debate the most illustrious of all Jewish sages of the time. Amid the heated discussion, the monarch himself even delivered an address, contravening one of the conditions established by the Jews. But in any event, such was the freedom of expression that Nahmanides was able to state that reason does not support Christian dogma on the nature of the Divinity and even predicted the destruction of the Christian kingdom. James I settled the debate by telling Nahmanides that it was better to leave things as they were "because I have not seen anybody who is not in the right argue his case as well as you have." After taking leave of the king, who gave him three hundred coins to reward him for his efforts, he returned to Gerona. The result of the debate failed to satisfy either side, and the Dominicans did all they could to have Nahmanides punished harshly for speaking his mind too freely. However, the king did not allow this.[43]

Of the other debates held, we know of that of Majorca in 1286 and, in particular, the famous Tortosa debate of 1413–1414.

We know of the Tortosa debate through the official acts, written in Latin, and different Jewish versions drawn up by the Hebrew debaters.[44] Yehosu'a ha-Lorquí, from Alcañiz, a scholar of *halakhah* and physician to Pope Benedict XIII, converted to Christianity in 1412, taking on the name of Jerónimo de Santa Fe. Moved by the zeal that characterized new *conversos*, he promised Benedict he would succeed in luring all the Jews to the baptismal font by basing his arguments

[41] It was he who persuaded Louis IX to pass a decree marking Jews wear the badge on their clothing.

[42] Nahmanides, also known as Bonastrug de Porta, 1190–1270.

[43] Earlier on in this article we refer to Nahmanides's flight to Jerusalem when Clement IV demanded his punishment.

[44] The full text of the protocol of the debate can be found in A. Palacios López, 1957. For the Jewish view of the dispute, I have taken Alisa Meyuhas Ginio's interpretation of the *Vara de Judah* by Solomon ibn Verga (2002).

Records of the Tortosa Debate, Tortosa, 1413–1414. Manuscript on parchment. Patrimonio Nacional, Biblioteca del Real Monasterio de San Lorenzo de El Escorial, Madrid (Ms. S–I–10).

on Jewish traditions, particularly the Talmud. At the end of 1412 all the Jewish councils of Aragon and Catalonia received a written order from the pope to each send two or four rabbis to the pontifical court of Tortosa by 15 January of the following year, where they would be instructed in the Christian religion. The sessions began on 7 February 1413 and lasted until December 1414.[45]

The pope originally received them politely and showed a certain amount of deference, promising to give them and their Christian opponents equal treatment. At the start of the session Benedict called them a "chosen people," stating that they were to blame for the Lord venting his anger on them. He also assured them they should not worry, "for as regards the debate the conditions are the same for all the contenders." However, the pope was unable to remain impartial: he had no doubt "as to which of the religions is the true one," and it turned out that the Jews had been invited merely to answer the arguments of Jerónimo de Santa Fe."[46] The same Jewish source praises the personal attention given to the arrangements for their stay: "The pope gave orders for them to provide us with suitable accommodation and to share with us his own bread or whatever we could eat according to our religion."

Jerónimo's reasoning was very simple: "The Messiah had already come and this could be perfectly proved in the Talmud itself." This argument sparked a flurry of replies and counter-replies and even the intervention of the pope, who, on more than one occasion, according to Jewish sources, reprimanded the Christian

[45] It lasted too long considering that the Barcelona debate was over in less than one week.

[46] Meyuhas, 2002, p. 29.

speaker. However, tension mounted. Benedict, arguing about the coming of the Messiah, rebuked the Jews as follows:

> O foolish people, contemptible people, mad followers of the Talmud! Should not Daniel who counted the time have said to himself "annihilate yourself"? Indeed, we see that you and they are sinners and rebels.

The Jewish representative's reply was a slap in the face of the Christians who aimed to identify the Jewish messiah with Christ on the basis of the Talmud:

> O our lord the Pope! If the followers of the Talmud are senseless in your opinion, why furnish proof that the Messiah has already come? Ask no proof from fools.[47]

Although opinions as to who won the debate differ, depending on the faith of the authors, the truth is that the sessions were ended hastily and many conversions took place. As Alisa Meyuhas Ginio comments, perhaps "it was not the arguments presented during the debate which tipped the balance against the Jews but rather the overall atmosphere on the Iberian peninsula, which led many, after a generations of persecution and furious preaching since 1391, to decide to convert to Christianity."[48] As a result of this prolonged dispute, the Christians drew up a set of bylaws for the Jews, which both the pope and the king enacted in 1415 — a further step towards the harassment and defeat of Jewish resistance to conversion. The Jewish side, plunged into a depression, either renounced their principles and assimilated or clung firmly to them. In any event, as ibn Verga reports in his chronicle, everything seemed to lead to an irremediable, anguished, and fatal despair:

> This far I found written; the end I did not find written, though I know from what I have heard that the delegates left with great honor, although they suffered much anguish, they and the communities who had pinned their hopes of their own salvation on them.

[47] Ibid., p. 31.
[48] Ibid., p. 28.

# The Legal Conflict: The "Law of the Kingdom" and the Religious Principles of the People of Israel

Not only did the conflict affect religious aspects — both dogmatic and doctrinal — of relations between the Jewish and Christian communities. It also posed problems in the daily application of laws. When referring to laws, we do not mean the internal rules governing the Jewish quarters but the laws enacted by the Christians for all inhabitants of the kingdom or those designed specifically to regulate relations between Christians and Jews. These were the "laws of the kingdom," and at times compliance with them raised serious problems of conscience for the people of Israel.

Although this chapter discusses the conflict arising from the interaction between Jews and Gentiles in medieval Spain, it should be pointed out that during this period the Sephardim were also troubled by internal strife, as many legal records illustrate.

## THE "LAW OF THE KINGDOM" AND JEWISH RELIGIOUS PRINCIPLES

We have already seen how, during the Diaspora, the Jews submitted to the authority of their new state, embodied in the figure of the king, taking Jeremiah and Nehemiah as their references in this connection.[1] The Talmud establishes the following rule in Aramaic:

> The law of the kingdom is law [for us]

The problem raised by such a general precept was how the Jewish *aljamas* or organized communities could adapt the laws of the Gentiles to their own religious law — possibly one of the most conservative aspects of the Jewish people. In order to settle these questions, the rabbis were consulted. Their *Responsa* are so diverse that it is sometimes difficult to find a coherent thread, for the arguments depend on the particular social circumstances of the time.[2] However, we can roughly outline the chief concerns.

On many occasions the Jews resorted to the laws of the kingdom to bring claims against other members of the community instead of doing so according to Hebrew law, when Hebrew law was less favorable to their interests. A certain father, on the basis of the king's laws, had claimed the dowry of his deceased daughter. Jewish inheritance law did not provide for such a claim unless previously stipulated. The *Responsum* of Rabbi Solomon ibn Adret of Barcelona (1235–1310),

[1] See the chapter on "Jews, Moors, and Christians under the King's Authority."

[2] No systematic research has been carried out in this area. However, a short but extremely useful paper provides an initial overall view (Orfali, 2002, pp. 143–152).

who was consulted on this matter, states very clearly that it is not lawful to seek the settlement of disputes between fellow Jews at the courts and according to the laws of the Gentiles:

> But truly, to act in this manner because such is the Law of the Gentiles seems to me to be unlawful, since it amounts to imitating the Gentiles. The Torah states: "[Now these are the ordinances which you shall set before them" (Exodus, 21: 1)], "before them," not before a Gentile court [...] Our people, who are the Lord's heirs, are forbidden by the Torah to honor the laws and ordinances of the Gentiles: and not only this, for it also forbids them to seek their courts, even for matters in which their legislation and the law of Israel are identical. Therefore we are amazed that in your city, a place of rabbinic justice and knowledge, such things as our Torah forbids can be done.[3]

The "law of the kingdom" posed an insurmountable obstacle when it clashed with religious laws: "by no means can those laws which contradict the Torah be accepted." Compared to its strict attitude towards religious affairs, the *halakhah* (Jewish private law) took a tolerant view of matters relating to royal revenues. The interpretations of the Jewish sages are unanimous and categorical in this respect. In his *Hilejot Zekiyá a-matana,* Maimonides states that:

> All the laws of the king on pecuniary matters are binding (Chap. I)[4]

This interpretation of the tax regulations took for granted that everyone was equal in the eyes of the law. However, on many occasions the Jews were obliged to pay special taxes depending on the personal needs of the king, "their lord and protector." As one would expect, these arbitrary impositions displeased the Jewish people, who were reluctant to pay. Sémahh Durán (1361–1444), in a more or less veiled manner, denounced the capricious taxes levied by certain monarchs, though acknowledging the duty to pay what is fair:

> Just as it is in only fair that he who is in debt should pay, he who evades the royal taxes is taking from the king what is just and should be given to him [...] And in all that is necessary for the well-being of the kingdom, such as felling trees, building bridges, developing the country, the royal laws are binding, but in cases where they are not for the well-being of the kingdom but merely arbitrary, albeit by royal decree, they should not be considered laws of the kingdom.[5]

Sémahh Durán's criticism of the excessive taxes levied by the kings has its origins in the writings of thinkers as important as Maimonides and Nahmanides. The latter, referring to these royal whims, stated categorically:

---

[3] Quoted by Orfali, 2002, p. 144.
[4] Ibid., p. 147.
[5] Ibid., p. 149.

This amounts to plundering by the king, and we should not regard it as a law in our Law.[6]

But these religious scruples were progressively shed. The anti-Jewish riots of 1391, which killed thousands, plunged the Jewish community into a profound moral identity crisis. In the view of many, the most lukewarm in their convictions, religious arguments no longer had the force of law and failed to convince them; more pragmatic recommendations were necessary. The Valladolid *taqqanot* (law of the Jewish community) of 1432 provide an enlightening testimony to this crisis:

> First, Jews should abide by their law on this; second, they will save themselves many costs and damages that they accumulate by frequenting non-Jewish courts; third, although the judges are great sages and men of justice, they are not sufficiently accustomed to our rights and laws as to be competent in them [...] Finally, we order that Jews or Jewesses not bring their companions or any other Jew before any mayor or other ecclesiastic or secular judge outside our law.[7]

The following words convey very clearly the startling materialism of this recommendation:

> Do not go to a court of the Gentiles. If not for your principles, at least for your money.

## GENTILES LEGISLATING ON JEWS

Any legislation drawn up specifically for an ethnic minority by the dominant majority of a nation entails major affronts to justice. Despite certain protectionist aspects, the laws formulated by the Christians of medieval Spain undoubtedly spring from the history of the conflict between both peoples. While it is not my intention to justify certain humiliating laws, it should nonetheless be stressed that there were times when the legislation was indulgent — and even egalitarian. Furthermore, when the wave of ecclesiastical radicalism, which had been applied through terrible secular laws elsewhere in Europe, began to spread to Spain, some kingdoms refused to adopt them fully.

The legal status of the Sephardic Jews in relation to the Christian community was gradually shaped through the charters, assemblies, and laws enacted by the king. All this constitutes what is known as the *fuero judiego* ("Jewish law code").[8]

## THE HARSHNESS OF THE LAWS OF GOTHIC SPAIN

As we have pointed out in previous chapters, the situation of the Jews in Gothic Spain was totally insecure. The first legal text dating from this period,

[6] Quoted by Diaz Esteban, 1985, p. 110.

[7] "Lo primero, que los judíos guarden su ley en esto; lo segundo, que quitarán de muchas costas e danios que les recrecen, andando en tribunales de no judíos; lo tercero, por cuanto los juezes aun que son grandes sabios e omes de justicia, non an usado en nuestros derechos e leyes pora que sean bien certificados en ellos [...] Por ende, ordenamos que algun judio o judia non traya a su compañero, nin a otro judio nin judia ante algún alcalde nin otro juez eclesiástico nin seglar de fuera de nuestra ley." Moreno Koch, 1987, p. 51.

[8] Villapalos, 1997, devotes a chapter to this (pp. 220–229). Fernando Suárez Bilbao has recently published an important monograph on this subject (see Suárez Bilbao, 2000).

the *Breviary of Alaric* (506), contains much of earlier Roman case-law concerning the Jews, particularly the Theodosian Code. Jews were granted jurisdiction in civil cases, whereas in criminal matters the Jewish courts were only allowed to handle religious offenses and could not impose the death penalty. For mixed disputes between Christians and Jews, the Jews submitted to Christian judges. As for contractual relations, there were a host of restrictions whenever Christians were involved: Jews were forbidden to hold any type of authority over them and banned from engaging in trade with them. Little is known about property law, only that there were restrictions on the possession of Christian slaves. Yet in many other aspects, the laws were tolerant: it came to be established that Jews should not be summoned to court on their feast days or obliged to work.

The Gothic monarchy's conversion to Catholicism put an end to all this. The growing intolerance that ensued, illustrated particularly well by King Euric's famous twenty-eight laws, is conveyed in the *Liber judiciorum*. Title II gives an idea of the nature and tone of the anti-Jewish doctrine of book XII, which is devoted entirely to the people of Israel:

> Since the laws were given to God's faithful we should make laws for the infidel.[9] Hitherto we have guarded against the faults of the Jews, which are many, and ordered that their evil acts, which are many and without measure, be remedied.[10]

## THE FIRST CENTURIES OF THE CHRISTIAN *RECONQUISTA*: JEWS AND CHRISTIANS ARE EQUAL

In the small Christian kingdoms which remained engaged in conflict with the Muslims, Jews had a say in the division of the territory. From the tenth century they acquired a legal status that practically placed them on a par with Christians. Law codes and charters allocating lands that kings or feudal lords granted to the populations of the newly conquered territories generally treat them equally. This is illustrated in law codes such as those of Castrogeriz (974) and León (1017–1020), on which so many others were modeled. The Leonese law code categorically stressed the need, whenever a dispute arose between members of the two religious communities, for both to be represented equally among those entrusted with the task of settling the suit and therefore recommended that "two Christians and two Jews be taken."

By the middle of the eleventh century, the restrictive laws of the Gothic monarchs had been practically abolished by Ferdinand I, king of Castile and León, though a few religious proscriptions still remained. The Council of Coyanza

[9] "Que después que las leyes fueron dadas a los fieles de Dios conviénenos á facer ley á los non fieles."

[10] "Fasta enesaquí [aquí] nos guardamos de las culpas de los judíos, que son muchas, é ordenamos cuemo fuesen enmendadas las sus maldades, que son muchas e sin mensura."

in 1050 reiterated the ban on engaging in close relationships with Jews, either at home or at meals:

> No Christian shall dwell with Jews in a house, or eat with them.[11]

The legislation derived from the settlement charters of this period is very diverse, given the variety of territorial and even municipal laws. Private and collective property such as synagogues and cemeteries was guaranteed. The taxation system only obliged Jews to pay royal taxes, which were levied directly by the king's treasury. They thus enjoyed judicial and administrative autonomy.

There is evidence that the Jews engaged increasingly in commerce from the twelfth century onwards. This clearly reflects the urban development that was taking place, which called for laws to regulate it. For example, moneylending became a thriving activity among Jewish bankers, and the law codes devote considerable attention to it, establishing limits on the interest that could be charged on loans, as we find in the laws of Cuenca and Teruel. A few legal restrictions also began to emerge in this century. Alfonso VII (1126–1157) banned Jews from testifying against Christians at trials. The Escalona law code of 1130 expressly banned Jews from trying Christians. But other aspects of the laws were kinder on the Jews. The Cuenca law code,[12] like many others, allowed Jews to swear oaths on the Torah, granting them the same value as Christian oaths sworn on the cross. It stated that disputes between Christians and Jews should be heard by a judge from each community.

As a rule, despite certain discriminatory measures inherited from Gothic legislation, we may agree with Suárez Bilbao that "the Jews came to enjoy a privileged situation that was comparable to that of minor nobles or clergy"[13] during the eleventh and twelfth centuries.

## THE RENEWAL OF THIRTEENTH-CENTURY LAWS AND THE POPES' JEWISH POLICY

Ferdinand III's conquest of the valley of the Guadalquivir marked a major geopolitical change in the kingdom of Castile: a huge expanse of territory with a considerable population of non-believers was incorporated. It was necessary to enact law codes for governing these newly conquered cities and towns. No doubt with a view to this expansion, in 1241 Ferdinand had commissioned the translation of the *Liber Judiciorum*, thereafter known as the *Fuero Juzgo*. But the circumstances were no longer the same as in the Gothic period: the Jews had become the kings' close collaborators. The entourage of victors who accompanied Ferdinand when he entered the city of Seville included

[11] "Nengunt christiano non more con judios en una casa, nen coma con ellos" (Cap. VI).

[12] This law code was adopted by Alfonso VIII in 1190 shortly after conquering the city.

[13] Suárez Bilbao, 2000, p. 55.

prominent Jews of Toledo, some belonging to families which had been forced to flee from the city in the past. This historical context explains why Ferdinand's laws established an equal civil status for Jews and the rest of the population.

The middle of the thirteenth century saw a major effort by the Spanish kingdoms to create a broader system of laws that established some sort of order and uniformity over the diversity of municipal codes. The greatest legislative endeavor, of far-reaching significance in subsequent years, was championed by Alfonso X and his team of jurists, who were responsible for drawing up codes such as the *Fuero Real, Leyes Nuevas, Espéculo* and *Las Partidas.* Together they constitute the most important body of legal doctrine on Jews in the whole of medieval Europe.

This legislation clearly displays the influence of the anti-Jewish ecclesiastical laws that were being introduced throughout Europe following the Fourth Lateran Council and Gregory IX's *Decretals.* However, the more extreme measures were softed, and even, as we have seen in other chapters of this book, some of the most humiliating ones were not actually put into practice. What is more, these Spanish law codes reproduced earlier laws providing protection and showing a certain tolerance of religious differences.

Let us now examine briefly some aspects of Jewish-related legislation in the *Partidas,* bearing in mind that, although this code did not enter into force until the following century,[14] as a whole it springs from a widespread state of opinion disseminated by the king among the population of thirteenth-century Castile. Title XXIV of *Partida* VII is devoted exclusively to the Jews and contains a total of eleven laws. Unlike the *Liber judiciorum,* the text does not begin with an accusation but merely points out their non-belief in Christ and the necessity of social intercourse with them:

> Jews are a type of men who do not believe in our Lord Jesus Christ, but the great Christian lords always endured their presence among them.[15]

The first and second laws explain who the Jews are and the manner in which they should live among Christians:

> Law I: What Jew means and where this name is derived from, and the reasons why the church and great Christian lords ceased to live among them.[16]
> Law II: The manner in which Jews must go about their life while residing among Christians, and what things they must not practice or do according to our law and what punishment is deserved by those who contravene this.[17]

In addition to recommending they abide by their own law, the lawmaker bans them from proselytizing:

[14] These laws were put into practice long afterwards, when they were enacted in the *Ordenamiento de Alcalá de 1348,* after being agreed upon and amended (*concertadas e emendadas*).

[15] "Judios son una manera de homes que como quier que non creen la fe de nuestro señor Jesucristo, pero los grandes señores de los cristianos siempre sufrieron que viviesen entre ellos."

[16] "Ley I: Que quier decir judio, et onde tomó este nombre, et por qué razones la eglesia et los grandes señores cristianos los dexaron vivir entre sí."

[17] "Ley II: En que manera deben facer su vida los judíos mientras vivieren entre los cristianos, et quáles cosas non deben usar nin facer segunt nuestra ley, et que pena merecen los que contra esto ficieren."

Meekly and without undue commotion must Jews live and lead their lives among Christians, abiding by their law and not speaking ill of the faith of our Lord Jesus Christ observed by the Christians. Furthermore they must take great care not to preach or convert any Christian to the Jewish faith by praising their law and reviling our own: and anyone who disobeys this shall be put to death as a consequence and lose what he has.[18]

The laws governing relations with the Christians are not new to Roman tradition:

Law III: No Jew may hold any office or rank in which he may compel Christians.[19]
Law VIII: How no Christian man or woman shall live in the house of a Jew.[20]
Law IX: What punishment is deserved by a Jew who lies with a Christian woman.[21]
Law X: What punishment is deserved by Jews who keep Christians as slaves or make their captives convert to their law.[22]

All these restrictive measures are based on a deep-rooted though naïve religious principle of preventing contagion through contact and ensuring that Christians' souls are not corrupted through magical practices or spells. The legislator gives a curious explanation of how this problem can be avoided by using the services of a Jewish physician:[23]

No Christian shall receive medicine nor remedy made by a Jew; but he may receive it on the advice of some Jewish sage, provided it is made by a Christian who knows and understands what things it contains.[24]

Another set of laws shows an interest in the Jews and establishes that their customs be treated with respect.

Law IV: How the Jews may have synagogues among Christians.[25]
Law V: How the Jews must not be compelled to work on the Sabbath and which judges can compel them.[26]
Law VI: How Jews who become Christians must not be compelled and how Jews who becomes a Christians are better, and what punishment is deserved by other Jews who do them ill or dishonor them for this reason.[27]

In these laws we find observations and expressions that denote a particular understanding of and sensitivity towards Jewish belief:

And because the synagogue is the house where the name of God is praised, no Christian shall dare destroy it, or remove or take from it any thing by force.[28]

[18] "Mansamente et sin bollicio malo deben vevir et facer vida los judios entre los cristianos, guardando su ley et non diciendo mal de la fe de nuestro señor Jesucristo que guardan los cristianos. Otrosi se deben mucho guardar de non predicar nin convertir á ningunt cristiano que se torne judio, alabando su ley et denostando la nuestra: et qualquier que contra esto ficiere debe morir por ende et perder lo que ha." (Partida VII, tit. XXIV, ley II.)

[19] "Ley III: Que ningunt judio non puede haber ningunt oficio nin dignidad para poder apremiar á los cristianos."

[20] "Ley VIII: Como ningunt cristiano nin cristiana non debe facer vida en casa de judio."

[21] "Ley IX: Qué pena merece el judio que yace con cristiana."

[22] "Ley X: Qué pena merecen los judios que tienen cristianos por siervos, ó facen sus cativos tornar á su ley."

[23] The jurist must have been aware that the most powerful men of the time had Jewish doctors.

[24] "Defendemos que ningúnt cristiano non reciba melecinamiento nin murga que sea fecha por mano de judio; pero bien la puede recebir por consejo de algunt judio sabidor, solamente que fecha por mano de cristiano que conozca et entiéndalas cosas que son en ella." (Partida VII, tit. XXIV, ley VIII.)

[25] "Ley IV: Cómo pueden haber los judios sinagogas entre los cristianos."

[26] "Ley V: Cómo no deben apremiar á los judios en dia de sábado, et quáles jueces los pueden apremiar."

[27] "Ley VI: Cómo non deben seer apremiados los judios que se tornan cristianos, et qué mejoria ha el judio que se torna cristiano, et qué pena merecen los otros judios que les facen mal ó deshonra por ello."

[28] "Et porque sinagoga es casa do se loa el nombre de Dios, defendemos que ningunt cristiano non sea osado de la quebrantar, nin de sacar nin de tomar ende ninguna cosa por fuerza."

One of the most degrading rules, inspired by papal policy, establishes that Jews should wear distinctive clothing in order that they may be identified by all:

> Law XI: How the Jews bear distinctive marks in order to be recognized.[29]

However, as we have stated in other sections of this book, this rule was not put into practice in the kingdoms of Castile and León during the thirteenth century.

The last of the laws relates to Christians who convert to Judaism. At the time this issue was not significant in its own right; it is mentioned in relation to the heretical Christian movements of the period:

> Law VII: What punishment is deserved by a Christian who becomes a Jew.[30]

The most immediate practical application of the theory that the *Partidas* contain on Jews was in the various law codes drawn up by Alfonso X's chancery.

The *Fuero Real*, possibly designed as the basis for municipal law codes, was drawn up around 1255 and remained in force until 1272. The most important laws on Jews are grouped together under Title II of Book IV and display the same spirit as the *Partidas*.[31] Some deal with the Jews' obligation to respect the religious laws of the Christians. Other provisions protect Jewish religious practice. They also lay down rules on loans and usury, though these do not apply merely to Jews but also to Christians and Moors.

Loans and usury are dealt with in greater detail in the *Leyes Nuevas,* compiled shortly after the *Fuero real.* They introduce a novelty: Jews are allowed to sell goods to Christians. The provision on the manner of swearing an oath is very interesting, as it illustrates the respect Alfonso's laws show:

> The manner in which Jews must swear an oath [...][32]
> Jews having to swear an oath must do so as follows: he who demands the oath of the Jew must go with him to the synagogue, and the Jew who has to swear the oath must place his hands on the Torah with which they pray, and there must be Christians and Jews present to witness how he swears.[33]

The *Espéculo,* enacted shortly before 1258, does not develop the laws on the Jews any further and deals with only a few aspects. It reiterates the type of oath laid down in the *Leyes Nuevas* and adds a restriction on witnesses:

> "A man of another law, be he a Jew, Moor, or heretic," may not be a witness against a Christian.[34]

Although Aragonese laws generally reflected a spirit of renewal that was partly inspired by the Castilian legal corpus, some aspects relating to the Jews were very

[29] "Ley XI: Cómo los judios deben andar señalados porque sean conocidos."

[30] "Ley VII: Qué pena merece el cristiano que se tornare judio."

[31] None of the laws that constitute this code goes against the Jews. Indeed, some are even clearly beneficial to this minority (David Romano, 1983, p. 271).

[32] "En qué manera deven yurar los iudios."

[33] "Iudios aviendo de yurar deven lo fazer desta manera; aquel que demanda la yura al iudio, debe yr a la sinagoga con él, e el iudio que a de yurar, debe poner las manos sobre la tora con que fazen oración, e deven seer delante cristianos e iudios para que vean como yura" (Ley XXVIII).

[34] "'Ome que sea de otra ley, como judío, moro o herege' no puede ser testigo contra cristiano."

From top to bottom: initial E: A man receives a bag of coins from a Jew in exchange for a goblet; initial N: Several men speak before a king and a man exchanges a goblet for money with a Jew; initial A: Two Jewish craftsmen at work; in *Vidal Mayor*, fols. 114r, 175v, 243, details. Los Angeles, The J. Paul Getty Museum (Ms. Ludwig xiv 6, 83. Mq. 165)

[35] This delightful manuscript is housed in the J. Paul Getty Museum (Los Angeles).
[36] The miniature illustrates the theme of profit or interest earned on capital. It indicates that nobody, regardless of his position, may claim interest from anybody else after his capital has been doubled by the interest.

harsh. Unlike Castile, the kingdom of Aragon did not refuse to enforce the terrible reforming laws of popes Innocent III and Gregory IX.

James I enacted a set of rules on the Jews in 1228: he established the interest rate on loans at twenty percent; abolished Jews' oaths as testimonial evidence in lawsuits over loans; and barred Jews from holding public office. Only thirteen years later, the Cortes of Gerona promulgated a set of laws banning usury. But in general, the worst part was the spirit of these laws, which can almost be described as anti-Semitic. In this connection, suffice it to compare the system of oaths set forth in the Alfonsine laws with the Catalan laws, which compelled Jews to swear their oaths before Christian judges instead of at the synagogue. Furthermore, the text of the oath they were made to swear contained many expressions that were offensive to the Jews.

When dealing with the laws of the kingdom of Aragon in the thirteenth century, mention should be made of the *Vidal Mayor*.[35] This is a collection of the law codes of Aragon compiled by Bishop Vidal de Canellas on the orders of King James I in 1247. As one might expect of feudal laws, it takes a very conservative stance with the Jews. However it is very interesting to note that Jews enjoy a fairly prominent role in the pictures which illustrate those laws. The Jews, in their characteristic pointed headdresses, are shown performing different activities; in a sense we might consider that these miniatures represent real genre scenes of the period.

Folio 114 recto illustrates the chapter on contracts between people of different religions, which must by drawn up by a scribe of the religion of the party which undertakes and promises to the other contracting party. It shows two Jews selling metalwork objects to two Christians, while the scribe — like the vendor, a Jew — draws up the contract. As one would expect, the traditional subject of usury is dealt with in the illustration on folio 175 verso. It depicts a Jew lending money to a Christian, who hands him a golden goblet as security. As they fail to agree on the interest rate, they subsequently appeal to the king's court to settle the dispute.[36] Other illustrations show Jews in their shops and workshops.

Owing to its close relations with France, Navarre was particularly affected by some of the restrictions imposed by papal policy. In 1234 Pope Gregory IX ordered the king to make the Navarrese Jews wear special clothing to differentiate them from the Christians, as he was under the impression that the rules of the general council were not being abided by. But whereas this indicates a certain degree of tolerance regarding compliance with some of the rules, others, such as those on usury, were observed very strictly. In 1256 Pope Alexander IV granted the king powers to prevent Jews engaging in usury and to strip them of the goods they had acquired by such means, which were returned to their owners or used for religious purposes. This was followed by further royal measures to crack down on Jewish usury throughout the rest of the century.

*Fuero de Estella*, Navarre, 1164, twelfth-fourteenth-century copy. Manuscript on parchment. Salamanca, Biblioteca General de la Universidad (Ms. 2652)

The *Fuero General de Navarra,* drawn up in the mid-thirteenth century, marked an attempt at introducing new laws. However, it proved unsuccessful, as population centers continued to operate by their own law codes. As most of these had been adopted in the twelfth century, the rules on the Jews were tolerant and egalitarian. One of these codes, that of Estella, illustrates how these laws had survived from remote times. King Sancho Ramírez had granted the code to the town around 1084. The text, now lost, was added to in 1164. Of this enlarged version there remains a delightful fourteenth-century copy containing illustrations. One of the most outstanding of these is a miniature depicting the crucifixion of Christ.[37] The chapter entitled *"De christiano et judeo,"* dealing with duties mutually incumbent upon people of both religions, is a good example of the earlier tradition of tolerance.

## CRISES OF THE FOURTEENTH AND FIFTEENTH CENTURIES

From the fourteenth century onwards, legislation grew increasingly restrictive as a new wave of anti-Semitism spread across Europe. Now the Jews no longer enjoyed such firm royal support as afforded by the thirteenth-century Castilian monarchs, and their freedoms and rights diminished.

The most important legal development of the century was the *Ordenamiento Real de Alcalá*.[38] This constituted a major legal reform, approved by the Cortes of

[37] Now held in the Biblioteca General, Universidad de Salamanca.

[38] The four surviving copies of this lawbook were produced by Nicolás González, the illuminator of the *Crónica Troyana.* The beautiful illustrations found in these codices include portraits of Alfonso X and Alfonso XI, the royal signum of Peter I, and monograms of Christ and royal coats of arms.

*Ordenamiento Real de Alcalá*, 1348.
Parchment. Madrid, Biblioteca Nacional
(Vit/15–7)

Alcalá de Henares in 1348, and was basically designed to settle the issue of debts owed to Jews. The cities' procurators had demanded a reduction in the debts owed to Jews and asked that payment of the outstanding sums be deferred. In response to these requests, the monarch, aware of his own need of the Jews' money, enforced his authority and only reduced one quarter of the legal debts. Only the debts considered by the *Ordenamiento de Alcalá* to be deceitful were to be trimmed by 75 percent.

The new law banned both Jews and Muslims from charging interest on loans and abolished all the privileges previously granted to Jews in this respect. The kingdom's officers were ordered not to collect Jewish debts, and it was proposed that the Church excommunicate anybody who failed to comply with the rule. Loss of the loan business and the reduction and deferral of existing debts would also have amounted to inability to lend money for taxes, and this would have irremediably led the Jewish power circles to lose influence at the court. But it seems that these rules were not put into practice, and the Cortes of 1351 requested they be repealed.

To make up for this substantial reduction in their income, the law authorized Jews to purchase lands belonging to the royal estate, in addition to the lands and houses they already owned.

From the beginning of the fifteenth century, Jews were progressively stripped of their rights with respect to the Christian community and the possibility of exercising their own laws among themselves.

At the 1405 meeting of the Cortes, the procurators stated that there were problems in lawsuits involving Jews if a witness from that community was involved, claiming that this was a "dishonor to and vituperation of the Christian faith." Henry III, following the instructions of the popes, agreed to their requests. This marked a significant loss of the protection the Jewish community had enjoyed hitherto.

# The Image of the Other

The long-drawn-out conflict between Christians and Jews led each group to shape an image of the other. This section deals with the image of Jews that was created by Christians as opposed to their real image, discussed in an earlier chapter, or the image of the "marked" Jews (who were required by law to wear a badge of identity), which was a reality. It is the image concocted by Christian minds out of all the anti-Jewish prejudices they harbored.

The host of images that spring from this view can basically be divided into two types: doctrinal and anti-Semitic. At times they overlap. Although these images were essentially negative, there were also some positive representations.

Anti-Semitic sentiment is conveyed through a conception of the Jews as a race of hypocrites, usurers, and misers whose deformed physical features are a result of their depraved moral conduct. We thus find an extremely stereotypical figure with such characteristics as a long, hooked nose, pointed teeth, and bulging eyes. Although dating from much earlier times, this image became widespread from the thirteenth century onwards. The society depicted in Alfonso X's *Cantigas* is full of Jews that fit this description.[1] Of a similar nature though more satirical are the illustrations from the fourteenth-century Catalan *Libri judeorum*. These notaries' registers of transactions involving Jews and Christians, which required a Christian scribe, are full of caricatures drawn by the notaries themselves: the drawing of Bishop Solomon Vidal in the Vic book is a typical example.

The views that spring from doctrine include two very different types of images of Jews: a positive one showing elegant and honorable

**Liber Judeorum, 1334–1340.
Manuscript on paper.
Vic (Barcelona),
Archiu Curia Fumada**

[1] Molina Figueras, 2002, p. 375.

*The Circumcision of Christ.* Late fifteenth century. Oil on wood. Palencia, Museo Diocesano

personages; and the negative ones depicting the Jews as the enemy of Christian doctrine.

Since they shared the Old Testament with the Jews, the Christians considered that certain eminent Jews ought to be respected. Accordingly, these Jews are shown with a noble appearance and generally attired in elegant robes that befit their status. The fifteenth-century Gothic Castilian panel painting depicting the circumcision of Jesus portrays the priests of the Temple in this manner.[2] There are many such images in Christian iconography.

[2] Here the Temple is shown as a centralized architectural structure as the painting draws a parallel between Jewish circumcision and Christian baptism.

The most interesting images are those which illustrate the doctrinal debate between Christians and Jews. The Church versus Synagogue controversy examined in this chapter is also represented in a large number of paintings. We have seen how the story of St. Stephen was involved in one of the earliest Spanish doctrinal disputes, on the island of Minorca. Paintings showing the saint preaching at the synagogue surrounded by Jews, as in Jaume Serra's panel painting, are very common. These compositions generally tend to emphasize the polemics of the encounter. But it was not long before the focus shifted from the theme of

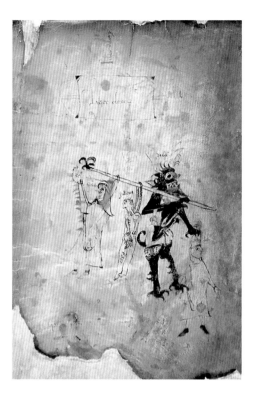

Cover of the *Cardona storybook,*
Barcelona, Biblioteca de Catalunya
(Archivo de la Bailía de Cardona,
B–VI–3)

evangelization to the depiction of the winning side, and we thus find images of the triumphant Church and vanquished Synagogue. In such pictures the Synagogue, blinded by its error and its flag torn as a sign of defeat, contrasts with the image of the victorious Church. Such images are numerous and greatly varied: particularly characteristic of thirteenth-century Castilian Gothic imagery is that of the Conventet collection. Those painted by Fernando Gallego in the Prado *Maiestas* are extremely beautiful.

As regards the Church/Synagogue controversy, the well-known *Fountain of Grace* attributed to Van Eyck[3] is of outstanding quality and significance. In the foreground of this panel painting, on either side of the fountain, are two groups: the Church and the Synagogue. While the members of the Church are led by the Pope, who bears the triumphal banner, the gesticulating members of the Synagogue appear despondent and shaken. Facing the group of Jews is the high priest wearing the breastplate with twelve precious stones; he is shown bearing the torn flag of the vanquished side and blinded by error. Although Van Eyck also portrayed the group of Jews in his famous Ghent polyptych, the emphasis is not on defeat as it is here. How do we account for this difference? I suspect that this painting was conceived soon after the Tortosa disputation (1413-14) in which it was said that the Church, led by Pope Benedict XIII himself, had defeated the scholars of the Synagogue.

Other images are more ideological. For example, since Romanesque times church iconography has featured. Cain as the embodiment of Jewish impiety, with all the stereotypical characteristics referred to earlier, and the compulsory marks on his clothing or headdress.[4] The Cardona storybook shows another image based on the idea of Jewish "error:" the Jew condemned to hell and conducted there by the devil himself.[5]

[3] A gift from Henry IV to the monastery of El Parral in Segovia (Yarza, 1993, pp. 124–125).
[4] Bango Torviso, 1993.
[5] Molina, 2002, p. 377.

# Expulsion

Devastating anti-Jewish riots in 1391, together with the monarchy's policy of isolating those who persisted in professing the faith of Moses, plunged the people of Israel into a terrible crisis. The long drawn-out confrontation between Spain's Christians and Jews came to an end one cold but sunny day in early spring 1492. A royal edict signed by Ferdinand and Isabella, the Catholic Monarchs, in Granada on 31 March ordered the expulsion of the Jews from Spain. The several surviving copies of this expulsion decree display slight differences. This has led specialists to disagree as to which one is most faithful to the spirit of the original edict.[1] The one addressed to the city of Burgos, published by Suárez, is generally considered the most faithful. However, Carrete Parrondo believes that the version published shortly after 1516 in the *Libro de bulas y pragmáticas de los Reyes Católicos* is the most reliable.[2] Quoted below is the text of the decree according to the edition by J. Ramírez in the *Libro en que están copiladas algunas Bullas et todas las pragmáticas (1503)*:[3]

King Ferdinand and Queen Isabella, by the grace of God, King and Queen of Castile, León, etc. […] To the prince Don Juan, our very dear and very beloved son, and to the Infantes, eminent clergy, Dukes […]. You know well, or should know, for we were informed, that in our dominion there are certain bad Christians who Judaized and committed apostasy against our Holy Catholic faith, much of it caused by the contract between Jews and Christians; in the Cortes held in the city of Toledo in the year fourteen hundred and eighty, we ordered that the Jews living in all the cities and towns and villages of our domains be confined to separate quarters, hoping that by segregating them the situation would be remedied. And we ordered that an Inquisition be established in such domains; as you know, during the twelve years it has existed, the Inquisition has found many people guilty. And we are informed by the Inquisition and many other religious and ecclesiastical and secular sources that the great harm done to the Christians persists, and it continues because of the involvement, conversations, and relations that they have with the Jews, who do their utmost to subvert and draw faithful Christians away from our holy Catholic faith and lure them to their own mistaken beliefs and opinions by instructing them in the ceremonies and observances of their Law, holding meetings to read to them and teach them what to believe in and the rules to be observed according to their law, attempting to circumcise them and their children, and giving them books with which to pray […] which has resulted in great damage, detriment, and dishonor to our holy Catholic faith.

[1] In 1886 Amador de los Ríos published a decree addressed to all the Spanish towns and cities, which was formerly held in the Biblioteca Nacional and is now lost. F. Fita published the one housed in the Archivo Municipal de Ávila, which is addressed expressly to this city. Baer improved on this edition in a well known publication (1936). However, the best transcription and interpretation was published by (León Tello 1963). A third decree, the one sent to the city of Toledo, was published by Torre, 1962, doc. 42. Another decree, this one addressed to the city of Burgos, was published by Luis Suárez (Suárez Fernández, 1964). M. A. Motis Dolader has published the text of a general decree housed in the Archivo de la Corona de Aragón (1985).

[2] Carrete Parrondo, 1992.

[3] Fols. 6v and 7r.

Don fernando e doña ysauel por la gracia de dios rrey
e rreyna de castilla de leon de aragon de se çilia de gra
nada de toledo de Valençia de galizia de mallorcas de
seuilla de çerdeña de corsega de corçega de murçia de jaen
de algarue de algezira de gibraltar e de las yslas de canaria
Con de condesa de barcelona e señores de bizcaya e de molyna
duq̃s de athenas e de neopatria condes de rrosellon
de çerdanya marq̃ses de oristan e de guçiano al prinçipe de
don juan mi muy caro e muy amado hijo e a los ynfantes
perlados duques marqueses condes maestres de las or
denes priores e ricos omes comendadores e alcaydes de los
Castillos e casas fuertes de los dichos nuestros reynos e señorios
e a los concejos corregidores alcaldes alguaziles merinos caualle
ros escuderos oficiales e omes buenos de la muy noble e
muy leal çibdad de burgos e de las otras çibdades e villas
e lugares de nuestros obispados e de los otros arçobispados e obispados
e dios de los dichos nuestros reynos e señorios e a las aljamas
de los judios de las dichas çibdades e burgos e de todas las otras
çibdades e villas e lugares de nuestros obispados e de todas las çibdades
villas e lugares de los dichos nuestros reynos e señorios
e a todos los judios e personas singulares dellos asi barones
como mugeres de qual quier hedad que sean e a todas las
otras personas de qual quier ley estado dignidades pre
minençia e condiçion que sean a quien lo de yuso en esta
nuestra carta contenido atañe o atañer puede en qual
manera salud e graçia bien sabedes o deuedes saber por
que nos fuymos ynformados que en estos nuestros reynos
auia algunos malos cristianos que judayzaban e apostataban
de nuestra santa fee catolica de lo qual era muncha causa la

And because we have previously been informed of much of this and know that the true remedy for all this harm and all these problems lies in severing all contact between the said Jews and the Christians and in sending them away from all our Kingdoms, we considered it sufficient to order the said Jews to leave all the cities and towns and villages of Andalusia where they appeared to have caused the greatest harm, believing that this would suffice to make those living in other cities and towns and villages in our Kingdoms and domains desist from causing the aforesaid harm. And because we have been informed that neither this, nor bringing some of the aforesaid Jews to justice and finding them guilty of the said crimes and transgressions against our holy Catholic faith, have been sufficient to fully remedy such great dishonor and offense to the Christian religion, and because every day we find and see that the said Jews increasingly persist in their evil and harmful ways wherever they live and lead their lives, and because it is time that our holy Catholic faith is offended no longer, among those whom God has wished to protect hitherto or among those who fell and mended their ways and returned to the holy Mother Church, since, because of the frailty of human nature and the diabolical temptation that continually batters us, this could easily occur if the principal cause is not removed by expelling the Jews from our Kingdoms. And because whenever a grave and heinous crime is committed by some members of a college or university, it is reasonable for that college or university to be dissolved and obliterated, and for youngsters to be punished by their elders; and because those who pervert the good and honest living in cities and towns by their contagion and could harm others should be expelled from the midst of the people, and even for minor causes that would be of harm to the Republic, this holds even truer for the worst and most dangerous and contagious of crimes like this one.

Therefore, with the advice and opinions of the eminent clergy and nobility and knights of our Kingdoms, and of other persons of learning and knowledge of our Council, after much deliberation, it is agreed and resolved that all Jews and Jewesses be ordered to leave our kingdoms, and that they never be allowed to return. And we further order in this edict that all Jews and Jewesses of whatever age who live and reside in our Kingdoms and domains, whether or not they were born there and for whatever reason they may have come to be there, leave with their sons and daughters, their Jewish servants and relatives, old and young, of whatever age, by the end of July of this year. And that they dare not return to our lands or to any part of them, either to live or in transit or in any other manner whatsoever. Jews who do not comply with this edict and are found in our Kingdoms and domains, or who trespass on them in any way, shall be put to death and all their belongings shall be confiscated by the royal Treasury. And they shall be punished without trial, judgment, or statement.

We further order that no person in our kingdom of whatever station or noble status dare receive, keep, or defend any Jew or Jewess, either publicly or secretly, from the end of July onwards, on their estates or in their homes or elsewhere in our Kingdoms and domains, upon punishment of confiscation of all their belongings, vassals, real property, and other hereditary privileges, in addition to confiscation of any *maravedís* of Ours they may have by the royal Treasury.

And in order that the said Jews and Jewesses may dispose of their households and belongings in the given period, we hereby provide our assurance of royal protection and safety so that, until the end of the month of July, they may sell and exchange their real and personal property and dispose of it freely as they wish; and that during the said time, no one may unlawfully cause harm or injury or injustice to them or to their goods, and anyone who violates our royal assurance shall be punished. Thus we grant permission to the said Jews and Jewesses to take their goods and belongings with them out of our kingdoms, either by sea or by land, with the condition that they not take out either gold or silver or minted money or any other items prohibited by the laws of the kingdom, save in the form of goods that are not prohibited or in bills of exchange.

And in order that this may be known to all and lest anybody should claim ignorance, we order that this Charter be proclaimed in the squares and market places and usual places of this city and of the main cities and towns and villages of its archbishopric, by a towncrier and before a public scribe [...]. Issued in the noble city of Granada on the thirty first of March, in the fourteen hundred and ninety second year of our Lord Jesus Christ. I, the King. I, the Queen. I, Johan de Coloma, secretary to the King and to the Queen, our lords, wrote it on their orders. Registered, Bernal Diañes, chancellor."

Most of the scholars who study this decree seek so many interpretations and analyses of the monarch's supposed intentions that they render it meaningless, offering instead a confusing, extensive theory of causes and effects. In the following pages we will explore a number of contemporary sources, including both opinions and direct accounts of the most significant events.

**THE ROYAL EDICT TAKES THE JEWS BY SURPRISE**

Traditionally, historians' analyses of the Jews' last two centuries in Spain generally describe a progressively worsening state of affairs leading to the expulsion edict. This approach seems to imply that the Jews would have been aware of the approaching calamity, a situation that might be called: "Sepharad 1492. An expulsion foretold." There is no basis for this theory, which has been examined by Carlos Carrete.[4] The Jews living in Spain continued to go about their daily lives as usual, unaware of what was in store. Everything seems to indicate that the monarchs' Jewish officials, who worked daily at close quarters with them, were not expecting such an outcome either. One of these officials was Isaac Abravanel, whose account of how he found out about the decree and his immediate reaction clearly conveys his surprise:"

[4] Carrete Parrondo, 1998.

At the time I was there, at the royal court, and I pleaded insistently until my throat was raw. I spoke to the monarch three times, as best I could, and I implored him saying: 'Please, King! Why do you act in this way with your subjects? Heap taxes upon us; a man of the house of Israel will give gold and silver and whatever he possesses for the sake of his country of birth'. I implored my friends, who enjoyed royal favor, to intercede on my people's behalf, and the nobility met to ask the sovereign forcefully to withdraw the proclamation of anger and wrath and to his abandon his plan to exterminate the Jews. And the queen, who was standing by his side to corrupt him, powerfully persuaded him to carry out and finish the deed. We worked earnestly but to no avail. I had no peace of mind, no rest. But the misfortune occurred.[5]

## THE DECREE AS INTERPRETED BY JEWS AND CHRISTIANS OF THE PERIOD

The decree is long and detailed, but it is obvious that the only arguments put forward are of a religious nature. Bernáldez, an acknowledged anti-Semite of the time, outlines the reasoning: the error of the Mosaic faith is based on a book of falsehoods, the Talmud; the Jews should remedy their error by converting to the Christian faith, in which they will be instructed; if they are not baptized, they must be expelled. Let us examine these explanations in Bernáldez's own words:

> While in the center of Granada in the year 1492, they ordered that the Holy Gospel and Catholic faith and Christian doctrine be preached to all the Jews throughout Spain and all its kingdoms, and that those who wished to be converted and baptized should remain in their Kingdoms as their vassals, with everything that was theirs, and that those who did not wish to convert should leave and depart from their Kingdoms and never return on pain of death, and that they take with them all their possessions, except for gold or silver, or sell them as they wish. And this edict was issued and sent to all the synagogues and town squares and churches, and the learned men of Spain preached to them the Holy Gospel and doctrine of our Holy Mother the Church, and proved using their very scriptures how the Messiah they await was our Redeemer Jesus Christ, who came at the right time, whom their ancestors evilly ignored […] deceived by the false book of the Talmud.[6]

Although this is the view of a fanatical Christian, it does not greatly differ from the accounts written by Jewish authors. The historical memory of the Jewish people in exile was fed by the belief that the causes for their expulsion were solely religious. In his well-known *Nomologia o discursos legales*, Rabbi Immanuel Aboah (1555-1628) gives only the following explanation for the decree of expulsion: "Seeing how the Jews of their states induced many Christians to Judaize, particularly the nobles of their Kingdom of Andalusia, they banished them for that reason under very harsh penalties."[7]

[5] Quoted by Carroto Parrondo, 1986.

[6] "Estando en el centro de Granada en el año de 1492, mandaron y ordenaron que a todos los judíos de toda España, e de todos los Reynos de ella, les fuese predicado el Santo Evangelio é fé católica, é doctrina cristiana, é que los que quisiesen se convertir é baptizarse, permanecieran en sus Reynos; asy como sus vasallos, con todo lo suyo, y los que no se quisiesen convertir; que dentro de seis meses se fuesen é partiesen de sus Reynos; é so pena de muerte no volviesen mas á ellos, é que llevasen todo lo suyo, ó vendiesen en lo que quisiesen, salvo no sacasen oro ni plata. E salido este edicto, é mandado en todas las sinagogas, é plazas é iglesias, por los sabios varones de España les fue predicado el Santo Evangelio é doctrina de nuestra Santa Madre la Iglesia, é probado por sus mismas escrituras como el Mesías que aguardaban era nuestro Redemptor Jesucristo, que vino en el tiempo convenible, el qual sus antepasados con malicia ignoraron [...] engañados por el falso libro del Talmud," Bernáldez, 1953, chapter CX, p. 651.

[7] "Visto como los Iudios de sus estados induzian a judaizar a muchos Cristianos, en particular a los nobles de su Reyno de Andaluzia, que por esso los desterrauan sobre grauissimas penas." (Quoted by Moisés Orfali, 2000.)

## THE DUAL REACTION OF THE JEWISH PEOPLE:
## FROM APOSTASY TO REAFFIRMATION OF THEIR FAITH

In 1510, just eighteen years after the expulsion, the chronicler Abraham bar Selomoh de Torrutiel wrote this moving account of the impact of the decree on the Jews:

> Adonai was inflamed with wrath against his people, and they were expelled from the towns of Castile by the king Don Her[n]ando and on the advice of his wicked wife Isabella and on the opinion of his advisors; in the first month, which is the month of *Nisan*, joy turned to affliction and pain. The town crier traveled around the whole kingdom of Sepharad, which was under their rule, and a messenger read out sternly: "To you, the Jews, who live throughout my kingdom, you are ordered to depart from my country within three months and anyone who refuses to do so, whoever disobeys a single clause of my edict shall be put to death'. In all the places where the king's word and mandate became known, the pain of the Jews was great, fasting and tears, hair shirts and ashes placed upon them; for many of them, there was bitter weeping on the first day of *Pesach* instead of *Haggadah*, devastation instead of *matzot* and bitter herbs. The people wept that night and there was great anguish."[8]

The account ends with the statement that "From Pesach to the feast of Tabernacles, the whole of Adonai's army departed from the country of Sepharad." However, not all the Jews chose exile. The monarchs sought their conversion, and this was the fate of the great majority, as Jewish sources acknowledge:

> Most of the Jews, the gentry, the lords, and the judges remained in their houses and exchanged their law for the law of the foreign god of the land; they abandoned the spring of living water and the King of the world and served other gods who were unknown or unrelated to them, being of wood and stone, and who do neither evil nor harm nor good. In charge of the multitude of apostates was the Rabbi Don Abraham Seneor, rabbi of the communities of Sepharad, he, his children and his whole family and like them thousands, a large number, were blotted out of the Book of the living, for they sinned and caused many others to sin, as the eyes of many were upon them and therefore the sin of many depends on them. Of the eminent people of Sepharad and their leaders, only a few resolved to die as martyrs and handed themselves over, some to death, others to punishment.[9]

[8] Abraham bar Selomoh [de Torrutiel], *Sefer ha-Qabbalah (Libro de la tradición)*, chapter III in *Dos crónicas hispanohebreas del siglo XV*, trans. by Moreno Koch, 1992, p. 104.
[9] Ibid., pp. 105–106.

The royal policy, which sought to achieve as many conversions as possible, turned the baptisms of certain prominent Jews into solemn and highly publicized ceremonies designed to attract others. The famous Abraham de Córdoba was baptized on 31 May with Cardinal Mendoza and the papal nuncio as his godfather. The Catholic Monarchs themselves were the godparents at the baptism of

Anonymous Spanish artist, *Our Lady of the Catholic Monarchs*, fifteenth century. Madrid, Museo Nacional del Prado (inv. 1260)

Abraham Seneor, chief rabbi of Castile and one of the monarchs' most faithful advisers. The ceremony took place at the convent of Guadalupe on 15 June 1492. The new Christian, who adopted the name Fernán Núñez Coronel, was appointed to posts of great prestige, such as alderman of Segovia, member of the Royal Council and chief accountant to the prince, Don Juan.

Unlike these apostates, "a few", as the chronicler Abraham bar Selomoh de Torrutiel reports, headed for exile, firm in their beliefs. Although sources of both religions stress that this was the choice of the lowliest Jews, some prominent Jews also chose this fate:

> The greatest of them all, the great man, the prince, the important, the great and wise rabbi Don Isaac Abravanel — may his memory be blessed — who sanctified the Name in public before the king and princes, he and the wise Don Solomon Seneor, the elder brother of the aforementioned rabbi [Abraham Seneor].[10]

As he himself states, Isaac Abravanel took it upon himself to be the "leader of my people," who "anxiously awaited my instructions, and would not have disobeyed my orders."[11] The Catholic Monarchs did their utmost to persuade Abravanel to convert so that he could remain in Spain; physical pressure was even brought to bear on some members of his family.[12] Isaac's son, the famous Yehuda, describes these ploys in verse:

> When the children of the diaspora
> were expelled from Spain,
> the King had me ambushed
> in order that I neither leave nor mix with the victims
> and ordered that the infant suckling my milk
> be taken from me
> and be instilled with his faith.[13]

## THE SUFFERING OF A PEOPLE ON THEIR WAY TO EXILE: DEPARTING FROM THEIR HOMELAND

The three months that elapsed between the issuing of the edict and the departure witnessed countless dramatic and agonizing situations. They Jews had to sell their houses and many of their belongings, often at a mere pittance. The bankers they turned to, particularly Italians, to provide bills of exchange that could be used abroad also took advantage of their plight by charging incredibly high interest rates. They had to resort to various means to get around the ban on removing gold and silver from the country. The scenes described by Bernáldez are particularly telling:

[10] Ibid., p. 106.

[11] Ibid., p. 228. Abravanel, with the help of a royal official, Luis de Satángel, and the Genoan banker Francisco Pinelo organized their departure by chartering ships.

[12] Although his son was to be secretly conducted to Portugal, he was in fact allowed to leave and granted certain special privileges to compensate for unpaid debts owed to him by the royal treasury.

[13] As quoted by Baer, 1998, p. 880.

The Christians bought their very many belongings and very rich dwellings and country estates for little money, and [the Jews] went around offering them and there was nobody to buy them, and they gave away a house in exchange for an ass, and a vineyard for a little cloth, because they could not take with them gold or silver; but the truth is that they secretly took away an incalculable amount of gold and silver, particularly many *cruzados* and ducats which they dented with their teeth and swallowed and carried them in their bellies past the points where they were searched, or the land and sea ports, and the women especially swallowed the most, each person was to swallow thirty ducats in one go.[14]

These poor people were frequently taken advantage of. Incidents such as those reported by the Jews of Ampudia were common all over the country:

> The mayors of the said town are doing them and have done them many wrongs and grievances; especially it is said that they do not allow them to sell their real and personal property, nor do they even pay them back the money that is owed to them though they are hastening and pressuring them to pay the debts which they owe, even though they are not yet due.[15]

Although the debts which the Christians owed the Jews were guaranteed, the abuses were so great that most of this money was not repaid. The Christians were not the only ones who took advantage of the situation — so did the *conversos*. Another major concern was the safety of the exiles during their journey to the Portuguese border or to the seaports. The Jews of Aranda de Duero describe these fears as follows:

> [They feared] as they or some of them traveled and passed though some cities or towns and places and open land and unpopulated places, that some people would wound or kill them or seize and steal their goods and possessions.[16]

To fulfill the promise of royal protection, many orders were issued to the royal officials to safeguard the Jews during their departure. They monarchs entrusted this task to people they could rely on. The nobleman Martín de Gurrea, baron of Argavieso, was put in charge of escorting the Jews of the kingdom of Aragon, on 14 May. Argavieso, considered by the king to be a person "in whose faith, goodness, integrity, and competence we greatly trust", was instructed to facilitate their passage through "any roads, mountain passes, and seaports."[17] In spite of these measures, there are reports of many unfortunate incidents, such as the attacks on the Jews of Huesca at La Ortilla plain, on those of Pina in Gilsa, and on those of Biel at the Isuerre mountain pass.[18]

Once again, despite his self-proclaimed anti-Semitism, it is Bernáldez who paints the most dramatic picture of the trials and tribulations of a people sadly heading for exile:

[14] "Ca ovieron los cristianos sus faciendas muy muchas, é muy ricas casas y heredamientos por pocos dineros, y andaban rogando con ellas, y no habia quien se la comprase, é daban una casa por un asno, y una viña por un poco paño e lienzo, porque no podían sacar oro ni plata; empero es verdad que sacaron infinito oro é plata escondidamente, y en especial muchos cruzados é ducados abollados con los dientes, que los tragaban é sacaban en los vientres, ó en los pasos donde habian de ser buscados, ó los puertos de la tierra é de la mar, y en especial las mujeres tragaban mas, cá á persona le acontecia tragar treinta ducados de una vez." Bernáldez, 1953, chapter CX, p. 652.

[15] "Los alcaldes de la dicha villa les fazian e han fecho muchas sinrazones e agravios especialmente diz que non les consienten nin dan lugar que vendan sus bienes muebles e raíces que tienen nin menos les quieren fazer e pagar las debdas que le son devidas e que las que ellos deven les apremian e fazen luego las paguen aunque los plazos non sean llegados." Suárez Fernández, 1964 pp. 465-466.

[16] "Yendo e pasando ellos o algunos dellos por algunas çidades o villas o lugares e yermos e despoblados que algunas personas los feriran op mataran o tomaran o robaran sus bienes e faziendas." Ibid., p. 447.

[17] "Qualesquiere caminos, passos e puestos por la mar y por la tierra." Ibid., p. 215.

[18] Motis Dolader, 1995, p. 214.

And they departed from the land where they were born, young and adults, old people and children on foot, and gentlemen on asses and other beasts, and in carts, and they each continued their travels to one of the ports they were to go to; and they travelled along roads and across fields with many hardships and fortunes, some falling, others picking themselves up, others dying, others being born, others falling ill, and there was no Christian who did not feel for them, and wherever they went they invited them to be baptized, and some were converted and stayed, but very few, and the Rabbis urged them on and bade the women and youths sing and play tambourines and drums to keep up the people's spirits, and so they departed from Castile.[19]

Given such terrible hardship, the only explanation for their leaving everything behind them and facing the ordeal of a pilgrimage to an uncertain destination is their firm conviction of their faith. The religious leaders made sure that the people held fast to their beliefs in order to overcome the difficulties. This is how we should interpret Bernáldez's testimony: the rabbis stirred up their people's feelings and raised their morale with music and song.

### THE NUMBER WHO LEFT

The last Jew departed from Spain on 31 July 1492 (7th day of *Av* of the Jewish year of 5252). According to a largely fabricated version based on legend, this occurred on the 9th day of *Av*, the anniversary of the destruction of the Temple of Jerusalem. The Jews were expelled from Portugal in 1496, and from Navarre in 1498.[20]

The person mainly responsible for organizing the exodus of the Jews, Isaac Abravanel, writes of the number of exiles in 1494:

> As the fear of God and the Honor of his Divine Presence are my witnesses, the number of Jews in the lands of the king of Spain the year in which Israel was stripped of its glory [i.e. the year the Expulsion took place] was three hundred thousand souls.[21]

Despite the many attempts at assessing the number of Jews who were expelled and estimating how many were living in Spain at the time the decree was issued, it is difficult to establish a figure. This task is even harder when dealing with accounts in which heart takes precedence over head. Estimates range from three hundred thousand to less than fifty thousand.

As it is not my intention to challenge any of the scholars who have examined this question, I will merely state the obvious fact that, whatever the real figure, the number of Jews who converted and stayed was far greater than those who left.

[19] "Y salieron de las tierras de sus nacimientos, chicos é grandes, viejos é niños, á piè y caballeros en asnos y otras bestias, y en carretas, y continuaron sus viajes cada uno á los puertos que habian de ir; é iban por los caminos y campos por donde iban con muchos trabajos y fortunas, unos cayendo, otros levantando, otros moriendo, otros naciendo, otros enfermando, que no habia christiano que no oviese dolor de ellos, , y siempre por do iban los convidaban al baptismo, y algunos con la cuita se convertían é quedaban, pero muy pocos, y los Rabies los iban esforzando, y facian cantar á las mujeres y mancebos, tañer panderos y adufos para alegrar la gente, y asi salieron fuera de Castilla." Bernáldez, 1953, chapter CXII, p. 653.
[20] Gampel, 1996.
[21] Quoted by Netanyahu, 2002, p. 227.

## A SINGLE NATION AND A SINGLE RELIGION: TOWARDS THE MODERN STATE

This section will end with a few observations on the causes and effects of the expulsion.

The root cause — and the only one — was religious. This is inferred from the arguments set forth in the edict and from the explanations given by both Jews and Christians. The main driving force was surely Queen Isabella; at least Hebrew sources contemptuously stress her as being the cause. In Abravanel's dialogue with the monarchs, the former clearly states that the queen is plainly pressuring her husband to stick to the decision: "And the queen, who was standing by his side to corrupt him, powerfully persuaded him to carry out and finish the deed". The adjectives used by the chronicler Abraham bar Selomoh de Torrutiel to describe the queen are harsher than those he reserves for her husband. This may indicate that Abravanel was expressing a widespread feeling among the people of Israel: "the advice of his wicked wife, Isabella the perverse" and "[Ferdinand] together with his wife, the detestable."

Who were the royal advisers quoted by the Jewish sources as influencing this decision? From what they say, it is obvious that very few were in on the secret, as very important people did not find out until the last minute. The language and reasoning of the edict are consonant with those used by the Inquisition, albeit somewhat less harsh. This seems to surprise some historians, even though it is very reasonable. The Inquisition was established by the Catholic Monarchs to preserve Christian faith; the inquisitors were people in whom they fully trusted. It is therefore understandable that on 20 March, eleven days before the decree was signed, Tomás Torquemada should have addressed a letter to the Infante of Aragon ordering the Jews to be expelled from the dioceses of Gerona. As Carlos Carrete has pointed out, there are obvious similarities between this document and the rules on expulsion set forth in the decree. Interestingly, Torquemada's letter is signed in the court, that is, at the time and place expulsion was brewing. Owing to his rank and the royal trust placed in him, the Inquisitor General would have been the person to provide the philosophical and theological arguments for expulsion. Nor should we forget the eagerness of some converts to compel their former brethren to convert in order to avoid expulsion.[22]

Were there any motives other than religion? If there were, they were certainly not economic. The utmost was done to persuade the Jews to convert, particularly the most powerful. If their estates were the objective, why bother persuading them to convert? Furthermore, by the time the decree was issued, Jewish-owned assets, although considerable, were less than they had once been. Certainly, as usual, the more powerful chose to preserve their material riches rather than their beliefs. As we have seen, the testimonies are numerous and indisputable.

[22] Little attention has been paid to this subject so far, though it must have been, important.

Expulsion brought about a major transformation in Spain's townscapes, though this had already begun at the end of the fourteenth century. Jewish quarters were rapidly converted into Christian neighborhoods[23] and synagogues into churches or other community buildings. Many ended up being transformed into town halls, and the sacred books were used to bind municipal documents; Jewish cemeteries were abandoned and declared out of bounds.[24]

As Luis Suárez points out in his well-documented *Expulsión de los judíos de España*, we should examine the expulsion of the Jews in the context of the shaping of the modern state. Unlike their medieval predecessors whose subjects practiced three religions, the absolutist Catholic Monarchs could not afford the unity of their kingdom to be marred by a religious division. The monarchs, themselves stalwart Christians, could not allow their subjects to continue to err and possibly undermine their reign. Joseph Pérez sees the Reconquest as the end of "religious tolerance:"

> Medieval tolerance — or what is generally known as such — can be explained by the situation of the Iberian Peninsula, which was divided into Muslim and Christian territory. By the end of the Reconquest the earlier tolerance had become pointless; Spain became yet another Christian nation, like all those that existed in Europe. It is no coincidence that the decree expelling the Jews was signed three months after the capture of Granada.[25]

[23] They started out as neighborhoods of new Christians, but fear of the Inquisition soon led the older families of *conversos* to abandon places that linked them to their Jewish origins.

[24] López, Santiago Palomero, and María Luisa Menéndez Robles have carried out a systematic study of the state of the Jews' property after the decree (1993).

[25] Pérez, 2002, p. 395.

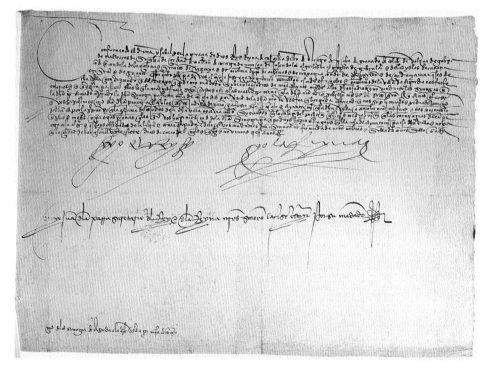

Letter from the Catholic Monarchs granting the synagogue left by the town's Jews following the Decree of Expulsion to the Council of Ágreda (Soria) as the premises for the Town Hall, Barcelona, 27 January 1493. From the Ayuntamiento de Ágreda (Soria). Ágreda (Soria), Archivo Municipal Sección Histórica (Cartas Redes no. 21)

*Decree of Expulsion of the Jews. Granada, 31 March 1492*

*Don Fernando e doña Isabel, por la gracia de Dios rey e reina de Castilla, de León, etc [...]*
*Al príncipe don Johan, nuestro muy caro y muy amado hijo, e a los Infantes, Perlados, Duques [...]*
*Bien sabedes, o devedes saber, que porque Nos fuimos informados que en estos nuestros Reinos avía*
*algunos malos christianos que judaizavan e apostatavan de nuestra sancta Fe cathólica, de lo qual*
*era mucha causa la comunicación de los judíos con los christianos, en las Cortes que fizimos en la*
*cibdad de Toledo el año passado de mil e quatrocientos e ochenta años, mandamoa apartar los*
*dichos judíos en todas las cibdades e villas e lugares de los nuestros Reinos e señoríos en las juderías*
*e logares apartados, donde biviesen e morassen, esperando que con su apartamiento se remediaría.*
*Otrosí, avemos procurado e dado orden cómo se hiziesse Inquisición en los dichos nuestros Reinos,*
*la qual, como sabeis, ha mas de doze años que se ha hecho e faze, e por ella se han fallado muchos*
*culpantes, segund es notorio; e segund somos informados de los inquisidores e de otras muchas*
*religiosas e eclesiásticas e seglares, consta e paresce el gran daño que a los christianos se ha seguido e*
*sigue de la participación, conversación e comunicación que han tenido e tienen con los judíos; los*
*quales, se prueva que procuran siempre, por quantas vías mas pueden, de subvertir e sustraher*
*de nuestra sancta Fe cathólica a los fieles christianos e los apartar della, e atraer e pervertir a su*
*dañada creencia e opinión, instruyéndoles en las cerimonias e observancias de su Ley, faziendo*
*ayuntamientos donde les lean e enseñen lo que han de creer e guardar segund su Ley, procurando*
*de circuncidar a ellos e asus hijos, dándoles libros por donde rezasen sus oraciones [...] lo qual ha*
*redundado en grand daño e detrimento e oprobrio de nuestra sancta Fe cathólica.*

*E como quiera que de mucha parte desto fuimos informados antes de agora, e conoscimos que el*
*remedio verdadero de todos estos daños e inconvenientes está en apartar del todo la comunicación de*
*los dichos judíos con los christianos e echarlos de todos nuestros Reinos, quisimos nos contentar con*
*mandarlos salir de todas las cibdades e villas e logares del Andaluzía, donde parescía que avían*
*fecho mayor daño, creyendo que aquello bastaría para que los de las otras cibdades e villas e logares*
*de los nuestros Reinos e señoríos cessassen de fazer e cometer losusodicho. E porque somos informados*
*que aquello, ni las justicias que se han fecho en algunos de los dichos judíos que se han fallado muy*
*culpantes en los dichos crímenes e delictos contra nuestra sancta Fé cathólica, no basta para entero*
*remedio para obviar e remediar cómo cesse tan grand oprobrio e offensa de la religión christiana; e*
*porque cada día se falla e paresce que los dichos judíos crescen en continuar su malo e dañado*
*propósito adonde viven e conversan, e por que no aya logar de mas offender a nuestra sancta Fe*
*cathólica, assí en los que fasta aquí Dios ha querido guardar como en los que cayeron e se*
*enmendaron e reduzieron a la sancta Madre Iglesia, lo qual segund la flaqueza de nuestra*
*humanidad e subjestión diabólica, que contino nos guerrea, ligeramente podría acaescer si la*
*principal causa desto no se quita, que es echar los dichos judíos de nuestros Reinos. E porque*
*quando algund grave e detestable crimen es cometido por algunos de algund colegio e universidad,*
*es razón que el tal colegio e universidad sea dissolvido e anichilado, e los menores por los mayores e*
*los unos por los otros sean punidos, e aquellos que pervierten el bien e honesto bivir de las cibdades*
*e villas por contagio, e pueden dañar a los tros, sean expelidos de los pueblos, e aun por más leves*
*causas que sean en daño de la República, quánto mas por el mayor de los crímenes e mas peligroso*
*e contagioso, como lo es este.*

*Por ende, Nos, con consejo e parescer de algunos perlados e grandes e cavalleros de nuestros Reinos*
*e otras personas de sciencia e consciencia del nuestro Consejo, aviendo avido sobre ello mucha*
*deliberación, acordamos de mandar salir todos los dichos judíos e judías de nuestros Reinos, e que*
*jamás tornen ni buelvan en ellos ni alguno dellos. E sobre ello mandamos dar esta nuestra Carta,*
*por la qual mandamos a todos los judíos e judías, de qualquier hedad que sean, que viven e moran*
*e están en los dichos nuestros Reinos e señoríos, así los naturales dellos como los no naturales que en*
*qualquier manera o por qualquier causa ayan venido e están en ellos, que fasta fin del mes de julio*

primero que viene deste presente año salgan de todos los dichos nuestros Reinos e señoríos, con sus hijos e hijas e criados e criadas e familiares judíos, assí grandes como pequeños, de qualquier hedad que sean. E que no sean osados de tornar a ellos ni estar en ellos ni en parte alguna dellos, de bivienda ni de passo ni en otra manera alguna, so pena que, si no lo fizieren e cumplieren assí, e fueren fallados estar en los dichos nuestros Reinos e señoríos o vinieren en ellos en qualquier manera, incurran en pena de muerte e confiscación de todos sus bienes para la nuestra Cámara e Fisco. En las quales penas incurran por esse mismo fecho, sin otro processo, sentencia ni declaración.

E mandamos e defendemos que ninguna ni algunas personas de los dichos nuestros Reinos, de qualquier estado, preheminencia e condición que sean, no sean osados de recebir e recebtar ni acoger ni defender, pública ni secretamente, judío ni judía, passado el dicho término de fin de julio, en adelante para siempre jamás, en sus tierras ni en sus casas ni en otra parte alguna de los dichos nuestros Reinos e señoríos, so pena de perdimientos de todos sus bienes, vasallos e fortalezas e otros heredamientos, otrosí de perder qualesquier maravedís que de Nos tengan, para la nuestra Cámara e Fisco.

E por los dichos judíos e judías puedan durante el dicho tiempo, fasta en fin del dicho mes de julio, mejor disponer de sí e de sus bienes e hazienda, por la presente los tomamos e recebimos so nuestro seguro e amparo e defendimiento real, e los aseguramos a ellos e a sus bienes, para que durante el dicho tiempo, fasta el dicho día fin del dicho mes de julio, puedan andar e estar seguros, e puedan entrar e vender e trocar e enajenar todos sus bienes muebles e raízes e disponer dellos libremente e a su voluntad, e que durante el dicho tiempo no le sea fecho mal ni daño ni desaguisado alguno en sus personas ni en sus bienes contra justicia, so las penas an que cahen e incurren los que quebrantan nuestro seguro real. E assímismo, damos licencia e facultad a los dichos judíos e judías que puedan sacar fuera de los dichos nuestros Reinos e señoríos sus bienes e haziendas, por mar e por tierra, con tanto que no saquen oro ni plata ni moneda amonedada, ni las otras cosas vedadas por las leyes de nuestros Reinos, salvo en mercadorías que no sean cosas vedadas o en cambios [...]

E por que esto pueda venir a noticia de todos e ninguno pueda pretender ignorancia, mandamos que esta nuestra Carta sea pregonada por las plazas e mercados e logares acostumbrados dessa dicha cibdad e de las principales cibdades e villas e logares de su arçobispado, por pregonero e ante escribano publico [...] Dada en la muy noble cibdad de Granada a treinta y un días del mes de marzo, año del Nascimiento de Nuestro Señor Jhesuchristo de mill e quatrocientos e noventa e dos años. Yo el Rey. Yo la Reina. Yo Johan de Coloma, secretario del Rey e de la reina, nuestros señores, la fize escrevir por su mandado. Registrada, Bernal Diañes de Almaçán, chanceller.

# THE INQUISITION

# The Inquisition

In the previous chapter we examined the history of the long course of the religious, and at times even racial, confrontation between Jews and Christians. This bitter, cruel, and unyielding conflict would eventually lead to the emergence of the Holy Office of the Inquisition, the ecclesiastic tribunal which, beginning in the thirteenth century was in charge of persecuting and condemning heresy.[1]

Towards the middle of the fifteenth century, there were opposing views with regard to the Jews. A large sector of society held very hostile attitudes against Jews. Their ideology is captured perfectly in Alonso de Espina's work *Fortalitium Fidei*, the first edition of which was published in 1460.[2] This Franciscan, the confessor to King Henry IV of Castile and himself inaccurately described as a converted Jew, held strong anti-Semitic opinions, a fact that is apparent in statements such as these:

> Then they entered, O Lord, into Your flock, the thieving wolves. No one thinks of the treacherous Jews, who blaspheme your name.

> It is more reasonable than profitable to put all of them to death or remove them from the world.

At the other end of the spectrum were those who defended the converted Jews, including some notable personages who were themselves *conversos*, such as the clerk Díaz de Toledo, Alonso de Cartagena, Lope Barrientos, and Juan de Torquemada[3].

Espina's words, "If a true inquisition were to be held in our time, countless people of those discovered Judaizing would be burned," speak for themselves about the keenness to see the Holy Office institutionalized. But this was not the worst of it, for, as we shall see, the Inquisition was also supported by many pro-converts. Sadly, Espina did not differentiate between Jews and Jewish converts and in the end clearly demonstrated his racial bigotry.

The other side, those who defended the *conversos*, readily accepted that converts who practiced Judaism ought to be punished. For this reason, Díaz de Toledo, referring to the new Christians, does not hesitate to state that if they turn from Christianity, "I will be the first to bring firewood to burn them and will set it alight." Even Alonso de Cartagena, in his *Defensorium sanitatis Christianae*, emphasized the need to punish those found Judaizing.

[1] The spread of the Albigensian heresy at the end of the twelfth century caused the popes to establish a coercive instrument to preserve the integrity of the Catholic faith. The Toulouse Council of 1229 established an ecclesiastic "inquisition" in charge of investigating unrepentants and turning them over to the civil courts for execution. From 1233, by order of Pope Gregory IX, the Dominicans were put in charge of investigating (inquisitio) the cases of heresy within each diocese. This was how the diocesan or ecclesiastic inquisitions came about, which, as we will see later, were sometimes called "the inquisitions of the inquisitors".

[2] The success of the book is apparent from the fact that four editions had been published by the end of the fifteenth century.

[3] This subject has been analyzed by Valdeón Baruque, 1994, pp. 35–45.

Alonso de Espina. *Fortalitium Fidei*. Castile, 1460; Lyon, Johannem de Romoys, 1511. Madrid, Biblioteca Nacional (R/27056)

[4] De Azcona, 1964, p. 367.

[5] Because of their proximity to the Albigensian heretics of southern France, Aragon and Catalonia adopted the ecclesiastic inquisition during the reign of James I (1213–1276). Its establishment was due to the decisive intervention of the Dominican Raimundo de Peñafort at the Council of Tarragona in the year 1242, whose canons included the organization and procedural rules for the inquisition. By the fifteenth century, the Aragonese Inquisition was in decline. In this Castilian kingdom during the fifteenth century there had been several attempts by the papacy to establish the Inquisition, although they had never actually taken root. In 1442 Eugenio IV sent a bull to this effect to Henry IV; in 1451, Nicholas V authorized the Bishop of Osma and the vicar of Salamanca to act in heresy trials; and in 1461 and 1465 several commissions asked the monarchs to establish the Inquisition.

[6] The original text of this bull is lost. Only several copies that were circulated by the early inquisitors are known.

[7] Torquemada's appointment included the presidency of the Council of the Supreme and General Inquisition, with authority over all the tribunals of Castile and all the Catholic Monarchs' dominions.

We must purify and thrust out the uncleanliness and filth of those who relapse into the blindness of Judaism.

Thus, both sides accepted the need for the Inquisition some because they saw it as an instrument for exterminating an entire race people, others because they regarded it as the only way to protect the truly sincere new Jewish converts to Christianity, given the radical nature of the confrontation. In this context, T. de Azcona stated emphatically that the monarchs did no more than follow the wishes of their subjects.

> It was not the Catholic Monarchs, but Castilian society itself, which, several decades earlier, had contrived this extraordinary measure for maintaining religious purity as a means of preserving Catholic unity, which was regarded as a crucial element of political unity at the time.[4]

After several previous attempts,[5] on 1 November 1478 Pope Sixtus IV, in response to a petition by the "Catholic Monarchs", issued the papal bull *Exigit sincerae devotionis affectus*, which can be considered the start of the Spanish Inquisition.[6] This bull authorized the Monarchs to appoint inquisitors throughout Castile. On 27 September 1480 they appointed two Dominican friars, a bachelor and a master of theology, inquisitors of Seville. These appointments were followed by the appointment of inquisitors in other places in Castile and León. In a bull of 1481, Pope Sixtus IV named such well-known inquisitors as Pedro de Ocaña, Tomás de Torquemada, Juan de Sancto Spiritu, and others, all of whom were either masters or bachelors of theology and members of the Order of St. Dominic. In autumn 1483 Tomás de Torquemada, prior of the monastery of Santa Cruz in Segovia and the queen's confessor, was named Inquisitor General by the Catholic Monarchs and the pope and given authority over all of Ferdinand and Isabella's kingdom and territories. This authority was recognized by a papal bull in the year 1485.[7]

On 7 May 1484, King Ferdinand informed the Cortes (Parliament) of Tarazona that, with his consent, the pope had decided to establish tribunals of the Inquisition in the kingdom of Aragon. To comply with this resolution, Torquemada appointed inquisitors for Saragossa (Zaragoza), who presided over the first auto-da-fé on 10 May. Torquemada's inquisitors arrived in Barcelona in July 1487. The Inquisition which began in Andalusia quickly spread throughout Castile, and was eventually adopted throughout the rest of the kingdoms of Spain. No other institution of its time was so structured and centralized in character, under the authority of the Inquisitor General, throughout all of the Catholic Monarchs' lands. At the time of Torquemada's death in 1498, the Inquisition's territorial organization consisted of sixteen tribunals: the early tribunals at Seville, Jaén, Ciudad Real, Toledo, Valencia, and Saragossa, which were followed by those at Cordoba (1482), Valladolid, Cuenca, León, and Palencia (1492), Teruel and Barcelona (1486), Majorca, and Murcia (1488). After a number of vicissitudes the kingdom of Navarre came under the authority of the Inquisitor General in 1518.

Scholars generally refer to the inquisition in Europe from its appearance in the thirteenth century as the Medieval Inquisition and the inquisition promoted by the Catholic Monarchs as the Modern Inquisition. According to the historian Kamen, the former cannot strictly speaking be described as an inquisition. It was rather a period during which inquisitors were active, but their activities were temporary and strictly local, with no structural organization laying down functions or precise regulations.[8] It was established specifically to fight heresy and employed legal methods that were orthodox at the time but much criticized, such as the death penalty,[9] torture, and the testimony of secret witnesses. The so-called Modern Inquisition, initially the Spanish Inquisition and subsequently from 1542 the Roman Inquisition, was an institution proper whose ultimate goal was to combat heresy and, unlike the Medieval Inquisition, maintained its organizational structure despite the appointment of different inquisitors.[10]

Reviewing the extensive bibliography on the Inquisition, one might conclude that it was a Machiavellian institution promoted primarily by Ferdinand the Catholic as a means of implementing his political designs. Other views of its origins are biased by certain historiographical views that spring from ethnic and religious prejudices.

The Spanish Inquisition was established according to a strictly medieval criterion: to combat heresy, that is, to protect the Catholic faith from the proponents of heterodox ideas, within the same faith, that might endanger it. It was also medieval in that the civil authorities were involved in its founding and its activities.

The persecution of Judaism is for many researchers the root cause of the Inquisition. It is quite clear that the Inquisition was supported both by strict anti-Semites and Jewish converts, but both groups probably had ulterior motives which were certainly not made public, and the decision makers merely followed what they believed to be the prevailing public opinion. Nor is it true that only Jews were persecuted, for early documents consistently mention both Jews and Muslims. According to inquisition documents, charges that merited investigation by the inquisition included "known Jewish or Moorish ceremonies, heresies, or manifest incitement."

The appointment of Torquemada, whose views were similar to much of Spanish society in that both hoped to segregate the Jewish community, marked a change.[11] In this respect, it is evident that the first Inquisitor General's

[8] Kamen, 1994, p. 55. By the same author, 1967.

[9] One of the most notable cases was the execution of Joan of Arc in 1431.

[10] In 1566 Fernando de Valdés, Inquisitor General and archbishop of Seville, initiated the collection and copying of all the papal documents that had been received by the Council since 1480, and this work continued through to the beginning of the eighteenth century. This documentation is currently contained in four volumes at the Archivo Histórico Nacional under the title of *Libros de registro de bulas y breves papales, dirigidos al Consejo de la Inquisición y a los reyes españoles, por asuntos de fe y costumbres* (1566–1706).

[11] As evidence of Torquemada's anti-Semitism, Pilar Huerga mentions the following points included in a memorandum sent to Queen Isabella: "That Jews not hold public office among Christians and that the Monarchs not bind their incomes except under very strict conditions, that Jews and Muslims be segregated and not allowed to live among Christians and that they wear signs by which they can be identified" ("Fray Tomás de Torquemada," 1987).

ideology was similar to that held by Alonso de Espina and which would result in the famous *Alboraique*.[12] In his famous *Instrucciones* of 1484 he clearly asserts that only Jewish heretics deserve persecution. However, in spite of all this, Jews were seldom persecuted for practicing their faith as Jewish converts were.

However, just as for centuries the Christian/Jewish and Muslim/Jewish conflict was not only the result of strictly religious factors but very complex social factors as well, the Inquisition was to become embroiled in the politics of the day. This is the opinion expressed by many historians who see the Inquisition as the principal political instrument of the policies of the Catholic Monarchs. According to B. Bennassar, there was full "complicity between the machinery of the state (the Spanish monarchy) and the Inquisition."[13] It went even further, in the opinion of J. Pérez, who regarded the Inquisition as "the first form of totalitarianism in modern times."[14] In another chapter of this book, the expulsion of the Jews is explained as the logical result of a policy of religious unity as an expression of a new concept of the state, which would come to be called the modern state by historians. Therefore, it could be said that by ensuring religious unity the Inquisition indirectly contributed to the emergence of the modern state. Some historians believe that the Catholic Monarchs used the Inquisitions as a weapon for doing away with the traditional privileges in some of their territories. The following extract reveals Ángel Alcalá's interpretation of inquisitorial proceedings in Aragon.

> In this design for the Castilianization of their kingdom and, in the long term, of the whole of the Aragonese Crown, the Inquisition was from the very start the most powerful and irrefutable weapon of the Monarchs, or rather, of the Church at the service of the Catholic Monarchs, as the most effective method of suppressing the traditional freedoms enjoyed by Aragon and of altering its ancient medieval statutes.[15]

To all this must be added — as many historians have done — another traditional source of Christian/Jewish conflict: the clash of economic interests between powerful groups, including the Jews.[16] Although most of these interpretations more or less reflect reality, they do not in themselves explain the origin of the Spanish Inquisition, for only after it was established did it become a completely centralized institution with legal authority across the complex map of Spain at the time and, as such, a useful means of furthering the interests of the monarchy.

[12] Entitled *Historia de las Comunidades de España, sacada de la Crónica del Emperador Carlos Quinto, escrita por Pedro Mexía, su cronista. Libro llamado el Alboraique*, it is a clear example of an anti-Semitic manifesto of the late fifteenth century. It was purported to have been written by followers of Torquemada. Alboraique or Alburac, the manuscript's nickname, is what Jewish converts were called in Llerena where the work was written.

[13] Bennassar, 1979, p. 76.

[14] Pérez, 1988, p. 349.

[15] Alcalá, 1984, pp. 32–33.

[16] Converted Jews regarded the Jews as collaborators of the tribunal of the Inquisition, and considered them to be dangerous enemies (Carrete Parrondo, 1998, p. 52).

ACTIVITIES OF THE INQUISITION

We have already mentioned the Inquisition's goal as well as the methods it used to accomplish them: denunciation, guaranteeing the anonymity of the accuser; the use of torture as a method for interrogating those who had partially confessed; and punishment, including the death penalty.

The rules established by Torquemada were not original; they followed the same guidelines previously set out by European inquisitors. Torquemada based his rules on the bulls issued by Innocent III and Innocent IV, as well as commentators such as Juan Teutónico and Tancredo, and most particularly the *Directorium Inquisitorum* by Nicolás Eymeric, an inquisitor in the last half of the fourteenth century.

The tribunals of the Inquisition consisted of two inquisitors, an advisor, a bailiff, a prosecutor, and the clerks, all of whom were salaried public officials. These officials, especially the inquisitors, were hated by some sectors of the public, especially the more prominent Jewish convert families. On the night of 15 September 1485, hired assassins in the pay of Aragonese Jewish converts murdered the inquisitor Pedro de Arbués, master of Épila, as he knelt in prayer inside the cathedral. Thereafter it became commonplace to see inquisitors surrounded by strict security measures. Whenever Torquemada travelled he was escorted by a troop of fifty "familiars" on horseback and another two hundred on foot to protect him from a possible attack.

What were the accusations? Jewish converts were accused of renouncing their new faith and, in the Inquisition's own words, reverting to "the law of Moses and the Jews." The other main charge was committing transgressions against the precepts the Catholic Church: performing parodies of Christian rites such as the Lenten and Eucharistic fasts; denying dogma such as the Holy Trinity or the presence of Christ in the sacrament of the Eucharist; and rejecting imagery, pilgrimages, and indulgences. These last charges gave religious fanatics a wide scope for fabricating false accusations. A later discussion of the Child of La Guardia will analyze one case of false accusations in detail.

Reading through the records of the proceedings, we find a series of charges that reveal what the these practices of the law of Moses entailed: possession of prayer books and having memorized prayers *(Semah,* the *Eighteen Benedictions,* the *Prayer of Dreams);* holding secret rites on the principal holy days; strict observance of the *Sabbath,* and meeting with others on the Sabbath to read stories from the Talmud and the Bible; secret ritual animal sacrifices in their homes; and baking unleavened bread on Fridays.

Torquemada was entrusted with the task of organizing the inquisitorial proceedings in accordance with a set of rules regulating the activities of Holy

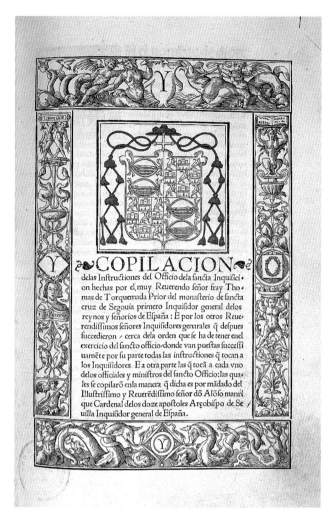

Office officials. To this end, he called a meeting of inquisitors and lawyers in Seville. In 1484 this synod published the *Compilación de las Instrucciones del Oficio de la Santa Inquisición,* which set forth all the rules into twenty-eight clauses.[17] The tactics of the Inquisition varied according to place and political conditions. In places where a new tribunal was established, the inquisitors would initially publish an edict of pardon allowing a thirty-or forty-day grace period in which they would hear voluntary confessions. Those who confessed would receive ecclesiastical punishment or fines. Between 1485 and 1498 Torquemada drew up new rules for the proceedings. Although further contributions were made by Diego de Deza and Jiménez de Cisneros, it was not until 1561 that the Inquisitor General Fernando de Valdés established a precise and systematic set of rules.

### The Place of Trial. The Houses of the Holy Office

The first stage of the trial was the inquest, which began with accusations made against a person for committing heretical acts. Only theologians could investigate these charges. The next stage was confinement, generally on the premises of the Holy Office itself, and confiscation of possessions. After this came the hearing and the prosecutor's indictment. It was at this stage that torture (rack, strappado, funnel, etc.) was used where deemed necessary. Although some scholars disagree, it is thought that the use of torture was not widespread.[18]

The houses of the Inquisition were places of suffering and horror, but in spite of the power of the Holy Office, their premises initially consisted of public buildings that had been converted for this purpose,[19] or buildings which were unsuited for their original purpose and were gradually enlarged to satisfy the growing demands of the increased number of trials. A plan drawn by Nicolás de Vergara on 14 July 1598 gives us a good idea of what the headquarters of the tribunal of the Inquisition at Toledo would have been like.[20] The accompanying documents and notes provide an insight into the improvised and shabby nature of the premises used when the tribunal was first set up in 1483.[21] The buildings were located on lands adjacent to the church of San Vicente. The

**Fray Tomás de Torquemada.**
*Instructions of the Holy Office.* **1485.**
**Cuenca, Archivo Diocesano**
**(inv. no. L–336)**

[17] We can see these instructions, edited and with comments, in the work by Miguel Jiménez Monteserin, Madrid, 1980.

[18] Bennassar, 1979, p. 116.

[19] In Seville it was located in the Dominican monastery of San Pablo, although it was later moved to the castle of Triana.

[20] The plan was part of a report written for the purchase of a house in order to enlarge the prison, which had become too small.

[21] Its first location was in Ciudad Real in 1483.

president of the tribunal and the second inquisitor had quarters within these premises; the latter described his dwelling as "extremely small"(letter M). A third inquisitor lived in a house outside the compound.[22]

The jail cells, which varied greatly in size and shape, occupied two floors in the central section of the building (marked with the letter G). At the time the report was written there were seventy-five prisoners, but due to lack of space they could not be kept incommunicado as stipulated by the Inquisition's regulations. Some cells even held more than one prisoner.[23] The court area proper consisted of a long room (D) with a chapel and a courtroom where prisoners were tried and sentenced. The tribunal would meet in an isolated "Secret" room to deliberate and hear accusations and witnesses' testimonies.[24]

Access was by way of a large entrance hall (A) with a monumental staircase that led to a courtyard (C ) connecting the court area with some of the cells. The quarters of the warden (B) who was in charge of the prison were adjacent to the entrance hall.

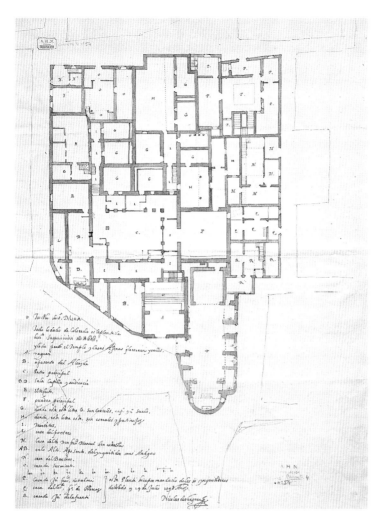

Ground plan of the house of the Toledo Inquisition drawn by Nicolás de Vergara, including a number of dwellings on the upper floor that could be purchased. 14 July 1598. Madrid, Archivo Histórico Nacional (Sección de Inquisición. Legajo 3081, Exp. 52)

[22] The rent was paid by the Holy Office.
[23] According to the charges, prisoners might be held incommunicado in prison or allowed to leave during the day to attend to their personal business and return at night.
[24] The name "Secret" clearly demonstrates how the inquisition proceedings, by keeping the identity of the witnesses secret, left the defendants absolutely defenseless.

## Proof of Charges

The trial consisted of a number of hearings in which lawyers and witnesses participated and the evidence was produced. The minutes of the proceedings meticulously record the charges and cases presented by prosecutors and lawyers as well as material evidence. This evidence, naturally, has not survived.

One exception is the handkerchief used in the proceedings against the clergyman Gonzalo de San Martín, who was charged with Judaizing in Cuenca. The handkerchief is housed in the city's Archivo Diocesano. It is made of a nearly square piece of linen. Two edges are embroidered in black herringbone stitch and the other two with the word "Almarya," the meaning of which is unclear, repeated four times on each side. This seemingly innocent object was one of the pieces of evidence that helped to convict the poor clergyman of the following charges: failure to fulfill his duties as a priest; ignorance of the formulas that proclaimed the virginity of Mary; ignorance of

Handkerchief used as evidence in an inquisitorial trial. Cuenca, before 1512. Cuenca, Archivo Diocesano (Legajo 45, exp. 712)

Latin; and the fact that his parents and grandparents had also been accused of Judaizing. In 1512 Gonzalo de San Martín was convicted and stripped of his office and benefice.

The trials would conclude with the prisoner being either acquitted or declared guilty and convicted. There were three categories for those found guilty: the *confitentes* or recanters, who were allowed to do penance, had their property confiscated, had to wear the penitential habit or *sambenito* and were sentenced to life imprisonment; the *pertinaces* or those who refused to recant, who were sentenced to be burned at the stake; and convicts, whose sentence consisted of abjuration, purge, or punitive torture.

While it is not fair to identify Spain with the Inquisition, we must nonetheless agree with the historian Pérez Prendes that "the trials of the Holy Office undermined the defendant's rights and strengthened the power of the court. They eliminated all personal dignity during interrogation by using deceit and torture."[25]

Although its priorities would change, the Holy Office survived until it was finally abolished in the nineteenth century. It was first suppressed under Joseph Bonaparte and abolished permanently by decree of Queen María Cristina de Borbón in Madrid on 15 July 1834.

### THE AUTO-DA-FÉ

Punishment became a solemn ritual, the auto-da-fé, whose principal goal was to serve as an example.[26] There were different categories of auto-da-fé: the general auto-de-fe, which was for a large number of prisoners of all types; the special auto-da-fé, which was for only a few prisoners and was less solemn and ceremonious; the individual auto-da-fé, which was for a single prisoner and was held in a church or at the public square; and the *autillo,* which was an individual auto-da-fé held in a court room, and could be either open- or closed-door.

The general auto-da-fé was a grand, lengthy public event with a complex protocol which ended by terrifing onlookers with its gruesome final scene of prisoners being burned at the stake. Paintings show us what these events looked like and how crowds of people flocked to witness the spectacle. The auto-da-fé painted by Pedro de Berruguete (ca. 1450–before 1504), although a depiction of a historical event,[27] gives us a glimpse of a ceremony that was still very medieval in nature and limited to the principal participants; the inquisitors and other officials of the tribunal of the Holy Office, the administrators of civil justice who were in charge of enforcing the sentence, and two categories of prisoner (recanters in penitent costume and the unrepentant who was to be burned at the stake). Because of lack of space, the audience was limited to a

25 Pérez Prendes, 1994, p. 187.

26 Maqueda, 1990.

27 This chart illustrates a passage in the life of St Dominic (Domingo de Guzmán), the founder of the order of preachers, who collaborated with the popes in their policy against heretics through preaching and inquisitions.

small number of spectators, contrasting with the ostentatious Inquisitor General's box.

What is not revealed in the painting is conveyed in descriptions dating from that period. Terror was used as the main instrument of conviction from the outset, following the same practices used by other European inquisitors. No descriptions survive of the early autos-da-fé held at Seville, but the accounts of Bernáldez, which refer to the first eight years of the Inquisition, are very explicit concerning the cruelty they entailed:[28]

> More than seven hundred people were burned and over five thousand recanted and were sentenced to life imprisonment, and they were held for four or five years or more and then released, and they had crosses placed on them and colored *sambenitos* on front and back which they wore for many years, and they finally removed them to avoid the spread of disgrace throughout the land by the sight of them.[29]

The historian tells us about the more notable personages and the charges against them, as well as their sentences:

> Three clergymen and three or four friars were burned, all converted Jews, and a Trinitarian monk named Savariego who was a great preacher, liar, and deceitful heretic and who had dared to preach on Good Friday having eaten his fill of meat. Countless bones were burned of converts buried on top of each other according to Jewish practice in the courtyards of the Trinitarian, and Augustinian, and Bernardine monasteries, and effigies were burned of many of the Jews who were found guilty but had fled.[30]

But the most terrible aspect of the Inquisition was the stake where heresy was purified by fire and even the bones of the unrepentant were burned, to symbolize the eternal fire that awaited them.

> Those early Inquisitors set up the stake at Tablada with four plaster prophets and there [heretics] were to be burned and shall continue to be burned as long as there is heresy.[31]

The first auto-da-fé that we learn about in detail took place at Toledo in the year 1486:

> And they brought them out on foot with hoods over their heads, dressed in cloaks of yellow linen with the names of each inscribed on their cloak. The inscriptions read so-and-so, convicted heretic, and their hands were tied behind their necks. And there they read aloud the charges against each one and the

[28] Bernáldez, t. LXX, pp. 567–788.

[29] "Quemaron mas de setecientas personas, y reconciliaron mas de cinco mil y echaron en cárceles perpétuas, que ovo tales y estuvieron en ellas quatro ó cinco años ó mas y sacáronles y echáronles cruces é unos San Benitillos colorados atrás y adelante, y ansí anduvieron mucho tiempo, é despúes se los quitaron porque no creciese el disfame en la tierra viendo aquello."

[30] "Quemaron á tres clèrigos de misa, é tres ó quatro Frailes todos de este linaje de los confesos, é quemaron un Dotor fraile de la Trinidad que llamaban Savariego, que era un gran predicador, y gran falsario, hereje engañador, que le contenció venir el Viernes Santo a predicar la Pasión y hartarse de carne [...] Quemaron infinitos güesos de los corrales de la Trinidad y San Agustín è San Bernardo, de los confesos que allí se habian enterrado cada unos sobre sí al uso judáico, é apregonaron é quemaron en estatua á muchos que hallaron dañados de los judios huidos."

[31] "Aquellos primeros Inquisidores ficieron facer aquel quemadero en Tablada, con aquellos quatro Profetas de yeso, en que los quemaban, y fasta que haya heregia los quemarán."

AVTO PVBLICO DFE EN LA SANTA ENQVISICION DE T. I. DEL AÑO 1651

**Anonymous Spanish artist.** *Auto-da-fé in Toledo's Plaza de Zocodover*, ca. 1656. Oil on canvas. Toledo, Museo de El Greco (inv. no. 131)

[32] "E sacáronlos en esta manera a pie, con coranzas en las cabezas, vestidos unos sambenitos de lienzo amarillo, escrito en cada sambenito el nombre de aquel. Dicie ansi: Fulano hereje condenado; las manos atadas con sogas a los pescuezos [...]; E allí, públicamente a voces leían el proceso de cada uno, e las cosas en que había judaizado; y en fin del proceso lo publicaban e condenaban por hereje, e remetían a la justicia y brazo seglar. Y estuvieron en pasar los procesos todos desde las seis de la mañana fasta las doce; y acabados de leer los procesos los entregaron a la justicia seglar; e de alli los llevaron a la vega, donde fueron quemados, que hueso dellos no quedó por quemar e facer ceniza."

things in which they had Judaized; and they announced the results of the trial and convicted them of heresy, and then they commended them to secular justice. And this went on from six in the morning to twelve and after the proceedings were read they were turned over to the secular authorities, and from there they were taken to the field where they were burned until nothing remained even of their bones but ashes.[32]

These accounts describing the brutal details of the events tell of the presence of prisoners and of the long duration of the ceremony at which the sentences were read aloud, ending with their being taken to the place of execution. There is no mention of facilities for spectators. Over time, the auto-da-fé became a public spectacle with an elaborate setting where the audience settled comfortably to watch the show. It was a truly baroque spectacle.

The painting by an anonymous artist, which, according to the sign that appears in it, depicts a *Public auto-da-fé at the Holy Inquisition of T.I in the year 1656*,[33] allows us a peek at this baroque spectacle. Although the performance was

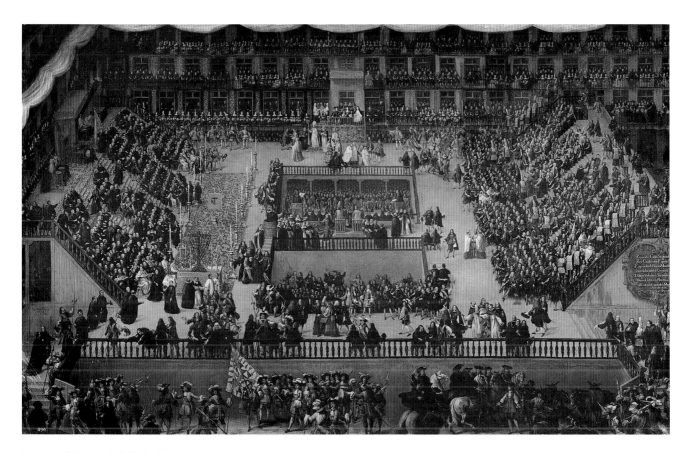

**Francisco Rizi, *Auto-da-fé in the Plaza Mayor in Madrid,* Madrid, Museo Nacional del Prado (Inv. 1126)**

[33] Gutiérrez, 2000, p. 203.

[34] Gómez Moreno identified the T of the sign with the imperial city of Toledo. With regard to the architecture of the square that was recognised by F. Marías, we see the following buildings: at the right of the painting, the Casa de la Carpintería with its columns and balconies, drawn by Juan de Herrera about 1589, at the back is the facade of Los Boteros, and on the left are the buildings on stilts which, according to the elevations submitted during the suit between the council and the town hall, still existed in the second half of the eighteenth century (idem).

undoubtedly harsh and cruel, for people of the time it had a certain amount of entertainment value. The spirit of the Counter-Reformation clearly considered these ceremonies exaltations of orthodox Catholic faith. The festive mood is emphasized by the painter: in the foreground he portrays a colorful procession with harquebusiers firing salutes and musicians playing. This is the procession of the Green Cross displaying the standard of the tribunal. As in Berruguete's painting, the Holy Tribunal sits beneath a canopy in the background. The altar stands on a large platform in the center of the composition, and gathered around it are the ecclesiastic hierarchy, the members of various religious orders, and the *Santa Hermandad* (rural police). On a stepped grandstand to the right are the defendants wearing their *sambenitos.* Members of all social classes are watching the event: ladies, gentlemen, and members of military orders stand on balconies of the houses around the square. Others are in boxes or stand on the platform around the stage. There are marked differences among the members of the public: the more privileged spectators are well-organized and seated in galleries or boxes, soberly dressed and severe looking, whereas crowded together in the street there are a number of clergymen, gentlemen, nuns, friars of all orders, and ladies, some of whom wear veils. The buildings allow to identify the exact spot where this auto-da-fé was held: the Plaza de Zocodover in Toledo.[34]

Anonymous Spanish artist. *Crucifixion of the Holy Innocent Child of La Guardia,* ca. 1550–1570. Oil on pine board. Madrid, Archivo Histórico Nacional (AHN, Inquisición. Objetos)

Years later, Francisco Rizi (1614–1685) painted his *Auto-da-fé in the Plaza Mayor of Madrid* as a record of the event held on 30 June 1683 in the presence of King Charles II of Spain his mother, and his wife. The baroque exaltation this work conveys relates to an extraordinary event held at the kingdom's capital in the presence of the king and queen.

Hardly anything remains of the early settings of the autos-da-fé. We only know that the stake mentioned by Bernáldez was a large stone platform erected in the fields of Tablada and that there were huge plaster statues of the prophets at each corner. We also know very little about the places used by the Toledo Inquisition. A plan of the burning platform, the *Brasero de la Vega,* can be seen in the famous painting *Map and View of Toledo.*

## A CASE OF SLANDER: THE HOLY CHILD OF LA GUARDIA

One of the most appalling instances of the cruelties and abuses committed by the Spanish Inquisition was the case of the Child of La Guardia. The painstaking, if at times confusingly obscure, record of the proceedings allows us to reconstruct the events in considerable detail. In June 1490 a *converso* by the name of Benito García was arrested at Astorga. Born in La Guardia (Toledo), he was a traveling wool carder by trade and was accused of a crime. He confessed to Judaizing and implicated several people from Tembleque (Toledo) by the name of Franco. They were all taken to prison at Segovia and after being subjected to the usual inquisition tricks and tortures, one of them, Yuce Franco, stated that, in La Guardia, "Alonso Franco told him that on a Good Friday he and several of his brothers had crucified a young boy in the same manner that the Jews had crucified Jesus." After a trial lasting little over a year, an auto-da-fé was held at Avila on 16 November 1491 and all the defendants were executed.

In their desire to stir up as much public indignation as possible, the prosecutors had fabricated a story entailing the torture of an innocent child victim. It also played upon the fears of Christians by stating that Jews were continuing to commit the same atrocities that they had done to Jesus, only now their victims were the most innocent of Christ's followers. In truth, the story was not very imaginative. It was the same timeworn, sinister tale — the old blood libel — about Jews sacrificing children after a ceremonial rite.

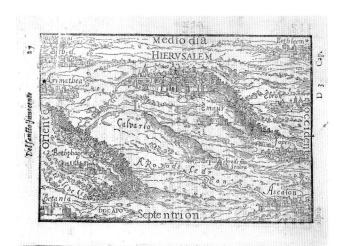 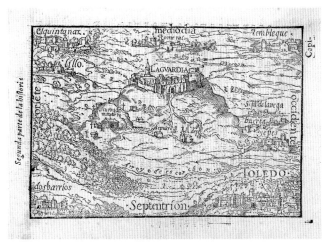

**"Views of Jerusalem and La Guardia"**, from Fray Rodrigo de Yepes, *Historia de la muerte y glorioso martyrio del Sancto Inocente que llaman de La Guardia, natural de la ciudad de Toledo* (1583), fols. 26r–27r. Madrid, Biblioteca Nacional (R 30981)

Stories of the ritual sacrifice of Christian children by Jews originated in Europe and spread to Aragon sometime before the middle of the thirteenth century. They were so universally accepted that they were soon commented on by all the anti-Jewish groups in Spain. Even the *Partidas* of Alfonso X held this practice to be true and severely condemned it:

> And we have heard that in some places on Good Friday the Jews commemorated and commemorate the Passion of Our Lord Jesus Christ mockingly by stealing young children and setting them up on a cross, or when they cannot obtain babies, by fashioning waxen figures and crucifying them. We order that if any such occurrence were heard of within our domains, all those involved in these acts shall be taken prisoner and summoned before the king, and when the truth is revealed, he shall order them all put to death in a degrading manner forthwith.[35]

The trial of the Jews of La Guardia in Toledo demonstrates how far the prosecutors of the Inquisition at the end of the fifteenth century would go in fabricating charges. It is well known that the use of torture can make anyone confess to even the most atrocious of crimes. During the sixteenth century the cult of the Holy Child of La Guardia became enormously popular. In 1523 Archbishop Alonso de Fonseca commissioned an altarpiece depicting the entire iconographical cycle: the abduction, the accusation, the flagellation, the capture of the Jews, their execution by burning at the stake, and the cure of the Holy Boy's mother's blindness. All these scenes are grouped around the central panel, which shows the boy's crucifixion and extraction of his heart.[36]

[35] "Et porque oyemos decir que en algunos lugares los judios ficieron et facen el dia del viérnes santo remembranza de la pasion de nuestro señor Jesucristo en manera de escarnio, furtando los niños et poniéndolos en la cruz, ó faciendo imágenes de cera et crucificándolas quando los niños non pueden haber, mandamos que si fama fuere daqui adelante que en algunt lugar de nuestro señorio tal cosa sea fecha, si se pudiere averiguar que todos aquellos que se acertaren en aquel fecho que sean presos, et recabdados et aduchos antel rey: et después que él sopiere la verdad, débelos mandar matar muy aviltadamente quantos quier que sean" (Partida VII, tit. XXIV, Ley II).

[36] Gutiérrez, 2002, pp. 419–421.

The Archivo Histórico Nacional houses a panel painting of the boy's crucifixion. This work is typical of mid-sixteenth-century folk art, and could have been used in the trial conducted by the Inquisition.[37] Shortly afterward, Fray Rodrigo Yepes wrote an account that would become the official version of the story and served as the basis for the cult: *Historia de la muerte y glorioso martirio del Sancto Inocente que llaman de la Guardia, natural de la ciudad de Toledo* (History of the death and glorious martyrdom of the Innocent Saint known as the Child of La Guardia, from the city of Toledo). In his enthusiasm to pattern the story on that of Christ, the author included two woodcut illustrations of Jerusalem and La Guardia to demonstrate the similarities between the passion of Jesus Christ and the death of the Holy Child.

[37] Several copies of the trial documents were made in 1569. The existence of holes for the cords of the packet of documents would appear to confirm the panel's function.

# Catalogue of Works

**Coins from Ampurias** [see p. 19]
1B.C.–A.D.1
Bronze. 1.5–1.7 cm
AMPURIAS, MUSEU D'ARQUEOLOGIA DE CATALUNYA-
EMPÚRIES (INV. NO. MAC-EMPURIES 6343-6352)

**Trough (pileta) with inscriptions in three**
**languages** [see p. 20]
5th–7th century (?)
White marble. 14 x 57 x 44 cm
From Tarragona
TOLEDO, MUSEO SEFARDÍ MINISTERIO DE EDUCACIÓN,
CULTURA Y DEPORTE (MUSEO DE SANTA CRUZ DE TOLEDO,
INV. NO. 89)

**Dentiscalpium** [see p. 72]
Silver. 6.8 x 1.6 x 0.8 cm
From Tesorillo I, found at Briviesca in 1938, near the
current cemetery
BURGOS, MUSEO DE BURGOS (INV. NO. 733)

**Pendant** [see p. 72]
Silver and traces of enamel. 4.3 x 3.3 x 0.6 cm
From Tesorillo I, found at Briviesca in 1938, near the
current cemetery
BURGOS, MUSEO DE BURGOS (INV. NO. 734)

**Shields** [see p. 66]
Gilded silver. 4.2 x 3 x 0.2 cm each
From Tesorillo I, found at Briviesca in 1938, near the
current cemetery
BURGOS, MUSEO DE BURGOS (INV. NO. 735)

**Shields** [see p. 66]
Gilded silver. 0.2 x 3 cm Ø
From Tesorillo I, found at Briviesca in 1938, near the
current cemetery
BURGOS, MUSEO DE BURGOS (INV. NO. 736)

**Sphere** [see p. 72]
Silver. 2 cm Ø
From Tesorillo I, found at Briviesca in 1938, near the
current cemetery
BURGOS, MUSEO DE BURGOS (INV. NO. 742)

**Ring with inscription** [see p. 71]
12th–13th century
Silver. Ring: 2 cm Ø; bezel: 1 x 1.2 cm
From the Cerro de los Judíos necropolis,
Deza (Soria)
SORIA, MONASTERIO DE SAN JUAN DE DUERO, MEDIEVAL
SECTION OF THE MUSEO NUMANTINO (INV. NO. 81/1/568)

**Ring with inscription** [see p. 71]
12th–13th century
Silver. Ring: 1.5 cm Ø; bezel: 1 cm Ø
From the Cerro de los Judíos necropolis,
Deza (Soria)
SORIA, MONASTERIO DE SAN JUAN DE DUERO, MEDIEVAL
SECTION OF THE MUSEO NUMANTINO (INV. NO. 81/1/569)

**Ring with inscription** [see p. 71]
12th–13th century
Silver. Ring: 1 cm Ø; bezel: 1 x 0.9 cm
From the Cerro de los Judíos necropolis, Deza (Soria)
SORIA, MONASTERIO DE SAN JUAN DE DUERO, MEDIEVAL
SECTION OF THE MUSEO NUMANTINO (INV. NO. 81/1/570)

**Decorated ring** [see p. 71]
12th–13th century
Silver. Ring: 2 cm Ø; bezel: 1.5 x 1.5 cm
From the Cerro de los Judíos necropolis, Deza (Soria)
SORIA, MONASTERIO DE SAN JUAN DE DUERO, MEDIEVAL
SECTION OF THE MUSEO NUMANTINO (INV. NO. 81/1/574)

**Decorated ring with inscription** [see p. 71]
12th–13th century
Bronze. Ring: 2.2 cm Ø; bezel: 1.4 cm Ø
From the Cerro de los Judíos necropolis, Deza (Soria)
SORIA, MONASTERIO DE SAN JUAN DE DUERO, MEDIEVAL
SECTION OF THE MUSEO NUMANTINO (INV. NO. 81/1/571)

**Silver bezel ring with glass paste** [see p. 71]
12th–13th century
Bronze. Ring: 2 cm Ø; bezel: 1 x 0.95 cm
From the Cerro de los Judíos necropolis, Deza (Soria)
SORIA, MONASTERIO DE SAN JUAN DE DUERO, MEDIEVAL
SECTION OF THE MUSEO NUMANTINO (INV. NO. 81/1/572)

**Ring with Hebrew inscription** [see p. 72]
13th–14th century
Gold. 1.5 cm Ø
From Montjuïc necropolis (Barcelona), tomb no. 51
TOLEDO, MUSEO SEFARDÍ-MINISTERIO DE EDUCACIÓN,
CULTURA Y DEPORTE (INV. NO. 83)

**Ring** [see p. 72]
13th–14th century
Gold. 1.8 cm
From Montjuïc necropolis (Barcelona), tomb no. 88
TOLEDO, MUSEO SEFARDÍ-MINISTERIO DE EDUCACIÓN,
CULTURA Y DEPORTE (INV. NO. 82)

**Ring** [see p. 72]
Silver. 1 x 2.2 cm Ø
From Tesorillo I, found at Briviesca in 1938,
near the current cemetery
BURGOS, MUSEO DE BURGOS (INV. NO. 738)

**Ring** [see p. 72]
Silver and reddish agate. 2 x 2.4 cm Ø
From Tesorillo I, found at Briviesca in 1938,
near the current cemetery
BURGOS, MUSEO DE BURGOS (INV. NO. 740)

**Ring** [see p. 72]
Silver. 1 x 2.4 cm Ø
From Tesorillo I, found at Briviesca in 1938,
near the current cemetery
BURGOS, MUSEO DE BURGOS (INV. NO. 739)

**Ring** [see p. 72]
Silver. 0.7 x 2 cm Ø
From Tesorillo I, found at Briviesca in 1938,
near the current cemetery
BURGOS, MUSEO DE BURGOS (INV. NO. 741)

**Ring** [see p. 72]
14th–15th century
Gold. 1 x 2.4 cm
From the Llanos de Santa Lucía Jewish necropolis
(Teruel)
TERUEL, MUSEO DE TERUEL (INV. NO. 594)

**Ring** [see p. 72]
14th–15th century
Gold. 0.8 x 2.1 cm
From the Llanos de Santa Lucía Jewish necropolis
(Teruel)
TERUEL, MUSEO DE TERUEL (INV. NO. 595)

**Necklace** [see p. 73]
14th–15th century
Silver. Several sizes
From the Llanos de Santa Lucía Jewish necropolis
(Teruel)
TERUEL, MUSEO DE TERUEL (INV. NO. 597)

**Seal** [see p. 70]
Toro, 14th century
Bronze. 1 x 3.2 x 3.2 cm
TOLEDO, MUSEO SEFARDÍ-MINISTERIO DE EDUCACIÓN,
CULTURA Y DEPORTE (INV. NO. 216)

**Bowl** [see p. 55]
Late 14th century
Teruel ceramic ware, green/purple series.
6 x 14 cm Ø
From the Casa del Judío, Plaza de la Judería, Teruel
TERUEL, MUSEO DE TERUEL (INV. NO. 2225)

**Bowl** [see p. 56]
Late 15th century
Teruel ceramic ware, blue series. 3.5 x 8.5 cm Ø
From the Plaza de la Judería, Teruel
TERUEL, MUSEO DE TERUEL (INV. NO. 5298)

**Bowl** [see p. 53]
Mid 14th–mid 15th century
Ceramic. 7 x 15.5 cm Ø
From the cloister of the church of San Pedro in Teruel
TERUEL, MUSEO DE TERUEL (INV. NO. 7577)

**Dish or carving platter** [see p. 55]
Second half of 14th century
Teruel ceramic ware, green/purple series. 10 x 27 cm Ø
From the site of the Archivo Provincial de Teruel
TERUEL, MUSEO DE TERUEL (INV. NO. 5053)

**Dish or carving platter** [see p. 53]
Second half of 14th century
Teruel ceramic ware, green/purple series. 12 x 34 cm Ø
From Teruel city centre
TERUEL, MUSEO DE TERUEL (INV. NO. 7156)

**Plate** [see p. 55]
Second half of 15th century
Teruel ceramic ware, blue series. 3 x 22.5 cm Ø
From Teruel city centre
TERUEL, MUSEO DE TERUEL (INV. NO. 7710)

**Bowl** [see p. 55]
Late 15th century
Teruel ceramic ware, blue series. 6 x 15 cm Ø
From the Plaza de la Judería, Teruel
TERUEL, MUSEO DE TERUEL (INV. NO. 5297)

**Mortar** [see p. 56]
Late 15th century
Teruel ceramic ware, green/purple series. 17 x 20 cm Ø
From the Plaza de la Judería, Teruel
TERUEL, MUSEO DE TERUEL (INV. NO. 5251)

**Mortar** [see p. 56]
Late 14th–early 15th century
Teruel ceramic ware, green/purple series. 14 x 16 cm Ø
From Calle Amantes, nos. 15–17–19, Teruel
TERUEL, MUSEO DE TERUEL (INV. NO. 18452)

**Jug with spout** [see p. 56]
Second half of 15th century
Teruel ceramic ware, green/purple series. 18 x 9.5 cm Ø
From Teruel city centre
TERUEL, MUSEO DE TERUEL (INV. NO. 7317)

**Saltcellar** [see p. 54]
Paterna, first half of 14th century
Glazed ceramic, painted in copper and manganese.
5 x 12.5 cm
VALENCIA, COLLECTION OF THE AYUNTAMIENTO DE
VALENCIA, IN DEPOSIT AT THE MUSEO NACIONAL DE
CERÁMICA «GONZÁLEZ MARTÍ» (INV. NO. 598)

**Fragment of leather scroll with Hebrew script
(fragment of Torah)** [see p. 100]
13th or 14th century
Manuscript on leather; ferrogallic ink. 55 x 29.5 cm
From Ágreda synagogue (Soria)
ÁGREDA (SORIA), ARCHIVO MUNICIPAL (SECCIÓN HISTÓRICA,
REG. 15/98; EXP. SO–165)

**Hanukkah lamp** [see p. 102]
14th century
Honey glazed pottery. 2.5 x 44 x 6.8 cm
From Santa María la Blanca (Burgos)
BURGOS, MUSEO DE BURGOS (INV. NO. 8.796/19.1)

**Book of Esther** [see p. 103]
14th or 15th century
Manuscript on parchment scroll. Total length:
265 cm; height: 11 cm; with wooden holder, 27 cm
From Toledo
MADRID, ARCHIVO HISTÓRICO NACIONAL-MINISTERIO DE
EDUCACIÓN, CULTURA Y DEPORTE (CÓDICE 1423B)

**Tesorillo de Briviesca** [see p. 104]
From Tesorillo III, found in 1988 in Calle
de Los Baños (Briviesca, Burgos)

Spoon, first half of 14th century
Silver. 17.1 x 4 cm; l g
BURGOS, MUSEO DE BURGOS (INV. NO. 8.782)

Spoon, first half of 14th century
Silver. 18.1 x 4.7 cm; l g
BURGOS, MUSEO DE BURGOS (INV. NO. 8.783)

Plate, first half of 14th century
Silver. 2.3 x 17 cm Ø
BURGOS, MUSEO DE BURGOS (INV. NO. 8.784)

Plate, first half of 14th century
Silver. 3.2 x 21 cm Ø
BURGOS, MUSEO DE BURGOS (INV. NO. 8.785)

Plate, first half of 14th century
Plate. 2.7 x 16 cm Ø
BURGOS, MUSEO DE BURGOS (INV. NO. 8.787)

Plate, first half of 14th century
Silver. 3.4 x 22 cm Ø
BURGOS, MUSEO DE BURGOS (INV. NO. 8.790)

**Plate** [see p. 104]
Gilded silver. 3 x 24.5 cm Ø
From Tesorillo I, found in Briviesca in 1938
near the current cemetery
BURGOS, MUSEO DE BURGOS (INV. NO. 745)

**Leaf from the Damascus Keter** [see p. 123]
1260
Manuscript on parchment. 32 x 28 cm
From Burgos
TOLEDO, MUSEO SEFARDÍ-MINISTERIO DE EDUCACIÓN,
CULTURA Y DEPORTE (INV. NO. 230)

**Hebrew Bible** [see p. 106]
Spain, second quarter of 15th century (?)
Illuminated manuscript on parchment; VIII + 478 +
IV folios; bound at a later date in red leather on
boards with gilt ornamentation, cloth lining,
marbled paper flyleaves. 33.5 x 26.5 x 12.5 cm
MADRID, BIBLIOTECA NACIONAL (VIT/26–6)

**Alba Bible** [see p. 107]
Maqueda, 1422
Manuscript on paper. 513 folios. 42.5 x 32.5 x 12.5 cm
MADRID, FUNDACIÓN CASA DE ALBA

**Translation of Books of the Old Testament
("Bible of Isabella 'the Catholic'")**
Castile, 13th century; copy dating from the first half
of the 15th century
Manuscript on parchment and paper; 258 folios
in 2 columns of 42-48 lines; bound at El Escorial;
leather on cardboard. 40 x 31 x 8.5 cm
PATRIMONIO NACIONAL, BIBLIOTECA DEL REAL MONASTERIO
DE SAN LORENZO DE EL ESCORIAL, MADRID (MS. I–I–5)

**Ketubah** [see p. 88]
Milagro, 1309
Manuscript on parchment with decorative border.
30 x 57 cm
PAMPLONA, ARCHIVO GENERAL DE NAVARRA (CÁMARA DE
COMPTOS, CAJA 192, NO. 54)

**Contract of dowry and marriage (ketubah)
between Rabbi Moses Amigo and Bienvenida,
Jews of Arévalo (Ávila)** [see p. 90]
Torrelobatón (Valladolid), 7 March 1479
Manuscript on parchment with Hebrew writing;
sepia and red ink and border decorated with
geometric motifs. 43 x 35 cm
VALLADOLID, ARCHIVO DE LA REAL CHANCILLERÍA-
MINISTERIO DE EDUCACIÓN, CULTURA Y DEPORTE
(PERGAMINOS, CARPETA 13, NO. 11)

**Records of the bet-din** [see p. 80]
Tudela, 1467
Manuscript on parchment; single 65-line sheet.
59 x 55 cm
TUDELA (NAVARRE), M. I. AYUNTAMIENTO DE TUDELA
(NAVARRE)-ARCHIVO MUNICIPAL (DH NO. 2)

**Fuero de Estella** [see p. 188]
Navarre, 1164; 12th–14th–century copy
Manuscript on parchment; 160 folios in 2 columns.
25 x 18 x 5.5 cm
SALAMANCA, BIBLIOTECA GENERAL DE LA UNIVERSIDAD
(MS. 2652)

**Fragment of epitaph** [see p. 109]
10th–11th century
Brick. 26 x 18 x 3 cm
From Toledo
Toledo, Museo Sefardí-Ministerio de Cultura,
Educación y Deporte (MS 2)

**Tombstone of Mar Selomó ben Mar David
b. Parnaj** [see p. 110]
15 July 1097
Marble. Traces of red paint inside the letters in the
last four lines. 38 x 31 x 7 cm (field 34 x 24.5 cm)
From the Castrum Iudeorum cemetery
(Puente Castro, León)
León, Museo de León (donated by the García de
Arriba family, inv. no. 2000/26)

**Cabbalistic amulet** [see p. 135]
Spain, 15th century
Manuscript on parchment; 1 folio. 25 x 25 cm
Cuenca, Archivo Diocesano

**Moré Nebujim** [see p. 136]
Moses ben Maimon (Maimonides)
(Cordoba, 1138-Cairo, 1204)
Fostat, 1190
Manuscript on paper; 1 folio. 35 x 28 x 1.2 cm
New York, The Library of The Jewish Theological
Seminary of America (MS. 8254.5)

**Sefer ha-hahasvaá** [see p. 131]
Jonah ibn Janah (ca. 985, Cordoba?)
Zaragoza, 11th century; 13th–14th–century copy
Manuscript on parchment; subsequently bound in
boards with gilt and clasp; 197 folios. 22 x 15.5 x 5.5 cm
Madrid, Biblioteca Nacional (MS. 5460)

**Medical aphorisms** [see p. 132]
Moses ben Maimon (Maimonides)
(Cordoba, 1138-Cairo, 1204)
Fostat, 1187-1190; undated copy
Manuscript on paper; 178 folios. 20 x 19.5 x 5 cm
Patrimonio Nacional, Biblioteca del Real Monasterio
de San Lorenzo de El Escorial, Madrid (MS. Árabe, 869)

**Model of the Samuel Halevi synagogue**
[see p. 117]
HCH Model, 2002
Polyurethane resin, acrylic paint (polychrome).
139 x 84.5 x 65.4 cm. Scale: 1/20
Owned by Seacex

**Model of Cordoba synagogue** [see p. 116]
HCH Model, 2002
Polyurethane resins, acrylic paint (monochrome).
52.5 x 57.5 x 45 cm. Scale: 1/20
Owned by Seacex

**Model of Santa María la Blanca synagogue**
[see p. 118]
HCH Model, 2002
Polyurethane resin, acrylic paint (monochrome).
75.5 x 58.5 x 20 cm. Scale: 1/40
Owned by Seacex

**Fragments of stuccowork with Hebrew
inscription** [see p. 115]
14th century
Stuccowork. 37 x 22 x 20 cm; 17 x 15 x 20 cm;
27 x 16 x 20 cm
From the synagogue in Cuenca that became the
church of Santa María la Nueva and, subsequently,
that of Santa María de Gracia, and was finally
demolished in 1912. There are archaeological remains
beneath the current Torre Mangana
Cuenca, Archivo Diocesano de Cuenca

**Fragments of stuccowork with Hebrew
inscription** [see p. 115]
14th century
Stuccowork. 52 x 49 x 20 cm
From the synagogue in Cuenca
Cuenca, Archivo Diocesano de Cuenca

**Capital with bilingual inscription** [see p. 114]
12th–13th century
Limestone. 26 x 16 cm; 42 cm Ø widest part and
10 cm Ø narrowest part
Toledo, Museo Sefardí-Ministerio de Educación,
Cultura y Deporte (On loan from the Museo
Arqueológico Nacional, inv. no. 25)

**Keys to the city of Seville** [see p. 142]
Mid–13th century
Iron and gilded silver. 10 x 0.5 cm and 7 x 0.5 cm
Seville, Cathedral (inv. nos. 112/68 and 112/69)

**El libro de ajedrez, dados y tablas** [see p. 155]
Seville, 1283
Manuscript on parchment. 41 x 31 x 5.5 cm
Patrimonio Nacional, Biblioteca del Real Monasterio
de San Lorenzo de El Escorial, Madrid (T.I.6)

**Libro de las formas et de las imágenes
que están en los cielos** [see p. 152]
1276–1279
Manuscript on parchment. 39.5 x 30 x 2 cm
Patrimonio Nacional, Biblioteca del Real Monasterio
de San Lorenzo de El Escorial, Madrid (MS. h–I–16)

**Records of the Tortosa Debate** [see p. 177]
Tortosa, 1413–1414
Manuscript on parchment; 409 folios; bound
at El Escorial. 36 x 24 x 9.5 cm
Patrimonio Nacional, Biblioteca del Real Monasterio
de San Lorenzo de El Escorial, Madrid (MS. S–I–10)

**Allegory of the Synagogue** [see p. 193]
Second half of 13th century
Polychrome woodcarving. 146 x 27 x 34 cm
From Palencia (?)
Barcelona, El Conventet Collection
(inv. no. 00954-CO)

**Decree of Expulsion of the Jews** [see p. 196]
Granada, 31 March 1492
Manuscript on paper; uncertified copy; 4 folios.
20.5 x 29.4 cm.
Simancas (Valladolid), Archivo General de Simancas-
Ministerio de Educación, Cultura y Deporte (PR. 28–6)

**Auto-da-fé in Toledo's Plaza de Zocodover**
[see p. 220]
Anonymous Spanish artist, ca. 1656
Oil on canvas. 167 x 123.5 cm
Inscription: «avto publico de fe en la santa
inquisición de t.i. del año 1656»
Toledo, Museo de El Greco (inv. no. 131)

**Handkerchief used as evidence in an
inquisitorial trial** [see p. 218]
Cuenca, before 1512
Linen. 33 x 37 cm
Cuenca, Archivo Diocesano (Legajo 45, exp. 712)

**Ground plan of the house of the Toledo
Inquisition** [see p. 217]
Nicolás de Vergara, 14 July 1598
Gouache plan and 2 sheets of text. Plan: 57.5 x 42.5
cm; text: 30 x 21.5 cm
Madrid, Archivo Histórico Nacional-Ministerio
de Educación, Cultura y Deporte (Sección de
Inquisición. Legajo 3081, exp. 52)

**Crucifixion of the Holy Innocent Child
of La Guardia** [see p. 222]
Anonymous Spanish artist, ca. 1550-1570
Oil on pine board. 32.5 x 20.5 cm
Madrid, Archivo Histórico Nacional-Ministerio de
Educación, Cultura y Deporte (AHN Inquisición.
Objetos)

**Historia de la muerte y glorioso martyrio del
Sancto Inocente que llaman de La Guardia,
natural de la ciudad de Toledo** [see p. 223]
Fray Rodrigo de Yepes, 1583
Volume in quarto. 21.5 x 16 x 2 cm
Madrid, Biblioteca Nacional (R/30981)

**Epitaph of Havaab** [see p. 27]
1156
Marble. 32 x 26 x 5 cm
From the church of San Miguel el Alto in Toledo
Toledo, Museo de Santa Cruz (inv. no. 235)

# Bibliography

Abraham bar Selomoh, 1992 • Abraham bar Selomoh [de Torrutiel], *Sefer ha-Qabbalah (Libro de la tradición), vid.* Moreno Koch, 1992.

Abraham Ibn Daud, 1990 • Abraham Ibn Daud, *Libro de la Tradición (Sefer ha-Qabbalah), vid.* Ferre, 1990.

Abraham M. Asan, 1990 • Abraham M. Asan, *Shul'han Aruj de Rabi Yosef Caro. Recopilación de las leyes prácticas y sus comentarios hasta los Sabios contemporáneos según la tradición sefardí,* 1990.

*Actas,* 1985 • *Actas del II Congreso Internacional Encuentro de las Tres Culturas,* Toledo, (1983) 1985.

Alba Cecilia, 2002 • Alba Cecilia, A., "Exégesis, normativa legal y cábala," in *Memoria de Sefarad,* Madrid, 2002, pp. 320–323.

Alcalá, 1984 • Alcalá, A., *Los orígenes de la Inquisición en Aragón. San Pedro de Arbués mártir de la autonomía aragonesa,* Zaragoza, 1984.

Alfonso, 2002 • Alfonso, E., "Los límites del saber. Reacción de intelectuales judíos a la cultura de procedencia islámica," in *Judíos en tierras de Islam...,* Madrid, 2002, pp. 59–83.

Amador de los Ríos, 1875–1876 • Amador de los Ríos, J., *Historia social, política y religiosa de los judíos de España y Portugal,* Madrid, 1875–1876 (facsimile ed. in 3 vols., Madrid, 1984).

Arco, 1949 • Arco, R. del, "Nuevas noticias de la aljama judaica de Huesca," *Sefarad,* IX (1949), p. 371.

Arco, 1954 • Arco, R. del, *Sepulcros de la Casa Real de Castilla,* Madrid, 1954.

Avello *et alii,* 2002 • Avello J. L., *et alii,* "Losa sepulcral de Mar Selomó ben Mar David b. Parnaj," in *Memoria de Sefarad,* Madrid, 2002, pp. 216–217.

Azcona, 1964 • Azcona, T. de, *Isabel la Católica,* Madrid, 1964.

Baer, 1929–1936 • Baer, F., *Die Juden im christlichen Spanien: Erster teil: Urkunden und regesten: I Aragonien und Navarra; II Kastilien, Inquisitionakten,* 2 vols., Berlin, 1929–1936.

Baer, 1981 • Baer, Y., *Historia de los judíos en la España cristiana,* 2 vols., Madrid, 1981.

Baer, 1998 • Baer, Y., *Historia de los judíos en la España cristiana,* 2 vols., Barcelona, 1998.

Bango García, 2002 • Bango García, C., "Un barrio de la ciudad: la judería," in *Memoria de Sefarad,* Madrid, 2002, pp. 63–70.

Bango Torviso, 1993–1994 • Bango Torviso, I. G., "San Pelayo de Perazancas," in *Homenaje al profesor Dr. D. José María de Azcárate y Ristori,* Madrid, 1993–1994, pp. 545–558.

Barkai, 1944 • Barkai, R., *Chrétiens, musulmans et juifs dans l'Espagne medieval,* Paris, 1994.

Benassar, 1979 • Benassar, P. de, *L'Inquisition Espagnole XV–XIX siècles,* Paris, 1979.

Bernáldez, 1953 • Bernáldez, A., *Historia de los Reyes Católicos don Fernando y doña Isabel,* in Biblioteca de Autores Españoles, LXX, 1953, pp. 567–788.

Blasco Martínez, 1988 • Blasco Martínez, A., *La judería de Zaragoza en el siglo XIV,* Zaragoza, 1988.

Blasco y Romano, 1991 • Blasco, A. y Romano, D., "Vidal (ben) Satorre, copista hebreo (1383–411)," *Sefarad,* LI (1991).

Blasco, 2002 (1) • Blasco, A., "La vida quotidiana al call," in *La Catalunya Jueva,* Barcelona, 2002, p. 134.

Blasco, 2002 (2) • Blasco, A., "Trabajo y ocio en el mundo hispanojudío," in *El legado de los judíos...,* Pamplona, 2002, pp. 103–133.

Bunes, 1998 • Bunes Ibarra, M. A. de, "Concepto y formación del patrimonio hispanojudío," in López Álvarez and Izquierdo Benito, 1998, pp. 79–91.

Cantera Burgos, 1973 • Cantera Burgos, F., *Sinagogas de Toledo, Segovia y Córdoba,* Madrid, 1973.

Cantera Burgos, 1984 • Cantera Burgos, F., *Sinagogas españolas, con especial estudio de las de Córdoba y la toledana del Tránsito,* Madrid, 1984 (re-ed.).

Cantera Montenegro, 2001 • Cantera Montenegro, J., "El Séfer Torah del archivo catedralicio de Calahorra," *Kalakorikos,* 6 (2001), pp. 115–128.

Cantera and Millás, 1956 • Cantera, F. and Millás, J. M., *Las inscripciones hebraicas de España,* Madrid, 1956.

Cantera, 1927 • Cantera, F., *Chebet Jehuda,* Granada, 1927.

Carrasco *et alii,* 1994 • Carrasco, J., *et alii, Los judíos del reino de Navarra. Documentos 1093–1333,* Pamplona, 1994.

Carrete, 1998 • Carrete Parrondo, C., "El judaísmo castellano en vísperas de la expulsión," in *Luces y sombras...,* Pamplona, 1996, pp. 161–182.

Carrete, 2000 • Carrete Parrondo, C., "Sefarad 1492: ¿una expulsión anunciada?," in *Movimientos...,* Pamplona, 2000, pp. 49–54.

Carrete, 2002 • Carrete Parrondo, C., "Reflexiones sobre el decreto de expulsión," in *El legado de los judíos...,* Pamplona, 2002, pp. 111–118.

Casanovas, 2002 • Casanovas, J., "Las necrópolis judías hispanas. Nuevas aportaciones," in *Memoria de Sefarad,* Madrid, 2002, pp. 209–215.

Castaño, 2000 • Castaño, C., J., "Traumas individuales en un mundo trastornado. El éxodo mediterráneo de R. Yeduhad b. Yaàqob Hayyat (1492–1496)," in *Movimientos...,* Pamplona, 2000, pp. 55–68.

Castaño González, 1995 • Castaño González, J., "Las aljamas judías de Castilla a mediados del siglo XV: La carta real de 1450," in *España Medieval,* 18 (1995), pp. 181–203.

Castillo, 2002 • Castillo, B., "Los Adornos," "Las piezas de una vajilla para la celebración de la Pascua," in *Memoria de Sefarad,* Madrid, 2002, pp. 111–113; 181–185.

Chazan, 1989 • Chazan, R., *Daggers of Faith,* Berkeley, 1989.

Chico, 2002 • Chico Picaza, M. V., "El *scriptorium* de Alfonso X el Sabio," in *Memoria de Sefarad,* Madrid, 2002, pp. 268–274.

*Convivencia,* 1992 • Mann, V., Glick, T. and Dodds, J. (eds.), *Convivencia: Jews, Muslims, and Christians in Medieval,* New York, 1992.

Díaz Esteban, 1985 • Díaz Esteban, F., "Aspectos de la convivencia jurídica desde el punto de vista judío en la España medieval," in *Actas del II Congreso Internacional Encuentro de las Tres Culturas,* Toledo, 1985, p. 110.

Díez, 1998 • Díez Merino, C., "San Isidoro de Sevilla y la polémica judeocristiana," in *La controversia...,* Madrid, 1998, p. 110.

Domínguez, 1982 • Domínguez, A. (ed.), *La Miniatura de El Lapidario,* Madrid, 1982.

*El legado de los judíos,* 2002 • *El legado de los judíos al Occidente europeo. De los reinos hispánicos a la monarquía española. Cuartos encuentros judaicos de Tudela,* Pamplona, 2002.

*El legado judío,* 2002 • *El legado judío en Hebraica Aragonalia,* Zaragoza, 2002.

Ferre, 1990 • Ferre, L., *Abraham Ibn Daud, Libro de la Tradición (Sefer ha-Qabbalah),* Barcelona, 1990.

*Fuero Real,* 1836 • *Fuero Real del Rey Don Alonso el Sabio. Copiado del Código del Escorial señalado ij. z–8,* Madrid, 1836.

Gampel, 1996 • Gampel, B. R., *Los últimos judíos en el suelo ibérico. Las juderías navarras, 1479–1498,* Pamplona, 1996.

García Avilés, 1996 • García Avilés, A., "Two Astromagical Manuscripts of Alfonso X," *Journal of the Warburg and Courtauld Institutes,* 59 (1996), pp. 14–23.

García Avilés, 2002 • García Avilés, A., "Los judíos y la ciencia de las estrellas," in *Memoria de Sefarad,* Madrid, 2002, pp. 335–343.

García Iglesias, 1978 (1) • García Iglesias, L., *Los judíos en la España antigua*, Madrid, 1978.

García Iglesias, 1978 (2) • García Iglesias, L., "Los menores de edad, hijos de judíos, en los cánones y leyes de época visigótica," *El Olivo*, 5–6 (1978), pp. 28 *et seq.*

García Iglesias, 2002 • García Iglesias, L., "Oscuro origen y avatares más antiguos de las comunidades judías en España," in *Memoria de Sefarad*, Madrid, 2002, pp. 31–41.

González Dávila, 1606• González Dávila, Gil, *Historia de las antigüedades de la ciudad de Salamanca: vidas de sus obispos y cosas sucedidas en su tiempo…*, Salamanca, Artus Taberniel, 1606.

González Jiménez, 1999 • González Jiménez, M., "Alfonso X rey de Castilla y Léon," *El Scriptorium,* 1999, pp. 1–15.

González, 1960 • González, J., *El reino de Castilla en la época de Alfonso VIII*, 3 vols., Madrid, 1960.

Gozálvez, 2002 • Gonzálvez Ruiz, R., "Un judío de Toledo transfiere la deuda de un tercero en beneficio de una señora mozárabe de Toledo," in *Memoria de Sefarad*, Madrid, 2002, p. 267.

Gutiérrez Pastor, 2000 • Gutiérrez Pastor, I., "Auto de fe en la plaza de Zocodover de Toledo," in *El mundo de Carlos V. De la España medieval al Siglo de Oro*, Madrid, 2000, p. 203.

Gutiérrez Pastor, 2002 • Gutiérrez Pastor, I., "Crucifixión del Santo Inocente Niño de la Guardia," in *Memoria de Sefarad*, Madrid, 2002, pp. 419–421.

Hilgarth and Narkis, 1961 • Hilgarth, J. N. and Narkis, B., "A list of Hebrew books (1300) and a contract to illuminate manuscripts (1335) from Majorca," in *Revue des Etudes Juives*, 3rd series, III, CXX (1961), pp. 316 *et seq.*

Huerga, 1987 • Huerga, P., "Fray Tomás de Torquemada," in Contreras, J. (ed.), *Inquisición. Nuevas aproximaciones*, Madrid, 1987.

*Inquisición y conversos,* 1994 • *Inquisición y conversos,* III Curso de Cultura hispanojudía y sefardí de la Universidad de Castilla-La Mancha, Madrid, 1994.

Izquierdo, 1998 • Izquierdo Benito, R., "Arqueología de una minoría: la cultura material hispanojudía," in *El Legado material hispanojudío*, VII Curso de Cultura Hispanojudía y Sefardí de la Universidad de Castilla-La Mancha, Cuenca, 1998, pp. 265–290.

Jiménez Monteserín, 1980 • Jiménez Monteserín, M., *Introducción a la Inquisición Española*, Madrid, 1980.

*Judíos en tierras del Islam,* 2002 • Fierro, M. (ed.), *Judíos en tierras del Islam I. Judíos y musulmanes en al-Andalus y el Magreb. Contactos intelectuales. Actas,* Madrid, 2002.

Kamen, 1967 • Kamen, H., *La Inquisición española*, Barcelona-Mexico, 1967.

Kamen, 1993 • Kamen, H., "La expulsión de los judíos y el contexto internacional," in *La expulsión,* 1993, pp. 15–26.

Kamen, 1994 • Kamen, H., "Orígenes de la antigua Inquisición en Europa," *Inquisición y conversos,* III Curso de Cultura hispanojudía y sefardí de la Universidad de Castilla-La Mancha, Madrid, 1994, pp. 53–59.

*La Catalunya Jueva,* 2002 • *La Catalunya Jueva*, Barcelona, 2002.

*La controversia,* 1998 • *La controversia judeocristiana en España (Desde los orígenes hasta el siglo XIII). Homenaje a Domingo Muñoz León*, Madrid, 1998.

*La expulsión,* 1993 • *La expulsión de los judíos españoles.* II Curso de Cultura Hispano Judía y Sefardí, Toledo, 1993.

*La sociedad medieval,* 1998 • Izquierdo Benito, R. and Sáenz-Badillos, Á. (coords.), *La sociedad medieval a través de la literatura hispanojudía*, Cuenca, 1998.

*La vida judía en Sefarad,* 1991 • *La vida judía en Sefarad*, Madrid, 1991.

Lacave, 1991 • Lacave, J. L., "Judíos en España," in *La vida judía en Sefarad*, Madrid, 1991, pp. 17–42.

Lacave, 1998 • Lacave, J. L., *Los judíos del reino de Navarra. Documentos hebreos (1297–1486),* Pamplona (Navarra Judaica, 7), 1998.

Ladero, 1971 • Ladero Quesada, M. A., "Las juderías de Castilla según algunos servicios fiscales del siglo XV," *Sefarad*, XXXI (1971), pp. 249–264.

Laguna, 2000 • Laguna, T., "La Capilla de los Reyes de la primitiva catedral de Santa María de Sevilla y las relaciones de la Corona castellana con el Cabildo hispalense en su etapa fundacional (1248–1285)," in *Maravillas de la España Medieval. Tesoro Sagrado y Monarquía, 1*, Madrid, 2000, pp. 235–249.

Lasker, 1998 • Lasker, D. J., "Polémica judeo-cristiana en al-Andalus," in *La controversia...,* Madrid, 1998, p. 170.

León Tello, 1963 • León Tello, P., *Judíos de Avila*, Ávila, 1963.

León Tello, 1979 • León Tello, P., *Judíos de Toledo*, 2 vols., Madrid, 1979.

Levi-Provençal, 1973 • Levi-Provençal, E., *Historia de España, V, España musulmana*, Madrid, 1973.

Levy, 1963 • Levy, I., *The Synagogue: its History and Function*, London, 1963.

Llama, 1932 • Llama, J. "Documentos para la historia jurídica de las aljamas hebreas de Toledo y Molina," *Religión y Cultura*, 19 (1932), p. 276.

López Álvarez and Izquierdo Benito, 1998 • López Álvarez, A. M.ª and Izquierdo Benito, R. (coords.), *El Legado material hispanojudío*, VII Curso de Cultura Hispanojudía y Sefardí de la Universidad de Castilla-La Mancha, Cuenca, 1998.

López Álvarez *et alii,* 1993 • López Álvarez, A., Palomero Plaza, S. and Menéndez Robles, M. L., "Consecuencias del decreto de expulsión sobre los bienes inmuebles de los judíos españoles," in *La expulsión de los judíos españoles*, II Curso de Cultura Hispano Judía y Sefardí, Toledo, 1983, pp. 149–173.

López Álvarez, 1998 • López Álvarez, A. M., "El ajuar hispanojudío: documentación y restos," in *El Legado material hispanojudío*, VII Curso de Cultura Hispanojudía y Sefardí de la Universidad de Castilla-La Mancha, Cuenca, 1998, pp. 219–246.

*Los caminos del exilio,* 1996 • *Los caminos del exilio. Segundos encuentros Judaicos de Tudela (1995),* Pamplona, 1996.

*Luces y sombras,* 1996 • *Luces y sombras de la judería europea (siglos XI–XVII), Primeros encuentros judaicos de Tudela (1994),* Pamplona, 1996.

Maíllo, 2002 • Maillo Salgado, F., "Los judíos y la ciencia en la Península Ibérica en el medievo," in *Memoria de Sefarad*, Madrid, 2002, pp. 279–291.

Maqueda, 1990 • Maqueda, C., *El auto de fe*, Madrid, 1990.

Martín, 1988 • Martín, E., "Inventario de bienes muebles de judíos bilbilitanos en 1492," *Sefarad*, XLVII, 1988, pp. 93–115 and 309–345.

Martínez, 1998 • Martínez Díez, G., *Bulario de la Inquisición española*, Madrid, 1998.

*Memoria de Sefarad,* 2002 • *Memoria de Sefarad,* Madrid, 2002.

Metzger, 1982 • Metzger, T. and Metzger, M., *La vie juive au Moyen Âge illustrée par les manuscrits hébraïques enluminés du XIIIᵉ au XVIᵉ siècle*, Fribourg, 1982.

Meyuhas, 2002 • Meyuhas Ginio, A., "La controversia de Tortosa (1413–1414) según Sebet Yehudad de Selomoh ibn Verga," in *El legado de los judíos...,* Pamplona, 2002, pp. 23–32.

Mirambell, 1988 • Mirambell Belloc, E., "Los judíos gerundenses en el momento de la expulsión," in *Per una historia de la Girona jueva*, Gerona, 1988, vol. II, p. 657.

Molina, 2002 • Molina, J., "Las imágenes de los judíos en la España Medieval," in *Memoria de Sefarad,* Madrid, 2002, pp. 373–379.

Montes, 1995 • Montes Romero-Camacho, I., "El antijudaísmo o antisemitismo sevillano hacia la minoría hebrea," in *Los caminos del exilio...,* Pamplona, 1996, pp. 73–157.

Montoya Martínez and Domínguez Rodríguez, 1999 • Montoya Martínez, J. and Domínguez Rodríguez, A. (coords.), *El Scriptorium Alfonsí: De los Libros de Astrología a las Cantigas de Santa María*, Madrid, 1999.

Moreno Koch, 1987 • Moreno Koch, Y., *Fontes Iudaeorum Regni Castellae. V De iure hispano-hebraico. Las taqqanot de Valladolid de 1432. Un estatuto comunal renovador*, Salamanca, 1987.

Moreno Koch, 1992 • Moreno Koch, Y., *Dos crónicas hispanohebreas del siglo XV*, Barcelona, 1992.

Moreno Koch, 1998 • Moreno Koch, Y., "El espacio comunal por excelencia: la Sinagoga," in López Álvarez and Izquierdo Benito, 1998, pp. 135–141.

Moreno Koch, 2002 • Moreno Koch, Y., "Organización de las aljamas españolas," in *El legado de los judíos...,* Pamplona, 2002, pp. 135–142.

Motis Dolader, 1985 • Motis Dolader, M. A., *La expulsión de los judíos de Zaragoza*, Zaragoza, 1985.

Motis Dolader, 1996 • Motis Dolader, M. A., "Caminos y destierros de los judíos de Aragón tras el edicto de expulsión," in *Los caminos del exilio...*, Pamplona, 1996, pp. 197–254.

*Movimientos, 2000* • *Movimientos migratorios y expulsiones en la Diáspora occidental. Terceros encuentros judaicos de Tudela (1998)*, Pamplona, 2000.

Narkiss, 1982 • Narkiss, B., *Hebrew Illuminated Manuscripts in the British Isles,* vol. 1, *The Spanish and Portuguese Manuscripts,* Jerusalem-London, 1982.

Netanyahu, 2002 • Netanyahu, B., *Los marranos españoles según las fuentes hebreas de la época (siglos XIV–XV)*, Valladolid, 2002.

Ojeda and Tabales, 1994 • Ojeda Calvo, R. and Tabales, M., "Estudio diacrónico de la ocupación del edificio islámico bajo el palacio Mañara (Sevilla): tres usos, tres culturas (siglos XII–XV)," in *IV CAME, Actas,* Alicante, 1994, vol. II, pp. 137–146.

Orfali, 2002 • Orfali, M., "La 'ley del reino' y las aljamas hispanohebreas," in *El legado de los judíos...*, Pamplona, 2002, pp. 143–152.

Ortega Martínez, 2002 • Ortega Martínez, A. I., "Yacimientos de Burgos," in *Memoria de Sefarad,* Madrid, 2002, pp. 133–140.

Ortega, 2002 • Ortega, J., *Operis terre turolii. La cerámica bajomedieval en Teruel,* Teruel, 2002.

Palacios, 1957 • Palacios López, A., *La disputa de Tortosa, Actas,* vol. II, Madrid, 1957.

Passini, 1998 • Passini, J., "La juiverie de Tolède: bains et impasses du quartier de Hamanzeit," in *El Legado material hispanojudío*, VII Curso de Cultura Hispanojudía y Sefardí de la Universidad de Castilla-La Mancha, Cuenca, 1998, pp. 301–326.

Peláez del Rosal, 1968 • Peláez del Rosal, J., *La sinagoga,* Cordoba, 1968.

Pérez Prendes, 1994 • Pérez Prendes, "El procedimiento inquisitorial (Esquema y significado)," in *Inquisición y conversos,* III Curso de Cultura Hispanojudía y Sefardí de la Universidad de Castilla-La Mancha, Madrid, 1994, p. 187.

Pérez, 1988 • Pérez, J., *Isabelle et Fredinand, Rois Catholiques d'Espagne,* Paris, 1988.

Pérez, 2002 • Pérez, J., "La expulsión de los judíos," in *Memoria de Sefarad,* Madrid, 2002, pp. 385–395.

Planas, 2002 • Planas, S., "Les comunitats jueves de Catalunya: l'area de Girona," in *La Catalunya Jueva,* Barcelona, 2002, p. 58.

Reyes, 1998 • Reyes, F., "El espacio privado: una casa en la judería de Alcalá de Henares," in *El legado material hispanojudío*, VII Curso de Cultura Hispanojudía y Sefardí de la Universidad de Castilla-La Mancha, Cuenca, 1998, pp. 181–216.

Rico, 1998 • Rico Sáez-Bravo, R., "Las juderías de Ocaña y Yepes," in *El legado material hispanojudío*, VII Curso de Cultura Hispanojudía y Sefardí de la Universidad de Castilla-La Mancha, Cuenca, 1998, pp. 209–233.

Romano, 1971 • Romano, D., "Le opere scientifiche di Alfonso X e l'intervento degli ebrei," *Oriente e Occidente nel medioevo: filosofia e scienza*, Rome, 1971, pp. 677–711 (now in idem., *De historia judía hispánica. Homenaje al profesor David Romano Ventura,* Barcelona, 1991, pp. 147–181).

Romano, 1985 • Romano, D., "Marco jurídico de la minoría judía en la corona de Castilla de 1214 a 1350," in *Actas del II Congreso Internacional Encuentro de las Tres Culturas,* Toledo, (1983) 1985, pp. 261–291.

Romano, 1994 (1996) • Romano, D., "Los hispanojudíos en el mundo científico...," in *Luces y sombras...,* Pamplona, 1996, pp. 17–56.

Romero, 1978 • Romero, E., *Castello, Selomo ibn Gabirol. Poesía secular,* Madrid, 1978.

Rosen, 1998 • Rosen, T., "Representaciones de mujeres en la poesía hispano-hebrea," in Izquierdo Benito, R. and Sáenz-Badillos, Á. (coords.), *La sociedad medieval a través de la literatura hispanojudía,* Cuenca, 1998, pp. 123–138.

Rubio Semper, 2001 • Rubio Semper, A., *Fuentes medievales sorianas. Ágreda II,* Soria, 2001.

Rucquoi, 1994 • Rucquoi, A., "L'Invective anti-juive dans l'Espagne chrétienne: Le cas de Martin de León," in *Atalaya. Revue d'Etudes Médiévales Hispaniques,* 1994, pp. 135–151.

Ruíz Souza, 2002 • Ruíz Souza, J. C., "Sinagogas sefardíes monumentales en el contexto de la arquitectura medieval hispana," in *Memoria de Sefarad,* Madrid, 2002, pp. 225–239.

Sáenz-Badillos, 1988 • Sáenz-Badillos, Á., *Historia de la Lengua Hebrea,* Sabadell, 1988.

Sáenz-Badillos, 1991 • Sáenz-Badillos, Á., *La literatura hebrea en la España Medieval,* Madrid, 1991.

Sánchez, 1963 • Sánchez, G., *El Fuero de Madrid y los derechos locales Castellanos,* Madrid, 1963.

*Santo Martino, 1987* • *Santo Martino de León. I Congreso Internacional sobre Santo Martino en el VIII Centenario de su Obra Literaria, 1185–1985,* León, 1987, pp. 513–549.

Sempere y Guarinos, 1788 • Sempere y Guarinos, J., *Historia del luxo y de las leyes suntuarias en España,* 2 vols., Madrid, 1788.

Silva, 1988 • Silva y Verástegui, S., *La miniatura medieval en Navarra,* Pamplona, 1988.

Suárez Bilbao, 2000 • Suárez Bilbao, F., *El Fuero Judiego en la España cristiana. Las fuentes jurídicas. Siglos V–XV,* Madrid, 2000.

Suárez Fernández, 1964 • Suárez Fernández, L., *Documentos acerca de la expulsión de los judíos,* Valladolid, 1964.

*Synodicon, 1994* • *Synodicon Hispanum, VI Ávila y Segovia,* Madrid, 1994.

Torre, 1962 • Torre, A. de la, *Documentos sobre las relaciones internacionales de los Reyes Católicos,* vol. IV, Barcelona, 1962.

Torres Balbás, 1985 • Torres Balbás, L., *Ciudades hispanomusulmanas,* Madrid, 1985, I, pp. 210–211.

Ulrich, 1991 • Ulrich, E., *Carmen Figuratum. Geschichte des Figurengedichts von den antiken Ursprüngen bis zum Ausgang des Mittelalters,* Cologne-Weimar-Vienna, 1991.

Valdeón, 1994 • Valdeón Baruque, Julio, "Los orígenes de la Inquisición en Castilla," in *Inquisición y conversos,* III Curso de Cultura Hispanojudía y Sefardí de la Universidad de Castilla-La Mancha, Madrid, 1994, pp. 35–45.

Valdeón, 2000 • Valdeón Baruque, J., *Judíos y conversos en la Castilla Medieval,* Valladolid, 2000.

Valle, 1998 • Valle, C. del, "La carta encíclica del obispo Severo de Menorca (a. 418)," in *La controversia...,* Madrid, 1998, pp. 62–76.

Villapalos, 1997 • Villapalos, G., "Justicia y monarquía," *La jurisdicción de moros y judíos,* Madrid, 1997, pp. 220–229.

Viñayo, 1948 • Viñayo González, A., *San Martín de León y su apologética antijudía,* Madrid, 1948.

Vives, 1963 • Vives, J., *Concilios visigóticos e hispano-romanos,* Barcelona-Madrid, 1963.

Yanguas y Miranda, 1964 • Yanguas y Miranda, J., *Diccionario de Antigüedades del reino de Navarra,* I, Pamplona, 1964.

Yarza, 1993 • Yarza Luaces, J., *Jan Van Eyck,* Madrid, 1993.

Yosef ben Saddiq, 1992 • Yosef ben Saddiq, *Capítulo cincuenta del Compendio Memoria,* vid. Moreno Koch, 1992.

# Catalogue

**PUBLISHED BY**

State Corporation for Spanish Cultural Action Abroad, SEACEX

**TEXT BY**

Isidro G. Bango

**TRANSLATIONS**

Jenny Dodman

Ann Canosa

Richard Connahay

**PRODUCTION**

Ediciones El Viso, Madrid

**BOOK DESIGN**

Fernando López Cobos

**U.S. EDITOR**

Rosemary Regan

**TYPESETTING & COLOUR SEPARATIONS**

Cromotex, S.A., Madrid

**PRINTED BY**

Brizzolis, S.A., Pinto (Madrid)

**BOUND BY**

Encuadernación Ramos, Madrid

ISBN: 84-96008-27-4

D.L.: M-19093-2003

Cover: "Passover seder," *Barcelona Haggadah,* fol. 28v, Barcelona, ca. 1350. London, The British Library (Ms. Add. 14761)

**PHOTOGRAPHS**

Alicante, José María Espí

Astorga, Imagen Más

Barcelona, Gasull fotografía

Barcelona, Ramón Manent

Barcelona, Museu d'Historia de Catalunya, Pepo Segura

Barcelona, Servei fotogràfic Museu Nacional d'Art de Catalunya, Calveras, Mérida, Sagristà

Berlin, Dietrich Graf

Budapest, Magyar Tudományos Akadémia

Burgos, Foto Santi

Calahorra, José Javier Varela

Cambridge, University Library

Copenhagen, Det Kongelige Bibliotek

Edimburgh, National Museums of Scotland

Gerona, Josep Maria Oliveras

Jerusalem, Israel Museum

Lisbon, Biblioteca Nacional

London, The British Library

London, Victoria & Albert Museum

Los Angeles, The J. Paul Getty Museum, Passela and Dupe

Madrid, Biblioteca Nacional

Madrid, Manuel Blanco

Madrid, Cuauhtli Gutiérrez

Madrid, Museo Nacional del Prado, José Baztán y Alberto Otero

New York, Suzanne Kaufman

Oxford, Bodleian Library

Palencia, Javier Marín

Palma de Mallorca, Jaume Gual

Pamplona, Larrión & Pimoulier

Paris, Bibliothèque nationale de France

Salamanca, Santiago Nodal

Saragossa, Ricardo Vila

Seville, Luis Arenas

Soria, Museo Numantino

Teruel, J. Escudero

Toledo, Antonio Pareja

Valencia, Francisco Alcántara

Vic, Archivo diocesano